Emotionally Indebted

Sabina Pultz

Emotionally Indebted

Governing the Unemployed People in an Affective Economy

Sabina Pultz
Department of People and Technology
Roskilde University
Roskilde, Denmark

ISBN 978-3-031-57155-8   ISBN 978-3-031-57156-5   (eBook)
https://doi.org/10.1007/978-3-031-57156-5

© The Editor(s) (if applicable) and The Author(s), under exclusive license to Springer Nature Switzerland AG 2024

This work is subject to copyright. All rights are solely and exclusively licensed by the Publisher, whether the whole or part of the material is concerned, specifically the rights of reprinting, reuse of illustrations, recitation, broadcasting, reproduction on microfilms or in any other physical way, and transmission or information storage and retrieval, electronic adaptation, computer software, or by similar or dissimilar methodology now known or hereafter developed.

The use of general descriptive names, registered names, trademarks, service marks, etc. in this publication does not imply, even in the absence of a specific statement, that such names are exempt from the relevant protective laws and regulations and therefore free for general use.

The publisher, the authors, and the editors are safe to assume that the advice and information in this book are believed to be true and accurate at the date of publication. Neither the publisher nor the authors or the editors give a warranty, expressed or implied, with respect to the material contained herein or for any errors or omissions that may have been made. The publisher remains neutral with regard to jurisdictional claims in published maps and institutional affiliations.

Cover illustration: Maram_shutterstock.com

This Palgrave Macmillan imprint is published by the registered company Springer Nature Switzerland AG.
The registered company address is: Gewerbestrasse 11, 6330 Cham, Switzerland

Paper in this product is recyclable.

To my daughters, Ellen and Ingrid.

Preface

Being unemployed is not just a matter of not having a job or losing salary—of *"deprivation"* (Boland & Griffin, 2015). For many, becoming unemployed gives rise to a fundamental doubt. Questions like 'is it my fault' or 'what have I done wrong' gradually appear as time goes by as unemployed.

The title "Emotionally indebted" is invented to signal an intimate relation between lived experiences and wider political structures. The main point is that how you feel as an unemployed person is shaped by your life history, your family system, personality etc., but contra-intuitively, these experiences are also largely influenced and constituted by larger structures located outside the individual. These structures encompass policies, cultural repertoires, and value systems to mentions a few. The book aims to foreground these psycho-political patterns in trying to understand unemployment experiences in what I call the affective economy.

Our feelings and lived experiences are influenced by how our labor markets are organized, how the welfare state governs unemployed people through particular social policies, how these policies are administered at the frontline, and finally how the underlying value systems tend to distribute dignity and respect unequally in society based on for example employment status. In other words, the focus of the book is the various ways that unemployed people are governed through affects and emotions. Receiving monetary currencies from the state while being unemployed involves making the unemployed person emotionally indebted. 'Emotional debt' is a term I use to refer to the special position unemployed people are put in. Emotional debt is a particular form of debt that unemployed people are placed in as a result of receiving money from the state and thus not living up to a very basic norm in society: being economically self-reliant. Emotional debt involves putting special emotional demands on the unemployed. The emotional debt also accumulates over time and challenges the well-being of the unemployed. The emotional demands are not communicated explicitly but are rooted in practices, policies, and understandings in the unemployment system, in the labor market and in society more broadly. Instead of paying money (unemployment benefit or social assistance) back, the unemployed are positioned in a pinch, where they are expected to pay back with other currencies than monetary. Here I examine the forms of expression these emotional demands take, and how they affect and are handled by the unemployed. The emotional demands are not unambiguous, and, in that sense, it is not possible to 'pay back' and 'get rid of' the debt. The demands also pull in opposing directions. Based on a thorough empirical study of the subjective and lived experiences of being unemployed, my analysis shows that these demands are contradictory and therefore difficult to honor. This gives rise to ambivalence and tension that manifest at the individual level as a challenge the unemployed person must grabble with.

The purpose here is to uncover the many different sides of the emotional debt. At the same time, the book is written in the understanding that such an analysis can never be exhaustive. I do strive to draw as complete a picture as possible foregrounding social psychological research. By exploring how the unemployed are managed in the Danish welfare state as well as how the unemployed manage themselves, the book gives an idea of timely and specific challenges unemployed people face. That knowledge is relevant for the unemployed themselves, for practitioners in the field, researchers, and decision makers. Furthermore, the theoretical contribution is relevant in other parts of the welfare state as well, where different types of monetary and affective currencies intertwine and in a certain sense shape what it is like to be a citizen in various situations. To some extent, the book addresses dynamics that also shape other groups in society who find themselves outside the normative script; that is, the immigrants, the poor, the single parents etc. Receiving help from the state often comes in the shape of a double-edged sword: providing necessary help, but also subjectifying, othering, and surveilling the individual citizen leaving them to grapple with emotional challenges.

I explore the specific expressions of emotional debt by zooming in on different foci. These foci cover self-responsibility and blame (Chap. 4), shame and managing shame (Chap. 5), a particular type of unemployed people who seek to escape the shame called 'unemployed by choice' (Chap. 6), networking technologies in Denmark and the US (Chap. 7), and lastly, experiences of unemployment during Covid-19 (Chap. 8). Below, each section will be briefly introduced.

As an unemployed person, you must be willing to engage in a self-critical process, where you identify different possible ways to work on yourself to optimize your chances on the labor market. These dynamics are explored in Chap. 4. You are required to demonstrate sufficient motivation and empowerment to refute the built-in mistrust of the unemployed people inherent in activation policies (with specific requirements for what it takes to be active and requirements for how to be available). You are entitled to receive unemployment benefit or social assistance based on a principle of conditionality, which means that you must perform particular duties to be deserving of the right to receive economic support. Deservingness does not come for free or as a natural effect of citizenship. The money is conditional on whether you, as an unemployed person, create yourself as sufficiently active, and thereby mitigate against the suspicion of inactivity or laziness associated with the prejudice against unemployed people. In addition to a built-in mistrust, or perhaps rather as another side of it, there are special technologies that target the unemployed person's ability to feel fear—you are encouraged (with small affective nudges) to fear that you do not live up to the rules (or that you could get caught not living up to the rules) so that you are constantly at risk of being financially sanctioned. The purpose of the fear technologies is that it should not be too comfortable to be financially supported by the state. That would be both too expensive on the welfare state's budget and it entails a potential demoralization of the workforce. Fear works. Consequently, a range of policies builds on the effect of 'threat' in an economic understanding, and while these policies have documented effects on behavior, they also shape how it feels being unemployed in a negative fashion (Eskelinen & Olesen, 2010).

For many reasons and many of them interlinked, it should 'suck enough' to be unemployed in the Danish welfare state. The policies and the governmental technologies applied target the unemployed people directly, but at the same time and perhaps more importantly—they also target the population more broadly in ways that protect and support a particular sense of morals and work ethics. Being unemployed is difficult or challenging for many, because not having a job tests a very basic sense of dignity. In Western societies work is intimately connected with identity. Who am I if I cannot exchange my labor for money on the market? When you become unemployed, an underlying value system is made visible that assigns dignity and status to those who work (to varying degrees) and leave those who do not empty handed. The rules and logics of the value system become visible to us when we step outside the path of normativity. For many, unemployment often gives rise to shame, and this is the focus of Chap. 5. Shame is defined as what happens when you step outside the normative script. However, the shame does not strike in any monolithic fashion and not everybody feels the emotional toll of having to deal with the stickiness that shame of unemployment comes with.

In Chap. 6, I focus on a group of creative young people who challenge the underlying value system in which paid labor is directly linked to dignity. These creative young people consider unemployment benefits to be entrepreneurial support and therefore do not see themselves as unemployed even though they formally belong to the social category. This positioning, which I call *unemployed by choice*, is connected to and made possible by an increasingly precarious labor market, which in many ways erodes the binary division between unemployed or in work. Today there is a vast gray zone offering a range of different positions such as solo-employed, freelancer, un- or underpaid work etc. This diversity offers new options for the unemployed in terms of how they behave and not least how they present themselves to others.

In addition to precariousness, there is a tendency in the labor market for us to bring our personality to work to a greater extent. Networking plays an increasingly important role in job search, and this is the center in Chap. 7. Networking as an unemployed person places special demands on the unemployed people, since cultivating and displaying passion is made difficult in the face of repeated rejections. Also, it requires walking a fine line to balance between being passionate enough about a job without falling into desperation or wanting it 'too much'. Since job searching involves networking, repeated rejections can often feel like rejections not only of one's professional identity or objective skills, but also as rejections of who one is as a person. Precisely that type of rejection affects the unemployed people's ability to participate naturally and with the emotional presence required when connecting with people in networking practices. I explore this emotional labor of the unemployed to understand another central facet of the overall pickle the unemployed find themselves in. The analysis is made as a comparison between Danish and American job seekers. That design enables an exploration of the extent to which the welfare state functions as a buffer for the experience of feeling exposed. I do not explore the question as a causal matter. Rather, I explore whether the Danish flexicurity system offers some sort of protection against these vulnerabilities compared to their American counterparts who are embedded in a liberal state. The analysis shows that unemployed people across countries experience the emotional labor as demanding and exhausting, but also meaningful and as productive in terms of instilling hope. In the American context, networking is naturalized to a greater extent, whereas several Danish unemployed people are critical of the meritocratic problem, that one's job opportunities are largely shaped by who you know and how charming you are, rather than solely depending on qualifications and merits. Merits are deemed more just, even though this idea can also be challenged (Sandel, 2020).

Last, in Chap. 8, I explore what it was like to be unemployed during Covid-19, during which the active labor market policies (ALMPs) were temporarily suspended, and hence the potent 'responsibility machinery' was set on hold. This event constitutes a natural experiment that allows us to learn about the meaning and workings of ALMPs through their very absence. The analysis documents that unemployed people experienced an enhanced sense of agency and without the ever-present surveillance and monitoring, they felt as if they got back into the driver's seat. In the political discourse, we witnessed a paradigmatic shift putting more weight on external factors alleviating some of the self-blaming pressure. New categories also emerged distinguishing between 'corona-unemployed' and 'old unemployed'; however, the newfound respect and understanding for unemployed people did not necessarily include all of the above equally.

Summing up, 'Emotionally indebted' is a book that tries to explore these different sides of the prism of unemployment separately, to synthesize how unemployed people are governed in the Danish welfare state linked to how they govern themselves. The book identifies some of the challenges unemployed people face that can stand in the way of the unemployed people getting closer to living the lives they want. My hope is that the book should lead to a greater understanding of the situation you are in as an unemployed person in a way that helps sharpen our understanding of how politics and psychology interact and relatedly, how we can turn the arrow outwards, rather than inwards.

Roskilde, Denmark   Sabina Pultz

References

Boland, T., & Griffin, R. (2015). The death of unemployment and the birth of job-seeking in welfare policy: Governing a liminal experience. *Irish Journal of Sociology, 23*(2), 29–48. https://doi.org/10.7227/IJS.23.2.3

Eskelinen, L., & Olesen, S. P. (2010). Beskæftigelsesindsatsen og dens virkninger set fra kontanthjælpsmodtagernes perspektiv. AKF. http://www.akf.dk/udgivelser/container/2010/udgivelse_1050/

Sandel, M. J. (2020). *The tyranny of merit: What's become of the common good?* Allen Lane.

Contents

1 Introduction — 1

2 Governing Unemployed People Through Technologies of Power and Those of the Self — 31

3 Setting the Scene — 61

4 Governing the Active Jobseeker — 73

5 The Sticky Shame and What to Do with It — 99

6 Resisting the Shame and 'Unemployed by Choice' — 125

7 The Intimate Dance of Networking — 141

8 Unemployment Experiences During Covid-19: A Little Less Blame? — 167

9 Synthetizing the Contributions	183
Conclusion	213
Index	217

1

Introduction

To explore and understand these practices, the book contributes with an original theoretical framework that allows a broader analytical scope addressing not only behavior but also how unemployed people are *affectively subjectified* in the unemployment system as well as in relation to cultural norms in society. Connecting the political level to the lived experience of unemployment allows the book to contribute with a fine-tuning of the understanding of the link between politics and psychology. The book addresses all these questions and, in doing so, it expands the analytical scope from focusing on behavior and linguistics to also addressing the more subtle and diffuse governmental technologies, invading and shaping how the person relates to oneself.

A key aim is also to understand how the unemployed person in various ways deals with the governmental technologies in ways that make sense for the individual. Unemployed people are governed based on governmental technologies but the meaning and effect of these emerge both at the front level of public employment services (PES), in relation to what the unemployed people actually do as well as in relation to how they conduct themselves in heterogenous ways. While ALMPs to some extent seem to be a catch-all problem-solver, this book dives deeper and critically explores both the intended and untended consequences of becoming unemployed in the affective economy. Employment policies are largely aimed at getting the unemployed person (back) into a job. While this intention at first glance seems both reasonable and understandable, taking a closer look into the specific ways this political goal is administered in the local practices at public employment offices, makes way for a richer narrative and understanding of what is going on.

The fundamental errand of (critical) social psychology is to understand the relationship between the individual and society and inspired by governmentality studies, I ask how young unemployed people are governed and how they govern themselves. The investigation is based on rich qualitative data sets consisting of field observations and in-depth interviews with unemployed people with the purpose of exploring their experience with the unemployment system, their own understanding of the demands they must meet as well as how they manage these. Based on updated analysis on data gathered during corona, the most recent historical events are taken into consideration which lays a solid foundation for pointing toward new research avenues. Covid-19 gave rise to a new language about unemployment emphasizing external factors as the reason for unemployment. Active labor market policies were temporarily suspended; and exploring the unemployment experience during this time brings about new insights into the workings of ALMP and their psychological consequences through their absence.

Consulting first-hand perspectives on how the management of unemployment is experienced by those who are in the system is a societally and psychologically relevant issue due to both large state expenditures and grave psychological consequences such as severe negative effects on mental and physical health as well as the elevated risk of mortality and suicide (Paul & Moser, 2009; Immervoll, 2012).

To explore these questions, I have gathered empirical material that uncovers these experiences.

I have prioritized breath, rather than depth in the sense that I have asked very open questions about the participants' lives. As a social psychologist focusing on the everyday life (Højholt, 2005; Schraube, 2010), it has been important for me to understand not only how experiences in Danish PES affect unemployed people, but rather how these interact with experiences in other domains in life, such as one's personal and social life.

Using interviews as the prime empirical material might shape the findings in the sense that conversations tend to enhance self-reflection and perhaps also self-critical reflections. Had I solely used observations or shadowing methods (Czarniawska, 2007) the main finding, that unemployment has been psychologized, might not have stood out so clearly. The method of interviewing also involves social desirability bias, that is; people present themselves as favorable as possible which also entails discussing and commenting on morality (see also Lamont, 2009, p. 256). Hence, there is a risk of overestimating moral aspect of their everyday life as unemployed linked to the method applied. It is impossible to get rid of such risk entirely. However, I have applied several methods relying on triangulation as a way of managing the risk in a qualified manner.

While the main finding of this book is that unemployment is psychologized and that this effect results in a particular emotional debt, it is also necessary to underline what goes against this overall finding. Among the interviewees, there were several people who did not struggle with the psychologization of unemployment. For example, I interviewed unemployed people who were educated as mechanical engineers with an unemployment rate at about 0 and they did not worry about their job chances or invest much energy in reflecting about the potential deficits in their personality or social competences. Insecurity and worry are a gateway to self-blaming and self-critical reflections and because this group did not really fear for the future, they did not face the same emotional struggles. These variations emphasize, for me, that while the methods in part produce what we are able to see as social scientists (Bramming et al., 2012), it is not only because of the interview as methods that I identified this finding. The interviewees in fact sometimes did dispute my finding clarifying the boundaries of it.

To allow the reader transparency I will shortly introduce the data that I rely on in this book. The first wave consists of interviews with 6 young, creative people who received unemployment benefit gathered in 2012. The second wave consists of in-depth interviews with 33 unemployed Danes and 15 unemployed people in Boston in 2014/2015 as well as a number of field observations made in both Danish unemployment funds and career centers in Boston. The empirical data also consists of survey data but this material is not used for the purpose of this book (see Pultz,

2017 for more). The third and final wave consists of 44 unemployed people receiving unemployment benefit and social assistance in 2020 and 13 of these made supplementary video diaries adding a more longitudinal perspective.[1]

Over the course of the last decade, I have gone from focusing on a particular segment among the unemployed, namely the young and well-educated who are recipients of unemployment benefit recipients, to broadening the scope and interviewing older unemployed people as well as social assistance recipients who in general struggle with more complex issues beyond not having a job (Danneris, 2018). Recruiting more heterogenous participants is also fruitful in terms of identifying the boundary of my finding. Talking to workers such as bus drivers during the third wave made me realize that not all unemployed people take it personally if they are unable to find a job. There are also substantial patterns linked to social classes, however this perspective has not been systematically pursued and thus here it suffices to note the contours of the limits to the generalizability of the findings.

The book gradually builds a narrative that unemployed people often come to doubt themselves when they are unemployed, and I will shortly unfold that narrative here. They experience self-blame, doubt, shame, and fear and have a hard time dealing with the insecurity of not knowing when they are able to find a job and for some of them questioning if they ever will find a job.

Beneath these experiences, I identify *psychologization* as the driving force.

Psychologization is intimately connected to individualization which suggests that people tend to think of unemployment in individualized terms,—meaning the individual carries the responsibility for being unemployed, rather than their blaming structural factors such as labor market dynamics or employment policies. However, psychologization contains the specific dimension of engaging one's personality and emotional life as the main explanation of why one is unemployed. When unemployment is *psychologized*, it means that unemployment is governed

---

[1] This data was gathered as part of a research project called "Unemployed in a time of crisis" financed by Velux Foundations and co-led with my colleague Magnus Paulsen Hansen.

in a way that focuses on psychological constructs such as motivation or passion leading to the question; what is wrong with me?

To illustrate this notion, I will briefly touch on an alternative way of thinking which is not psychologized, but is still individualized: a person who analyzes the needs of the labor market and realizes that his or her educational or professional profile does not fit in terms of what is asked for on the labor market. Rather than questioning what is wrong with me, that person identifies that their objective skills are not sufficient, and they need to requalify to enhance job opportunities. While this is also tied to the individual reflecting on their own human capital and working on improving it, psychologization is characterized by an emotional dimension and by a focus on a psychological construct such as an aspect of one's personality (motivation, passion, self-assertiveness, self-esteem etc.) or relational and social skills in interpersonal dynamics.

Before delving into the depth of the analyses, I will briefly situate the book within the wider landscape of unemployment studies. The literature on unemployment is abundant and thus I selectively choose literature that allows me to position this contribution within the larger terrain.

Eroding the Binary Category of Un/employment

First of all, we need to ask, what is unemployment? How was it invented historically and how is that tied to research on the topic?

Various attempts have been made to categorize, conceptualize, and construct unemployment as a relatively 'pure' and objective issue. The widely used definition offered by the International Labour Organization (ILO) unemployment is "the share of the labor force that is without work but available for and seeking employment". This definition of unemployment is directly linked to what is established as the solution to the problem: finding a job. Accordingly, Organisation for Economic Co-operation and Development (OECD) defines unemployment as the absence of a contractual working relationship based on a social ordering of society in a capitalist economic system. Being unemployed not only entails a lack of employment, but it is also a highly regulated space intimately tied to the governing of welfare states as well as the organization of the labor market.

The 'pure' category of unemployment is challenged by labor market dynamics eroding the clear-cut boundaries between being either employed or unemployed (Chen et al., in press). Precarization has enabled a plethora of categories of 'in-between'—that is, project work, underemployment, unpaid labor—and includes cultural labor or caretaking of children and elderly or other undervalued or marginalized positions in the labor market. Changing the wider structures and working conditions carry a tremendous effect in terms of setting the stage for unemployed people and their possibilities for governing themselves in various ways.

The 'pure' category obscures the diversity and the variety of problems that unemployed people face, such as dealing with other issues like poverty and mental illness (Waldmann et al., 2019). Wiertz and Chaeyoon (in press) suggests giving up on the historical binary positioning between being employed or unemployed and instead contributes with an understanding of the complexity of possible positions on today's labor markets as well as the transitions between these manifold positions.

Producing knowledge about unemployment is a particularly pressing issue at a time in which periods of unemployment are becoming increasingly normal as part of what has been termed the 'flexible' or 'precarious' labor market (Kalleberg, 2013; Standing, 2011). The globalization and technological advances have radically changed the labor market, and consequently organizations today have to rapidly adjust and accommodate to changed circumstances at an accelerated pace (Pultz & Dupret, 2023, pp. 1–2; Rosa, 2013). One of the ways organizations have met the demand for acceleration is by turning away from heavy bureaucratic ways of organizing and instead securing flexibility, that is, by cutting down expenses on permanent staff and hiring and firing casual workers as needed (Campbell & Gregor, 2004; Rubery, 2015). Over the course of the last couple of decades there has been an increase in short-term, temporary or project work, reshaping the contours of current labor markets, especially for knowledge workers (Eurofond, 2015; Kalleberg, 2008, 2009, 2013; Standing, 2011, 2014). This diversification of contracting has especially been covered in the literature on the precariat (Standing, 2011), precarization (Gleerup, 2018), precarious work (Hewison, 2016), the gig economy (Fleming, 2017), flexible employment (Isaksson, 2010; Kornelakis, 2014), boundary-less careers (Kamoche et al., 2011), etc. Due to lack of standard rights associated with the protection of permanent workers and the absence of these among casual workers, some researchers suggest that casual workers are treated as second-class citizens in the labor market (Alberti et al., 2018; Campbell & Burgess, 2001; Fudge & Owens, 2006; Vallas, 2015).

Well-educated people are currently interesting regarding unemployment as the relationship between education and unemployment is dramatically changing. Contemporary analyses show that unemployment occurs irrespective of skill and education level and thus education is no longer the employment guarantee that it used to be (Scarpetta et al., 2010). Higher qualification levels would earlier have predicted a good professional trajectory, but today well-educated people face an uncertain future characterized by austerity (Atkinson, 2010). This is in alignment with Standing's label termed the 'academic precariat', covering a growing segment of individuals with a good education who are unable to secure safe labor market positions (Standing, 2011). Deleuze and Guattari (1987) note that this insecure labor market involves "micropolitics of little fears" suggesting an affective dimension of the new way the labor market is organized. When people cannot feel safe in their jobs, the sense of security shifts. Either it is replaced by focusing on employability—that is a person's ability to find a job, or it continues to be a challenging condition in (work)life.

In the literature on precarity, the negative consequences of being in non-standard contracts have largely been covered (Du Gay & Morgan, 2013; Kalleberg, 2013; Knights & Clarke, 2014; Standing, 2014; Vallas & Cummins, 2014; Vallas & Kleinman, 2008; Vallas & Prener, 2012; Vives et al., 2011). For some casualized workers, however, there are great opportunities to change jobs or to establish portfolio incomes by working for numerous employers, and increasingly these professionals advance not only vertically in organizations but also laterally intra- and interorganizationally (Kamoche et al., 2011; Kattenbach et al., 2014). These labor market changes do not only affect the professionals who are currently working on temporary contracts. Prior studies have explored the different work related effects of permanent versus casualized employment and found poorer outcomes in terms of job satisfaction and job performance for casualized workers despite doing similar work tasks at the same organization (Wickramasinghe & Chandrasekara, 2011). Ward and Greene (2018) show that employment status also makes a difference in terms of how people experience a shared emotional arena with particular feeling rules by exploring the managerial task of affectively managing volunteers. In the creative industries, precarious and casualized employments have long been an integral and characteristic part of the labor market (Flew & Cunningham, 2010; Kalleberg, 2009). It is however underexplored how these dynamics affect the people outside of and in-and-out of precarious employment and these voices need to be heard.

Governing Unemployment in the Welfare State

While the labor market has changed the last decades, the administration and governing of unemployed people have remained rather stable for a very long time, drawing on the same or similar ideas of governing. Since the 1980s, there has been a shift, internationally, toward expanding activation policies at a supranational level such as the EU and the OECD (Lindsay & Daguerre, 2009). This active turn is constituted by ALMPs which are the primary backbone of policies implemented today across OECD countries, including Denmark (Immervoll, 2012; Weishaupt, 2011). In a Danish context, the active labor market policies have been introduced since the 1990s and unemployment benefits have been made increasingly conditional in the sense that people must partake in several job search activities to become entitled to unemployment benefits (Weishaupt, 2011), and failing to meet the requirements potentially results in being economically sanctioned (Hansen, 2019). This shift has often been described as a move from protective to corrective or even punitive welfare policies (Dwyer, 2004, 2019; McGann, 2023; Grover & Stewart, 1999).

Especially sociological and social policy research pinpoint how unemployed people for decades have been governed by policies arising from what has been termed "the activity paradigm" aimed at constructing the "active jobseeker" (Bengtsson et al., 2015; Bonoli, 2010). "The active turn" refers to a move in employment policies from supporting unemployed individuals passively toward an active turn shaping them as active jobseekers and conditioning unemployment benefits and social assistance on the unemployed person's ability to live up to certain demands (Andersen, 2020). This shift has been linked to at least two different policy paradigms: the neoliberal and the social investment policy paradigm. The activation paradigm is associated with elements from neoliberal policies, largely characterized as political rationality based on deregulation and privatization as well as the various ways in which social phenomena are conceived and thought of in economic terms (Brown, 2015; Dean, 2013; Lazzarato, 2009). Neoliberalism both denotes an ideology and associated policies but also refers to a particular configuration of subjectivity which, in an unemployment context, relates to the specific processes constructing people as active job seekers rather than dependent and passive recipients of unemployment benefits. The active labor market policies are also linked to ideas from the social investment paradigm according to which the goal of the welfare state is to enhance growth and prosperity in a society by investing in citizens' human capital and thus ensuring global competition (Morel et al., 2013; Esping-Andersen et al., 2002). By this token, policies are designed to invest in human capital to optimize future labor market opportunities (Jenson, 2011) such as with profiling systems (Gallagher & Griffin, 2023; Pultz, 2016, in press). Special technologies are also designed to be able to predict better as to who among the unemployed people are deemed worthy of investment and who able to get back into employment on their own and in that sense direct resources where best used.

Overall, the Danish PES can be described as a mix or a hybrid in terms of social policies and welfare and the specific context and the structural conditions they provide for unemployed people are elaborated on in Chap. 3.

Related to the diversification of employment, there has been a discursive recoding of the unemployment issue evident in the written material in the system as well as in relation to how people talk about unemployment in lay terms. Since the 1990s, the Danish term for 'unemployed' was substituted by 'ledig' which is the Danish word for 'available'. Other new words appeared in dialogue with management and enterprise vocabularies such as job seekers, people in transition or in-between jobs, open to new possibilities, etc. These newer categories can be interpreted as attempts to counteract some of the stigma associated with unemployment in many western societies (Boland & Griffin, 2015; Fryer & Stambe, 2014). These vocabularies tend to downplay the negative aspect of unemployment and can thus be viewed as being in line with what has been described as a 'positivization' of society characterized by the emergence and dispersion of positive psychology in many arenas in the welfare state (Brinkmann & Eriksen, 2005). Moreover, the new words align well with the virtues of flexibility and malleability which are valorized in neoliberal societies needed in austerity (Hartmann & Honneth, 2006). This discursive recoding prepares the ground for a particular self-management in which the unemployed person conducts him- or herself as a freelancer associated with enterprise culture (Rose, 1999). Interestingly, hiding, masking, or covering up unemployment seems to be one of the most fertile ways of dealing with unemployment today and this recoding plays an important role here.

Researching Unemployment

How people think and feel about themselves and behave in everyday life is entangled with politics and policies, from public discourses to encounters with street-level bureaucracy (Brodkin & Marston, 2013). However, investigating unemployed people within a restricted disciplinary perspective tends to neglect some of the social dynamics shaping lived experiences. Namely, an isolated focus on the individual (i.e., personality traits or coping strategies) tends to neglect political dimensions of the unemployment experience (Uysal & Pohlmeier, 2011) while studies focusing solely on the relationship between welfare institutions and the citizen tend to overestimate the influence of the system hereby blindsiding important dimensions of everyday life (Van Parys & Struyven, 2018). Last, a strict policy analysis overlooks the actual lived effects of specific policies and thus misses the unintended effects of the policies and how they interact with other spheres in the lives of unemployed people (Benda et al., 2019).

Inspired by Foucault (2010), a range of governmentality studies examine how people are governed and how they govern themselves (Dean, 1995; Pultz, 2017; Walters, 1994). These studies have also paved the way for a more contextual understanding of unemployment by zooming in on the concrete ways that unemployed people are encouraged to govern themselves relying on both discipline and rules as well as normative ideals and pressures. Studies inspired by Foucault's work on governmentality (Foucault, 2008) have thus shown how the active turn has led to the (re)invention of a plethora of instruments designed to conduct the behavior of the unemployed and create a certain kind of subject (Dean, 1995; Pultz, 2017; Walters, 1997) such as the "job seeker" (Boland & Griffin, 2015), the "at risk client" (Caswell et al., 2010; Pultz, 2016), the responsible self (McDonald & Marston, 2005) and the indebted self (Lazzarato, 2012). This move installs new dynamics in the encounters between the PES, often embodied in the job counselor or social worker at the employment office, and the unemployed (Garsten & Jacobsson, 2004; McDonald & Marston, 2005). From this perspective these encounters involve "subjectification" (Pultz, 2016) and "roleplaying" (Boland, 2015), using the vocabulary of Foucault and Goffman, that have an effect within as well as outside of the walls of the employment office. They may lead to self-blame (Pultz, 2017; Sharone, 2013b), stigma (Patrick, 2016; Whelan, 2021), shame (Pultz, 2018), loss of social citizenship (Dwyer, 2010), restricted agency and work first values (Eschweiler & Pultz, 2021) as well as to occasional resistance (Baker & Davis, 2018; Peterie et al., 2019).

The burgeoning literature based on a street-level bureaucracy approach adds a fine-tuning of the meaning of the meeting between the citizen and the system. Lipsky (2010) argues that there is a discrepancy between the political level defining official laws and rules on one hand and the actual implementation of these into everyday practices on the other. By the term "street-level bureaucrats", Lipsky (2010) refers to social workers on the frontline who become the manifestation of the meeting between the citizen and the state. While laws might have one type of meaning inscribed, the daily practices and coping strategies of frontline workers might result in a different set of meanings. While policy analysis does give some indications of how a certain group in society is treated, politics truly emerge as they materialize in day-to-day practices in the welfare state. Zacka (2017) suggests the concepts politics as written versus politics as performed to illustrate the important translations from policy level to what actually happens when the "state meets the street". How the caseworker at street level communicates and interprets a given set of laws is key to how the citizen experiences being met and governed (Lipsky, 1980; Brodkin, 2015; Hupe, 2019; Zacka, 2017).

In a Danish context, especially Caswell et al. (2010) have taken up the street-level bureaucratic framework, gradually contributing with key insights into how policies affect unemployed people lived life. Similarly, Nielsen (2021) analyzes the worth's of unemployed citizens viewed from a social worker's advancing our understanding of the micropolitical interactions in PES. The many bureaucratic rules can hinder the success of delivering service to citizens (Madsen, 2022; Madsen & Mikkelsen, 2022). Building on these important insights about the meeting between the system and the citizen, this contribution distinguishes itself by broadening the analytical scope encompassing not only what happens at PES and how that relates to citizens' lives, but by exploring the social psychology of everyday life of unemployed people.

Working *on* or *with* Unemployed People[2]

While psychological research in general moves one step closer to the subject compared to adjacent disciplines, there is often the risk of losing sight of the institutional setting and power relations. Within psychological research, I identify two overall strands, each representing unemployment in very different ways and hence also affording different ways of managing unemployment, both politically and individually (see also Pultz, 2024).

The first strand is called working on. This track is characterized by focusing on intra-psychological constructs and measuring these based on quantitative scales and closed-ended answer categories—what I term

---

[2] An earlier version of this is (Pultz, 2024).

objectifying unemployment research. An objectifying approach is defined as treating the participants as objects. Objectifying research largely reproduces the categories applied and excels at quantifying relations between various variables, such as personality traits and job search (Boyce et al., 2015), and is predominantly deductive in nature. Applying such a restricted view to the individual foregrounds intra-psychological constructs, such as motivation and self-efficacy (Wanberg et al., 1999) or mental health (Mckee-Ryan et al., 2005). Saks (2006) notes that most studies on unemployment are quantitative, relying on pre-defined scales and leaving little or no room for considering situational surroundings or circumstances as meaningful parts of the unemployment experiences.

Eisenberg and Lazarsfeld (1938) conducted a review regarding the psychological effects of unemployment and identified adverse reactions such as resignation, depression, lowered self-esteem, self-doubt and apathy, and early reports associated unemployment with shame (Bakke, 1933). Since then, the literature has expanded rapidly, and even though the context of unemployment since the 1930s has changed rather dramatically, these themes are still relevant today. Self-blame and shame, for instance, have long existed as themes in the unemployment literature. Psychological costs of unemployment are documented in a substantial number of meta-reviews (Paul & Moser, 2009; McKee-Ryan et al., 2005). The negative impact of unemployment on psychological characteristics such as self-esteem, self-efficacy, and clinical measures of depression, anxiety, and stress and also physical health, suicide, and mortality rates is also convincingly documented (Baum et al., 1986; Ezzy, 1993; Feather, 1990; Goldsmith et al., 1996). To clarify the relationship between unemployment and mental and physical health, research has been conducted in many economically developed countries (Feather, 1992; Janlert & Hammarström, 1992; Paul & Moser, 2009; Vansteenkiste et al., 2005; Warr, 1987). Research in the 1970s and 1980s was particularly focused on the question of whether poorer mental health led to unemployment ('drift' or 'selection' hypothesis) or whether healthy people who are unemployed become less mentally healthy ('social causation'). Studies provide empirical support based on both cross-sectional and longitudinal as well as epidemiological studies. It is certainly the case that mental health problems sometimes predispose individuals to lose their jobs; however, the empirical support for the so-called drift or selection hypothesis is not nearly as strong as the 'social causation hypothesis' (see e.g., the review of Murphy & Athanasou, 1999). These findings raise important and relevant issues when investigating unemployed people.

Recent unemployment research has focused specifically on job search and the predictors and outcomes, and perhaps not surprisingly, people who spend more time on job search tend to find jobs more quickly (Wanberg et al., 2000) and specific personal traits have been associated with better job outcomes such as Extroversion, Openness to experience, and Conscientiousness (Kanfer et al., 2001). As also noted by Wanberg et al. (2012), a close examination of the job search literature characterizes it as being focused on personality traits and biographical variables with only limited attention devoted to the job seekers' situations or other contextual variables (Saks, 2006; Wanberg et al., 2012). I concur with Fryer's characterization of the field when he notes that "in general, recent research has been dominated by decontextualized quantitative cross-sectional and longitudinal survey research" (Fryer in Kieselbach et al., 2006, p. 22). In much unemployment research, unemployment is conceived of as 'deprivation', problematized as a lack or loss of work, and according to Boland and Griffin (2021, p. 31), this is problematic because it tends to reduce, simplify, and overlook important aspects of how the unemployment experience is shaped in society: "Effectively, it theorises un-employment negatively, as a lack or absence of work, and therefore fails to explore or interpret what this experience is in itself. Furthermore, it neglects the ways in which the experience of unemployment is shaped by governmental institutions". In addition, it is problematic because it falls within, rather than questions, the morality that underpins the active turn (Fryer, 2019).

The deprivation theory is also evident in what Rose (1999) terms "psysciences" encompassing knowledge from psychology and adjacent disciplines such as pedagogy, psychiatry etc. that tend to establish a link between unemployment and poorer mental health, either as a result of unemployment or as one of the explanatory factors leading to unemployment, or both: "The above, dominant, approaches position both "unemployment" and "mental health" as "real" and independent and then claim a causal relationship between them which is truthed by means of "psy science", thus legitimating psy as a science capable of demonstrating real causal relationships between real "things."'" (Fryer, 2019, p. 290). In alignment with Fryer's (2019) critique, the aim here is not to identify hidden causal relationships between reified categories, nor to explore unemployment as a pathology (Boland & Griffin, 2015). Rather, the aim is to explore the experience of unemployment as it is lived, felt, and thought in all its complexity and ambiguity, by the unemployed people themselves.

Viewed from a social-psychological perspective, this literature does not sufficiently elaborate upon how unemployed people are influenced by their institutional embeddedness and, equally importantly, how they influence the system. Such focus on the individual only makes possible a very restricted view on the unemployment experience, far removed from how unemployment is lived in messy realities of front-level PES and everyday lives and also it risks hiding the impact of structural conditions and power dynamics. The objectifying element is linked to the choice of method, as Danneris (2018, p. 356) notes:

> The existing research within the field reveals a great skewing, favoring a range of quantitative outcome measure and a linear understanding of causality, which fails to address the dynamic effects of ALMP and rarely takes into account the diversity of the clients being served and the variety of challenges they confront.

While more traditional and mainstream psychological research dominates the unemployment field, a whole range of inspiring studies exist, and, in the following chapters, I will engage with these to further develop the framework.

The other strand within psychological research is called 'working with', which is based on consulting the people who are involved (such as the unemployed people) to understand the complexity of situated experiences. This line of research excels at identifying new and overlooked aspects of the research field and is predominantly inductive or abductive in nature. In an unemployment context, that entails exploring unemployed people's job search, the unemployment system but also the private side and the emotional work involved. It involves exploring how unemployed people navigate the labor market in a broader sense and examining other activities than job searching itself, such as volunteer work, unpaid work, and caretaking. As opposed to working on unemployed people, conducting research with unemployed people involves incorporating a more dynamic and inherently social-psychological way of doing research by exploring the link between the individual and the surrounding society (Asplund, 1983).

Building on or inspired by the iconic Marienthal study conducted by Marie Jahoda and colleagues in a small city in Austria in the 1930s, a range of studies apply sociographic or ethnographic methods in exploring various facets of unemployment (Jahoda et al., 1933; Jahoda, 1982). These studies are conducted with the purpose of understanding the role of the community in shaping a social phenomenon such as unemployment (Fryer, 1986). A given community does not determine how unemployment is experienced; however, looking at the community level rather than the individual opens the field of unemployment toward other explanations and allows for an understanding of the unemployment as well as of subjective experience as much more embedded in local communities (Fryer, 1986; Jahoda et al., 1933).

Exploring the meaning of unemployment from the vantage point of the subject without limiting the analytical scope to the individual level allows the researcher to look 'with' and 'at' the surroundings, the institutions, the communities, the practices of everyday life. That involves exploring what people do and how they think and feel about themselves and their life as unemployed. The object of research is not the individual perspective per se, but rather the conditions under which unemployed people live and conduct themselves. That involves taking the subjective standpoint as a starting point to understand subjectivity and how individuals are embedded in concrete contexts and practices that allow them particular conditions for conducting themselves as they do. These conditions are shaped as much from macropolitical structures to the more proximate and intimate level referred to as meso- and micro-levels of interaction by Bronfenbrenner (1979) (see also Pultz & Hviid, 2018).

Social Psychological Approach

The book takes its departure in the unemployment research literature and offers an alternative social psychological approach as a way of studying young unemployed people with a focus on the link between societal conditions and how they influence, and are influenced by, self-management. In order to produce social psychological knowledge, it is not sufficient to focus on either the isolated individual, or the structural or sociological context. It is indeed the link and entwinement between them that is key here, working with unemployed people, rather than on them.

While bottom-up and participatory approaches have been developed and established within a range of disciplines, theoretical frameworks such as critical psychology and action research have paved the way for exploring subjective perspectives, not for the sole purpose of gaining insight into the phenomenological experience but also to put subjective standpoints in clear relation to historical, structural and cultural relations (Schraube, 2010). Højholt (2005) argues that looking with entails looking at the lifeworld of the subject by exploring the social practices a person is involved in as well as analyzing and exploring across various spheres of everyday life. Similarly, working with unemployed people should not be mistaken as an endeavor to look into the person, as is the case in much individual-focused psychological research. Højholt (2005) argues that, in fact, exploring the subjective perspective is a matter of looking "with" and "from" a person's situated stance. Rather than resulting in an individualization, "looking from" enables a nuanced exploration of the everyday life focusing on the manifold practices people are involved in across their life trajectories. In Højholt's case, looking with and from children's perspectives creates a foundation for identifying dilemmas and social conflicts that allows for an understanding of their complex and historical conditions rather than simply looking on children (Højholt, 2005; Højholt & Kousholt, 2018). While critical psychology and governmentality studies have different epistemological and ontological premises, they share the common aim of relating subjective perspectives to societal and structural conditions guiding the analytical endeavor here as well.

By approaching the social psychological figure through governmentality studies, I wish to improve our understanding of the inherent and implicit entanglement between the individual and society and thus to contribute with a timely and context-sensitive understanding of not only how unemployed people are governed and govern themselves. As I will unfold later, I have a particular interest in the various ways that unemployed people "are not governed quite so much or at that cost" (Foucault & Lotringer, 2007, p. 45) thus exploring the agentic aspects of self-governing. Governmental technologies do not work in a uniform fashion but emerge as effects of social practices put in place both by the people who work at the frontline of the welfare state as well by the ways unemployed people experience and manage the rules and demands they meet in the system.

With inspiration from governmentality studies, I illuminate how certain practices and ways of thinking are established as 'natural' and 'necessary' as well as my capacity to open up a critical space around these. It can be viewed as part of what Fryer and Stambe (2014) term 'critical unemployment studies' as the research ambition here is to challenge the truths or the identities taken for granted, often associated with literature focusing on consequences at an individual level (see also Walters, 1994). Poststructural and sociocultural approaches excel at documenting how a given understanding and practice came into life with the important notion that these understandings and practices could in fact have been in another way. Making visible the contingency of unemployment relates it to the mantra "everything could always be different". That mantra does not only point backward to the past or sideways to the present, but in fact also remind us that unemployment can indeed be something different in the future. Research is part of developing that idea and imagery.

Aims and Contributions

The book has a threefold aim. The first aim is to uncover the specific subjectification mechanisms involved in the unemployment system in a Danish context, renowned for its generous social security system and its success in implementing active labor market measures (ALMPs). The second aim is to finetune our understanding of the subtle and affective pushes toward getting people to conduct themselves in specific ways. Ways that do not only identify appropriate behavior, but extends to loosely defining appropriate ways of feeling, about the situation, about the labor market and not least—how one feels about oneself. The third aim is to synthesize the theoretical and empirical findings into an overall framework that updates social analyses in terms of understanding what kind of subjectification processes are at play. Besides contributing to a fine-grained understanding of what happens in the Danish PES, the book also contributes to discussions about citizenship and morality as it unpacks the relationship between psychology and politics.

The book is firstly, motivated by the lack of critical discussion and research into the unemployment experience during the activation paradigm. Understanding how people experience and manage governmental technologies is crucial to understand how politics intertwine with psychology. Individualizing unemployment by identifying the individual as the sole reason why one becomes unemployed as well as the solution to the unwanted situation of unemployment, sometimes leads to psychological answers of self-blame. Blaming oneself and not feeling deserving or worthy in a society does not necessarily create better jobseekers. Rather, the opposite is true. Secondly, the book is motivated by a problematic tendency in the unemployment literature which tends to objectify unemployed people by asking them to respond to pre-defined scales rather than getting their unfiltered and rich descriptions about how they experience being unemployed—both encompassing being in the unemployment systems as well as being job seekers in the current labor market. The book aims at filling that void—giving voice to unemployed people themselves as a foundation for critically discussing both the intended and the unintended consequences of active labor market measures and moral evaluations of unemployed as either deserving or undeserving in the Danish society.

Analyzing diverse and rich qualitative data based on working with, rather than on unemployed people and applying a social psychological perspective constitutes an important contribution in terms of qualifying our knowledge about how best to govern unemployed people in ways that enable more agency, not less. Developing this knowledge demands that we are attentive toward the various ways we are governed through emotions.

Building knowledge from the vantage point of the subjective experiences allows me to scrutinize and explore governmental technologies and their consequences from an inherently micropolitical level. Looking with and from the unemployed person allows me not only to understand the individual and personal circumstances but also involves looking *out* and *at* various institutional surroundings such as the educational system, the employment system, and the labor market. Building from and viewing society from the perspective of the individual allows for a more comprehensive understanding of the actual workings of various policies.

The different and partly constricting technologies create ambivalences and tensions that must be managed by the individual. An affective economy, meaning an economy not based exclusively on monetary elements but rather intertwined with affects, increasingly put into play, and co-constituting the subjectification process. Being unemployed and receiving money from the state comes with an 'affective price'. The individual has to balance an uncertainty about the future, and, at the same time, they have to cultivate a repertoire of positive feelings and affects by working on motivations, passion, and enthusiasm which are identified as key currencies in the contemporary Danish labor market.

Structure of the Book

Each chapter can be read independently, however the individual chapters also each contribute to an overall comprehensive picture documenting the pickle that unemployed people find themselves in and have to grapple with. Chapter 3 establishes the theoretical stance of the book uniting a governmentality studies approach with a specific social psychological stance placing affects and emotions in the foreground of the governmental practices.

Chapter 4 describes the Danish context and welfare state with a brief historical overview up until the politics in the employment field during the pandemic. Chapters 5–8 constitute the main body of analysis. Chapter 5 zooms in on the self-blaming dynamics linking the activation policies to the psychological dynamics of responsibilization and psychologization. Chapter 6 focuses on the workings of shame and othering dynamics. Chapter 7 explores a subgroup among unemployed people, namely the creative, young people I refer to as unemployed by choice. Chapter 8 focuses on the emotional labor involved in networking among both Danish and American unemployed jobseekers. This comparative analysis allows me to wrestle with some of the specific Danish cultural expressions as well as speculating tentatively about the role of welfare state. Chapter 9 explores what happened during the pandemic when activation policies were suspended, and we had the opportunity to explore the meaning of activation policies through their absence relying on experiences from unemployed people who tried being unemployed before and after this suspension. Chapter 10 synthesizes across the various analytical chapters. It gathers the picture which allows the reader to have a more comprehensive and nuanced understanding of the specific challenge of being unemployed in the Danish welfare state and in an affective economy.

References

Alberti, G., Bessa, I., Hardy, K., Trapmann, V., & Umney, C. (2018). In, against and beyond precarity: Work in insecure times. *Work, Employment and Society, 32*(3), 447–457.

Andersen, N. A. (2020). The constitutive effects of evaluation systems: Lessons from the policymaking process of Danish Active Labour Market Policies. *Evaluation, 26*(3), 257–274.

Asplund, J. (1983). *Tid, rum, individ och kollektiv*. LiberForlag.

Atkinson, W. (2010). The myth of the reflexive worker: Class and work histories in neo-liberal times. *Work, Employment & Society, 24*(3), 413–429.

Baker, T., & Davis, C. (2018). Everyday resistance to workfare: Welfare beneficiary advocacy in Auckland. *New Zealand. Social Policy and Society, 17*(4), 535–546.

Bakke, E. W. (1933). *The unemployed man: A social study*. Nisbet.

Baum, A., Fleming, R., & Reddy, D. M. (1986). Unemployment stress: Loss of control, reactance and learned helplessness. *Social Science & Medicine, 22*(5), 509–516. https://doi.org/10.1016/0277-9536(86)90016

Benda, L. (2019). Understanding active labour market policies: An institutional perspective on intended and unintended consequences.
Bengtsson, T. T., Frederiksen, M., & Larsen, J. E. (2015). *The Danish welfare state, a sociological investigation*. Palgrave Macmillan.
Boland, T. (2015). Seeking a role: Disciplining jobseekers as actors in the labour market. *Work, Employment and Society, 30*(2), 334–351.
Boland, T., & Griffin, R. (2015). The death of unemployment and the birth of job-seeking in welfare policy: Governing a liminal experience. *Irish Journal of Sociology, 23*(2), 29–48. https://doi.org/10.7227/IJS.23.2.3
Boland, T., & Griffin, R. (2021). *The reformation of welfare: The new faith of the labour market*. Policy Press.
Bonoli, G. (2010). The political economy of active labor-market policy. *Politics & Society, 38*(4), 435–457.
Boyce, C. J., Wood, A. M., Daly, M., & Sedikides, C. (2015). Personality change following unemployment. *Journal of Applied Psychology, 100*(4), 991.
Bramming, P., Hansen, B. G., Bojesen, A., & Olesen, K. G. (2012). Imperfect pictures. Snaplogs in performativity research. *Qualitative Research in Organization and Management: An International Journal, 7*, 54–71. https://doi.org/10.1108/17465641211122346
Brinkmann, S., & Eriksen, C. (2005). Selvrealisering, kritiske diskussioner af en grænseløs udviklingskultur (1. udg.). Klim.
Brodkin, E. (2015). Street-level organizations and the "real world" of workfare: Lessons from the US. *Social Work and Society, 13*(1), 1–16.
Brodkin, E. Z., & Marston, G. (2013). *Work and the welfare state, street-level organizations and workfare politics*. Georgetown University Press.
Bronfenbrenner, U. (1979). *The ecology of human development*. Harvard University Press.
Brown, W. (2015). *Undoing the demos, neoliberalism's stealth revolution*. The MIT Press.
Campbell, I., & Burgess, J. (2001). Casual employment in Australia and temporary employment in Europe: Developing a cross-national comparison. *Work, Employment and Society, 15*(1), 171–184.
Campbell, M. L., & Gregor, F. (2004). *Mapping social relations, a primer in doing institutional ethnography*. AltaMira Press.
Caswell, D., Marston, G., & Larsen, J. E. (2010). Unemployed citizen or 'at risk' client? Classification systems and employment services in Denmark and Australia. *Critical Social Policy, 30*(3), 384–404.

Chen, V. T., Pultz, S., & Sharone, O. (in press). Introduction. In V. Chen, S. Pultz, & O. Sharone (Eds.), *Handbook on unemployment and society*. Edward Elgar Publishing.

Czarniawska, B. (2007). *Shadowing: And other techniques for doing fieldwork in modern societies*. Copenhagen Business School Press.

Danneris, S. (2018). Ready to work (yet)? Unemployment trajectories among vulnerable welfare recipients. *Qualitative Social Work, 17*(3), 355–372.

Dean, M. (1995). Governing the unemployed self in an active society. *Economy and Society, 24*(4), 559–583. https://doi.org/10.1080/03085149500000025

Dean, M. (2013). *The signature of power, sovereignty, governmentality and biopolitics*. SAGE.

Deleuze, G., & Guattari, F. (1987). *A thousand plateaus: Capitalism and Schizophrenia* (B. Massumi, Trans.) (1st ed.). University of Minnesota Press.

Du Gay, P., & Morgan, G. (2013). Understanding capitalism: Crises, legitimacy, and change through the prism of the new spirit of capitalism. New spirits of capitalism? *Crises, Justifications, and Dynamics*, 1–40.

Dwyer, P. (2004). Creeping conditionality in the UK: From welfare rights to conditional entitlements? *Canadian Journal of Sociology/Cahiers canadiens de sociologie, 29*(2), 265–287. https://doi.org/10.2307/3654696

Dwyer, P. (2010). *Understanding social citizenship: Themes and perspectives for policy and practice* (2nd ed.). Policy Press.

Dwyer, P. (Ed.). (2019). *Dealing with welfare conditionality: Implementation and effects*. Policy Press.

Eisenberg, P., & Lazarsfeld, P. (1938). The psychological effects of unemployment. *Psychological Bulletin, 35*(6), 358–390. https://doi.org/10.1037/h0063426

Eschweiler, J., & Pultz, S. (2021). Recognition struggles of young Danes under the work first paradigm: A study of restricted and generalised agency. *Human Arenas*. https://doi.org/10.1007/s42087-021-00200-7

Esping-Andersen, G., Gallie, D., Hemerijck, A., & Myles, J. (2002). *Why we need a new welfare state*. Oxford University Press.

Eurofond. (2015). *Sixth European Working Conditions Survey*. https://www.eurofound.europa.eu/surveys/europeanworking-conditions-surveys/sixth-european-working-conditions-survey-2015

Ezzy, D. (1993). Unemployment and mental health: A critical review. *Social Science and Medicine, 37*(1), 41–52.

Feather, N. T. (1990). *The psychological impact of unemployment*. Springer-Verlag.

Feather, N. T. (1992). Expectancy-value theory and unemployment effects. *Journal of Occupational and Organizational Psychology, 65*, 315–330.
Fleming, P. (2017). The human capital hoax: Work, debt and insecurity in the ear of uberization. *Organization Studies, 38*(5), 691–709. https://doi-org.ep.fjernadgang.kb.dk/10.1177/0170840616686129
Flew, T., & Cunningham, S. (2010). Creative industries after the first decade of debate. *The Information Society 26*(2), 113–123. https://doi.org.ep.fjernadgang.kb.dk/10.1080/01972240903562753
Foucault, M. (2008). *The birth of biopolitics, lectures at the College de France, 1978–1979*. Palgrave Macmillan.
Foucault, M. (2010). *The government of self and others, lectures at the Collège de France 1982–1983*. Palgrave Macmillan.
Foucault, M., & Lotringer, S. (2007). *The politics of truth*. Semiotexte.
Fryer, D. (1986). Employment deprivation and personal agency during unemployment: A critical discussion of Jahoda's explanation of the psychological effects of unemployment. *Social Behavior, 1*, 3–23.
Fryer, D. (2019). Applied social psychologies, the neoliberal labour-market subject and critique. In K. C. O'Doherty & D. Hodgetts (Eds.), *The SAGE handbook of applied social psychology* (pp. 278–296). SAGE Publications.
Fryer, D., & Stambe, R. (2014). Neoliberal austerity and unemployment. *Psychologist, 27*(4), 244–248.
Fudge, J., & Owens, O. (2006). Precarious work, women, and the new economy: The challenge to legal norms. In J. Fudge & R. Owens (Eds.), *Precarious work, women, and the new economy: The challenge to legal norms* (pp. 3–28). Hart Publishing.
Gallagher, P., & Griffin, R. (2023). Accuracy in algorithmic profiling of the unemployed—An exploratory review of reporting standards. *Social Policy and Society*, 1–14. https://doi.org/10.1017/S1474746423000428
Garsten, C., & Jacobsson, K. (2004). *Learning to be employable: New agendas on work, responsibility and learning in a globalizing world*. Palgrave Macmillan.
Gleerup, J., Nielsen, B. S., OlsØn, P., & Warring, N. (2018). *Prekarisering – og Akademisk Arbejde*. Frydenlund Academic.
Goldsmith, A. H., Veum, J. R., & Darity, W., Jr. (1996). The psychological impact of unemployment and joblessness. *The Journal of Socio-Economics, 25*(3), 333–358. https://doi.org/10.1016/S1053-5357(96)90009-8
Grover, C., & Stewart, J. (1999). 'Market workfare': Social security, social regulation and competitiveness in the 1990s. *Journal of Social Policy, 28*(1), 73–96.

Hansen, M. P. (2019). *The moral economy of activation: Ideas, politics and policies*. Policy Press.
Hartmann, M., & Honneth, A. (2006). Paradoxes of capitalism. *Constellations, 13*(1), 41–58. https://doi.org/10.1111/j.1351-0487.2006.00439.x
Hewison, K. (2016). Precarious work. In S. Edgell, H. Gottfried, & E. Granter (Eds.), *The SAGE handbook of the sociology of work and employment* (pp. 428–443). Sage.
Højholt, C. (2005). Præsentation af praksisforskning. In *ForældrIsamarbejde: Forsknng i fællesskab* (s. 23–46). Dansk Psykologisk Forlag.
Højholt, C., & Kousholt, D. (2018). Children participating and developing agency in and across various social practices. *International handbook of early childhood education*, 1581–1597.
Hupe, P. (2019). The ground floor of government in context: An agenda for street-level bureaucracy research. In *Research handbook on street-level bureaucracy* (pp. 484–506). Edward Elgar Publishing.
Immervoll, H. (2012). Activation policies in OECD countries: An overview of current approaches (Social Protection and Labor Policy and Technical Notes No. 71903). The World Bank.
Isaksson, K. (2010). Flexible employment and temporary contracts: The employer's perspective. In *Employment contracts, psychological contracts, and employee well-being*. Oxford University Press. ViewGoogle Scholar
Jahoda, M. (1982). *Employment and unemployment*. Cambridge Books.
Jahoda, M., Lazarsfeld, P. F., & Zeisel, H. (1933). *Marienthal*. Al-dine-Atherton.
Janlert, U., & Hammarström, A. (1992). Alcohol consumption among unemployed youths: Results from a prospective study. *British Journal of Addiction, 87*(5), 703–714. https://doi.org/10.1111/j.1360-0443.1992.tb02716.x
Jenson, J. (2011). Redesigning citizenship regimes after neoliberalism: Moving towards social investment. In *Towards a social investment welfare state?* Policy Press. https://doi.org/10.1332/9781847429247.003.0003
Kalleberg, A. L. (2008). The state of work (and workers) in America. *Work and Occupations, 35*(3), 243–261. https://doi.org/10.1177/0730888408320463
Kalleberg, A. L. (2009). Precarious work, insecure workers: Employment relations in transition. *American Sociological Review, 74*(1), 1–22. https://doi.org/10.1177/000312240907400101
Kalleberg, A. L. (2013). *Good jobs, bad jobs* | Russell Sage Foundation. https://www.russellsage.org/publications/good-jobs-bad-jobs

Kamoche, K., Pang, M., & Wong, A. L. Y. (2011). Career development and knowledge appropriation: A genealogical critique. *Organization Studies, 32*(12), 1665–1679. https://doi.org.ep.fjernadgang.kb.dk/10.1177/0170840611421249

Kanfer, R., Wanberg, C. R., & Kantrowitz, T. M. (2001). Job search and employment: A personality–motivational analysis and meta-analytic review. *Journal of Applied psychology, 86*(5), 837.

Kattenbach, R., Schneidhofer, T., Lücke, J., Latzke, M., Loacker, B., Schramm, F., & Mayrhofer, W. (2014). A quarter of a century of job transitions in Germany. *Journal of Vocational Behavior, 84*(1), 49–58. https://doi.org.ep.fjernadgang.kb.dk/10.1016/j.jvb.2013.11.001

Kieselbach, T., Winefield, A. H., Boyd, C., & Anderson, S. (Eds.). (2006). *Unemployment and health: International and interdisciplinary perspectives.* Australian Academic Press.

Knights, D., & Clarke, C. A. (2014). It's a bittersweet symphony, this life: Fragile academic selves and insecure identities at work. *Organization Studies, 35*(3), 335–357. https://doi.org/10.1177/0170840613508396

Lamont, M. (2009). *The dignity of working men: Morality and the boundaries of race, class, and immigration.* Harvard University Press.

Lazzarato, M. (2009). Neoliberalism in action inequality, insecurity and the reconstitution of the social. *Theory, Culture & Society, 26*(6), 109–133. https://doi.org/10.1177/0263276409350283

Lazzarato, M. (2012). *The making of indebted man: An essay on the neoliberal condition.* Semiotext(e).

Lindsay, C., & Daguerre, A. (2009). Active labour market policies and welfare reform: Europe and the US in comparative perspective. *Journal of Social Policy, 38*, 180–182. https://doi.org/10.1017/S0047279408002638

Lipsky, M. (2010). *Street-level bureaucracy: Dilemmas of the individual in public services* (30th anniversary expanded edition.). Russell Sage Foundation.

Madsen, J. K. (2022). *Experiencing administrative burden: Investigating the interplay between state actions, individual resources, and outlook on (un)employment.* Roskilde Universitet. FS & P Ph.D. afhandlinger.

Madsen, J. K., & Mikkelsen, K. S. (2022). How salient administrative burden affects job seekers' locus of control and responsibility attribution: Evidence from a survey experiment. *International Public Management Journal, 25*(2), 241–260. https://doi.org/10.1080/10967494.2021.1951905

McDonald, C., & Marston, G. (2005). Workfare as welfare: Governing unemployment in the advanced liberal state. *Critical Social Policy, 25*(3), 374–401.

McGann, M. (2023). *The marketisation of welfare-to-work in Ireland: Governing activation at the street-level* (p. 191). Policy Press.

Mckee-Ryan, F. M., Song, Z., Wanberg, C. R., & Kinicki, A. J. (2005). Psychological and physical well-being during unemployment: A meta-analytic study. *Journal of Applied Psychology, 90*(1), 53–76. https://doi.org/10.1037/0021-9010.90.1.53

Morel, N., Palier, B., & Palme, J. (2013). The social investment welfare state in Europe, 1990s and 2000s: Economic ideas and social policies.

Murphy, G. C., & Athanasou, J. A. (1999). The effect of unemployment on mental health. *Journal of Occupational and Organizational Psychology, 72*(1), 83–99. https://doi.org/10.1348/096317999166518

Nielsen, M. H. (2021). Money, competences or behaviour? On the many worths of the unemployed. *European Journal of Cultural and Political Sociology (Print), 8*(2), 124–150. https://doi.org/10.1080/23254823.2020.1860785

Patrick, R. (2016). Living with and responding to the 'scrounger' narrative in the UK: Exploring everyday strategies of acceptance, resistance and deflection. *Journal of Poverty and Social Justice, 24*(3), 245–259.

Paul, K. I., & Moser, K. (2009). Unemployment impairs mental health: Meta-analyses. *Journal of Vocational Behavior, 74*(3), 264–282. https://doi.org/10.1016/j.jvb.2009.01.001

Peterie, M., Ramia, G., Marston, G., & Patulny, R. (2019). Emotional compliance and emotion as resistance: Shame and anger among the long-term unemployed. *Work, Employment and Society, 33*(5), 794–811.

Pultz, S. (2016). Governing homo economicus: Risk management among young unemployed people in the Danish welfare state. *Health, Risk & Society, 18*(3–4), 168–187.

Pultz, S. (2017). *It's not you, it's me: Governing the unemployed self in the Danish welfare state*. Copenhagen University.

Pultz, S. (2018). Shame and passion: The affective governing of young unemployed people. *Theory & Psychology, 28*(3), 358–381. https://doi.org/10.1177/0959354318759608

Pultz, S. (2024). Working with, not on unemployed people: How to explore subjective unemployment experiences in the affective economy. In *The Routledge international handbook of innovative qualitative psychological research* (pp. 249–260, 1st ed.). Routledge. https://doi.org/10.4324/9781003132721-24

Pultz, S. (in press). Profiling and subjectification. In R. Griffin, M. P. Hansen, & J. Lescke (Eds.), *Digital PES in action*. Polity Press.

Pultz, S., & Dupret, K. (2023). Emotional status and emotional labour: Exploring the emotional labour among casualised and tenured knowledge workers. *Culture and Organization, Latest articles.* https://doi.org/10.1080/14759551.2023.2258433

Pultz, S., & Hviid, P. (2018). Imagining a better future: Young unemployed people and the polyphonic choir. *Culture & Psychology, 24*(1), 3–25. https://doi.org/10.1177/1354067X16660853

Rosa, H. (2013). *Social acceleration: A new theory of modernity.* Columbia University Press.

Rose, N. S. (1999). *Powers of freedom, reframing political thought.* Cambridge University Press.

Rubery, J. (2015). Change at work: Feminisation, flexibilisation, fragmentation and financialisation. *Employee Relations, 37*(6), 633–644.

Saks, A. M. (2006). Multiple predictors and criteria of job search success. *Journal of Vocational Behavior, 68*(3), 400–415. https://doi.org/10.1016/j.jvb.2005.10.001

Scarpetta, S., Sonnet, A., & Manfredi, T. (2010). *Rising youth unemployment during the crisis: How to prevent negative long-term consequences on a generation?* OECD Social, Employment and Migration Working Papers, No. 106, OECD Publishing. https://doi.org/10.1787/5kmh79zb2mmv-en

Schraube, E. (2010). Første-persons perspektivet i psykologisk teori og forskningspraksis. *Nordiske Udkast, 38*(1/2), 93–104.

Sharone, O. (2013a). *Flawed system/flawed self: Job searching and unemployment experiences.* University of Chicago Press.

Sharone, O. (2013b). Why do unemployed Americans blame themselves while Israelis blame the system? *Social Forces, 91*(4), 1429–1450. https://doi.org/10.1093/sf/sot050

Standing, G. (2011). *The precariat, the new dangerous class.* Bloomsbury Academic.

Standing, G. (2014). Understanding the precariat through labour and work. *Development and Change, 45*(5), 963–980. https://doi.org/10.1111/dech.12120

Uysal, S. D., & Pohlmeier, W. (2011). Unemployment duration and personality. *Journal of Economic Psychology, 32*(6), 980–992.

Vallas, S. (2015). Accounting for precarity: Recent studies of labour market uncertainty. *Contemporary Sociology: A Journal of Reviews, 44*(4), 463–469. https://doi.org/10.1177/0094306115588484a

Vallas, S., & Cummins, E. R. (2014). Re-configuring worker subjectivity: The shifting meaning of work in an age of precarity. http://citation.allacademic.com/meta/p_mla_apa_research_citation/7/2/5/3/5/p725357_index.html

Vallas, S., & Prener, C. (2012). Dualism, job polarization, and the social construction of precarious work. *Work and Occupations, 39*(4), 331–353. https://doi.org/10.1177/0730888412456027

Vallas, S. P., & Kleinman, D. L. (2008). Contradiction, convergence and the knowledge economy: The confluence of academic and commercial biotechnology. *Socio-Economic Review, 6*(2), 283–311. https://doi.org.ep.fjernadgang.kb.dk/10.1093/ser/mwl035

Van Parys, L., & Struyven, L. (2018). Interaction styles of street-level workers and motivation of clients: A new instrument to assess discretion-as-used in the case of activation of jobseekers. *Public Management Review, 20*(11), 1702–1721.

Vansteenkiste, V., Lens, W., De Witte, H., & Feather, N. T. (2005). Understanding unemployed people's job search behaviour, unemployment experience and well-being: A comparison of expectancy-value theory and self-determination theory. *British Journal of Social Psychology, 44*(2), 269–287. https://doi.org/10.1348/014466604X17641

Vives, A., Vanroelen, C., Amable, M., Ferrer, M., Moncada, S., Llorens, C., Muntaner, C., Benavides, F., & Benach, J. (2011). Employment precariousness in Spain: Prevalence, social distribution, and population-attributable risk percent of poor mental health. *International Journal of Health Services, 41*(4), 625–646. https://doi.org.ep.fjernadgang.kb.dk/10.2190/HS.41.4.b

Waldmann, T., Staiger, T., Oexle, N., & Rüsch, N. (2019). Mental health literacy and help-seeking among unemployed people with mental health problems. *Journal of Mental Health, 29*(3), 270–276.

Walters, W. (1994). The discovery of 'unemployment': New forms for the government of poverty. *Economy and Society, 23*(3), 265–290. https://doi.org/10.1080/03085149400000006

Walters, W. (1997). The 'active society': New designs for social policy. *Policy and Politics, 25*(3), 221–234.

Wanberg, C. R., Kanfer, R., & Rotundo, M. (1999). Unemployed individuals: Motives, job-search competencies, and job-search constraints as predictors of job seeking and reemployment. *Journal of Applied Psychology, 84*(6), 897–910. https://doi.org/10.1037/0021-9010.84.6.897

Wanberg, C. R., Kanfer, R., & Banas, J. T. (2000). Predictors and outcomes of networking intensity among unemployed job seekers. *Journal of Applied Psychology, 85*(4), 491–503. https://doi.org/10.1037/0021-9010.85.4.491

Wanberg, C., Basbug, G., Van Hooft, E. A. J., & Samtani, A. (2012). Navigating the black hole: Explicating layers of job search context and adaptational responses. *Personnel Psychology, 65*(4), 887–926. https://doi.org/10.1111/peps.12005

Ward, J., & Greene, A. (2018). Too much of a good thing? The emotional challenges of managing affectively committed volunteers. *Nonprofit and Voluntary Sector Quarterly, 47*(6), 1155–1177.

Warr, P. (1987). *Work, unemployment, and mental health.* Clarendon Press.

Weishaupt, J. T. (2011). From the manpower revolution to the activation paradigm: Explaining institutional continuity and change in an integrating Europe.

Whelan, J. (2021). *Welfare, deservingness and the logic of poverty: Who deserves?* Cambridge Scholars Publishing.

Wiertz, D., & Chaeyoon, L. (in press). The impact of joblessness on civic engagement: Longitudinal evidence from the United States. In O. Sharone, V. Chen, & S. Pultz (Eds.), *Handbook of unemployment and society.* Edward Elgar Publishing.

Wickramasinghe, V., & Chandrasekara, R. (2011). Differential effects of employment status on work-related outcomes. A pilot study of permanent and casual workers in Sri Lanka. *Employee Relations, 33*(5), 532–550. https://doi.org.ep.fjernadgang.kb.dk/10.1108/01425451111153899

Zacka. (2017). *When the state meets the street: Public service and moral agency.* Harvard University Press. https://doi.org/10.4159/9780674981423

2

Governing Unemployed People Through Technologies of Power and Those of the Self

The Social Psychological Figure and Governmentality Studies

As one of my interview participants, John, expressed regarding being unemployed, "it is as if the state has moved inside my living room". Apparently, John experiences being unemployed as an intrusion of the state into his private life. Even though he and others recently received student grants while studying at university and thus have been economically dependent on the welfare state before, being supported financially as unemployed is somehow different. Now his livelihood is conditional on his ability to live up to the demands and requirements of PES. This experience is widely reflected in the empirical material and thus unemployment seems to be a fruitful field to investigate the focal point in social psychology; namely, the link between the individual and the society.

By exploring the fundamental social psychological question through governmentality, we see the individual and society as inherently intertwined, something also highlighted by many social psychologists (Andersen & Mørch, 2000, 2005; Asplund, 1983; Giddens, 1992). This characterization is, similarly, the key focus of attention in Foucault's later work focusing on what he terms the 'becoming of subjects' in a matrix between technologies of power and those of the self taken up in governmentality studies (Foucault et al., 1988). The link between social psychology and governmentality studies is not new but rather widespread internationally (Blackman, 2013; Greco & Stenner, 2013) as well as in a Danish context (Staunæs, 2011; Staunæs & Pors, 2015; Staunæs & Bjerg, 2014; Staunæs & Søndergaard, 2006, 2008; Søndergaard, 2006) and I contribute to these endeavors. Asplund (1983) defines the main fundamental social psychological issue as the relationship between the individual and society, and he characterizes this as a 'problematic' relationship (p. 53). By this, Asplund implies that the individual does not just adopt to the norms in society complacently, but also transforms them by their active use and actions. This understanding is in contrast to, for instance, socialization theories such as Parsons (1956). According to Andersen and Mørch (2000), this problematic relationship raises the issue of how the individual is socially integrated in society in a dialectic relationship in which the individual, through participation, influences, and changes society.

While social integration refers to many different phenomena such as societal cohesion, belonging to a community or simply having a social network (Kristensen et al., 2007), here it denotes that the individual partakes and participates in society and, in so doing, alters society. This fits nicely with my ambition to avoid simplifications, either romanticizing the resisting subject or denouncing the docile ditto.

Elias (1997) point out that emotions play an important role in these social integrative processes in the sense that an individual who feels ashamed tends to conform to prescribed codes of behavior. Consequently, shame serves a socializing or disciplining function. Feeling ashamed of being unemployed is linked to social integrative processes in which supporting oneself financially is deemed a crucial value in society. Emotions are important sites of government when investigating social integrative processes. In social psychological literature, traditional social institutions such as school, family, and work, have been identified as important social integrative contexts (Andersen & Mørch, 2000). Not having a job is viewed not as an absence of social integration—as a vacuum of managing the relationship between the individual and society; interestingly, unemployment becomes a social integrative context in which citizens are more intimately aware of their dependence on the state and thus their embeddedness in society. Unemployment does not only imply an absence of a job; it is a highly regulated space serving particular economic and societal interests. This governed space impacts citizens' ways of relating to themselves tremendously.

Governmentality Studies as the Theoretical Backdrop

Governmentality studies were introduced by Michel Foucault and further developed by scholars such as Peter Miller, Nikolas Rose, and Mitchell Dean (Burchell et al., 2003; Dean, 2007, 2010; Miller & Rose, 1995; Rose & Miller, 2010; Rose et al., 2006; Rose, 1996, 1999). It offers an analytical approach that lends itself well to shedding light on self-government and its relation to social institutions and regulations of human conduct toward ends, such as the goal of full employment in the 'competition state' (Pedersen, 2011). In a wider sense, governmentality studies address the question of how we think about the nature and practice of governing in various fields. This means identifying how the space of government is orchestrated. We should try to understand governmental practices as particular ways of conceptualizing a problem that call for specific solutions. Solutions are formulated in relation to these as specific interventions reflected in specific programs (Lemke, 2001). For instance, activation programs aimed at unemployed people are tied to an understanding of unemployment as a lack of activity or even sometimes with an understanding of unemployed people as lazy and undeserving (Dwyer, 2004; Whelan, 2021). The underlying assumption in a governmentality studies approach as well as other socio-cultural approaches is that subjects and subjectivities are constituted in social processes through heterogeneous systems of discourse, institutionalized practices, and semiotic systems of norms, standards, and ideals such as in Butler's queer theory (1997, 2007); Goffman's symbolic interactionism (1968); in Latour's Actor-Network Theory (2005) and Valsiner's cultural life course theory (1997).

According to Dean (2010), the main questions in Foucault's analyses are: What is identity and what does it have to do with politics? What are the potential unemployed identities and how are they specifically orchestrated and enacted in the unemployment system as well as by the unemployed people themselves? As such, the approach shares an ambition to deconstruct many diverse poststructuralist endeavors (Brown & Stenner, 2009; Clough, 2008; Deleuze & Guattari, 1987; Latour, 2005). Foucault and governmentality studies influenced many and diverse disciplines such as political science, sociology, geography, organizational studies and psychology and across a range of empirical fields such as social welfare (see e.g., Dean, 1995; Cruikshank, 1994, 1999; McDonald & Marston, 2005; Marston & McDonald, 2006), education (Ball, 1990; Juelskjær et al., 2013), social work (Bank, 2016; Mik-Meyer & Villadsen, 2013; Thomas & Davies, 2005) and crime (Garland, 1999). Governmentality studies constitute an inherently interdisciplinary approach as the method involves a questioning of the demarcations between various disciplines and offers a way of thinking and analyzing that cuts across these demarcations. This interdisciplinary feature is pivotal in the context of this book, which moves across psychological, social psychological, sociological, pedagogical, organizational, and political disciplines.

In short, this analytic has been applied and further developed by different people in ways that are not entirely consistent (Mckee, 2009). Rutherford (2007, p. 292) characterizes many governmentality studies as "decidedly 'un-Foucauldian'" and supporting this claim, McKee (2009) writes: "as such, they [the critiques] would be more accurately directed at secondary commentators who have interpreted and applied Foucault's work, rather than his original analysis, which does provide the conceptual apparatus to engage with these issues" (p. 4). Inspired by this criticism, I principally take Foucault's own statements as a starting point for my analysis.

Foucault used governmentality to denote a diffuse and heterogeneous form of power that, in various ways, dispositions a possible action field by promoting and restraining specific behaviors and understandings rather than determining them (Foucault, 2008; Foucault et al., 2007). When Foucault uses governmentality in relation to neoliberalism or advanced liberal states, the term refers to the multiple ways in which societies are organized with decentered power, where citizens play an active part in their self-government (Foucault, 2008). This active self-governing is also inherent in Foucault's definition of governmentality which is also widely quoted in the expression 'conduct of conduct' characterizing governmentality as a diffuse power that works 'at a distance' (Burchell et al., 2003) crucial in the configuration of the active job seeker. Foucault (1995) makes visible the contingency and historical specificity of a particular knowledge production and its effect on how people are offered ways of understanding and relating to themselves. For instance, many interview participants say that they experience a pressure from within to work on their ability to be more outgoing to improve their networking skills. They are not sanctioned if they fail to become more extroverted, however, many feel inclined to engage in this type of self-work and thus they play an active part in the governing through self-management. They experience the need to work on themselves, and I explore the various ways they are encouraged or affectively pushed toward such self-management. The current power works as much through shaping desires and normative ideals as much as it works by prohibiting behavior through discipline.

Technologies of Power and of the Self

In order to address the problematic relationship between the individual and society, Foucault offers useful concepts of technologies of power and those of the self to uncover the key dynamics in governmentality. For analytical purposes, I separate the units in the research question, differentiating between technologies of power on the one hand, and technologies of the self on the other, even though my approach implies that they are inherently intertwined. He defines technologies of power being able to "determine the conduct of individuals and submit them to certain ends or domination, an objectivizing of the subject" (Foucault, 1988, p. 18). Technologies of the self are defined as various activities and "operations on their own bodies and souls, thoughts, conducts, and ways of being that seek to reach a state of happiness, purity, wisdom, perfection, or immortality" (Foucault et al., 1988, p. 18). Here, the link between the management of society toward desired ends, such as full employment, is intertwined with self-management. Foucault elaborates and further defines governmentality as, "the contact point where individuals are driven by others is tied to the way they conduct themselves" (Foucault, 1993, pp. 25–26) and thus he highlights the strategic role played by the relationship one has to oneself (Lorenzini, 2016). The installation of the individual choice calls upon a self-governing actor and this creates a space for the subject to act upon him- or herself. Being offered various psychological ways of understanding unemployment, for instance as a lack of motivation, promotes ways of relating to oneself and supports a certain cultivation of motivation as well as improving one's ability to show this to others.

According to Raffnsoe et al. (2014), governmentality denotes a new configuration of a heterogeneous power assemblage in addition to law and discipline, and thus it does not substitute law and discipline but rather there has been a "shift of emphasis" (Foucault et al., 2007, p. 363). Thus, discipline has not vanished as is also evident in the control and surveillance systems in the unemployment system, but governmentality overlays discipline and the two coalesce. To approach the content of governmentality and the analytical tools, I will briefly consider this very compact and frequently quoted passage, in which Foucault refers to three main characteristics of governmentality as a fundamental alliance between power, identity, and truth (2007, p. 108):

> By 'governmentality' I understand the institutions, procedures, analyses, and reflections, calculations and tactics that allow the exercise of this very specific, albeit very complex, power that has population as its target, political economy as its major form of knowledge, and apparatus of security as its essential technical instrument.

Three important features of governmentality are highlighted here and below I show the features one can distinguish in the governing of the unemployed:

1. governmentality denotes a power that governs the entire population.
2. governmentality rests on economy as the primary power/knowledge.
3. governmentality works through a heterogeneous apparatus of security.

The first notion is linked to notions of bio-politics; that is, how the entire population is the object of governing rather than a particular segment, such as is the case with disciplining criminals, the pupils and the mentally ill (Foucault, 1995). Governing the unemployed is not secluded but should rather be viewed as a disciplining of the entire workforce, as also indicated by interview participant Michael who states, "We don't do it to change the criminals but so that we can all say, I do not want to go to prison".

The second notion is related to the workings of neoliberalism and the idea that unemployed people are governed as homo economicus who should have incentives to find a job either based on incentives in the shape of the 'carrot or the stick'. That implies investing in human capital and optimizing labor market chances through such social investment.

Last, the third notion is elsewhere referred to as the 'dispositive of security' (Foucault et al., 2007) which is characterized by a focus on calculations of risk and probabilities and on mitigating against various insecurities, such as unemployment. This technology is closely linked to the use of profiling systems that will be elaborated on later. By psychologizing unemployment risk management shifts from structural conditions toward the individual, increasingly making unemployment the individual's headache.

The Challenges of Governmentality Studies

Despite Foucault's own rigorous and meticulous empirical work, particularly in reading historical documents, governmentality studies have been criticized for losing empirical sensitivity by primarily focusing on the 'blueprints of governing' meaning the ideas and political rationality underpinning governing that sometimes diverge—quite dramatically— from the messy and muddy reality of everyday life. But how is it possible to analyze this messy reality equipped with analytics from governmentality studies? To answer my research question and elucidate the dynamics of self-management and how this is orchestrated institutionally from a social psychological perspective, it would not suffice to analyze the 'blueprints of governing'. To avoid losing sight of how unemployed people are actually governed and how they experience it from their point of view, I have thus chosen an eclectic range of methods consisting of interviews, field observations and video diaries combined with document analysis. In so doing, I depart from the more traditional genealogical methods usually conducted. In that sense, I conduct an analysis that more closely resembles what Stenson (2005, 2008) termed a 'realist governmentality approach' by which he stresses the importance of investigating actual practices. According to McKee (2009), this line of research meets some of the identified challenges and limitations of traditional governmentality studies in accordance with the research ambition of this book which is, in fact, to develop an empirical sensitivity to outline the various ways in which unemployed people are governed and govern themselves. Similarly, Mackenzie and McKinlay (2021) note that a limitation of Foucauldian readings of governmentality is often "abstract in nature" and lacks "reference to individual or collective agents". Mackenzie and McKinlay (2021, p. 1857) note that people do not 'live with' an enterprise economy; rather, "our analysis highlights how people 'live through' and struggle inwardly with neoliberal categories that attempt to define, animate and subsume them as 'entrepreneurs of the self'". It is exactly the lived experiences of the agents I am interested in uncovering in a way that balances between the poles of overestimating docility or resistance but in fact pertains to the messy middle.

Exploring governmental practices from the vantage point of unemployed people also involves what Haraway calls 're-tooling' described here:

> you can turn up the volume on some categories, and down on others. They are foregrounding and backgrounding operations. You can make categories interrupt each other. All these operations are based on skills, on technologies, on material technologies. They are not merely ideas, but thinking technologies that have materiality and effectivity. These are ways of stabilizing meanings in some forms rather than others, and stabilizing meanings is a very material practice (…) I do not want to throw away the category formation skills I have inherited, but I do want to see how we can do a little re-tooling.

Thinking categories are, in a sense, 'keys' that one can use to unlock the empirical material and the specific choice of categories as well as the weight they are given in the analysis co-constituting the specific knowledge production (Haraway, 1988, 2000; Søndergaard, 2002; Staunæs & Bjerg, 2014). As my research errand is social psychological, rather than sociological, I, so to say, "turn up the volume" of the concepts allowing me to get closer to the micro-political level. Certainly, this movement implies less sensitivity in other domains. Making a genealogy relying on historical documents describing changes in policies governing unemployed people in Denmark would probably have led to some of the same insights. However, it would also probably have contributed with new knowledge that I unquestionably silence or obscure.

As my research endeavor entails investigating the link between the technologies of power and those of the self, I supplement the traditionally used methods in governmentality studies by enlarging the micro-political level. As mentioned, Foucault's thinking has predominantly been used in historical and genealogical readings of documents, policies, and blueprints of governing (Clarke, 2005, 2008). Hacking (2004) explores the problem that Foucault does not fully cover, namely the micro-genetic processes of analysis, and he suggests integrating Foucault and his abstract focus on systems of thoughts with Goffman's concrete methods focusing exclusively on the micro-political social interaction in everyday life. While recognizing Hacking's fruitful contribution, its limitation is in failing to fully incorporate Foucault's later work that does get closer to the subject through such concepts as technologies of the self and care of the self which are the focal points in this book (Foucault, 2010; Foucault et al., 1988).

Indeed, Foucault studied first-hand perspectives, reading the letters and diaries of Ancient Greek and Roman philosophers, in order to uncover how people related to and conducted themselves (Besley, 2005; Foucault et al., 1988). My empirical material contains detailed descriptions of first-hand experiences and I argue that there is no need to regard subjective experiences as off-limits as do some Foucauldian traditions (Triantafillou & Nielsen, 2001). In governmentality studies, the personal experience of lived experience is often neglected, and consequently the transformative capacity of subjects is frequently overlooked (Brodkin &

Marston, 2013). Precisely this transformative capacity is crucial when addressing the social psychological figure based on an assumption of an active and agentic subject, reflected for instance, in the practice of those I call unemployed by choice. Attending to agentic endeavors as more subtle than acts of resistance involves looking at behaviors such as hesitations, reluctance, questioning etc. demands cultivating a certain sensitivity in the researcher.

Subjectification and the Art of Not Being Governed Quite So Much

Related to the notion above, the lack of empirical sensitivity, Foucault and specific receptions of his work have been criticized as overly deterministic. The deterministic reception probably has to do with the massive influence of Foucault's disciplinary model even though he himself tried to surpass this by his exploration of (neoliberal) governmentality. As pointed out, Foucault has been used differently by different scholars; however, there has been a preponderance of studies focusing on discipline, largely inspired by the seminal work 'Discipline and Punish' (Foucault, 1995) despite the fact that Foucault was only rarely occupied with control in contemporary societies (Lopdrup-Hjorth et al., 2013). Thomas and Davies (2005) rightfully criticize a bias toward subjugation in the reception of Foucault's dynamic concept of subjectification: "Foucauldian-influenced studies have been criticized for being too deterministic and totalizing, focusing on subjectification as subjection" (p. 686). There certainly are exceptions with scholars focusing on agency not merely conceived of as oppositional resistance (Katarzyna & McKernan, 2011), but also as an interest in people's active self-fashioning (Barratt, 2008, p. 516). This book builds on this strand of research emphasizing the active role of subjects unfolded below.

Subjectification constitutes a viable way of approaching the micro-level of analyses often taken up in, for instance, pedagogical psychology (Davies, 2006), in feminist literature (Butler, 2007; Søndergaard, 2006) and organizational psychology (Staunæs, 2011). I use these scholarly

2 Governing Unemployed People Through Technologies… 41

endeavors as a departure point in developing my approach and, in alignment with them, I stress the subject's agentic capacity. Turning to Foucault himself, he, in fact, defines subjectification as a process by which free subjects are constituted in the link between technologies of power and technologies of the self; that is, how the subject relates to, appropriates, and transforms these (Foucault, 1982, p. 790). One of the key features of Foucault's concept of subjectification is the double-nature described in the often cited quote here:

> this form of power applies itself to immediate everyday life which categorizes the individual; marks him (sic) by his own individuality, attaches him to his own identity, imposes a law of truth on him which he must recognize and which others have to recognize in him. It is a form of power which makes individuals subjects. There are two meanings of the word subject: subject to someone by control and dependence; and tied to his own identity by a conscience or self-knowledge. Both meanings suggest a form of power which subjugates and makes subject to. (Foucault, 1982, p. 781)

I highlight two key aspects from the quote. The first is that knowledge and discursive resources pose certain constraints and possibilities for the production of subjectivity in a specific context. These enabling and constricting conditions frame the becoming of the subject that must be culturally recognizable and understandable in a particular society (Butler, 2007; Søndergaard, 2006). Secondly, power is not repressive but indeed a productive force constituting subjects. Foucault (1978) characterizes resistance or counter-conduct as immanent in relation to power, noting, "where there is power, there is resistance, and yet, or rather consequently, this resistance is never in a position of exteriority in relation to power" (Foucault, 1978, p. 95). This notion is not to be mistaken for resistance as a refusal of technologies of power offered, but more as an understanding of subjects as being free to experiment and to twist and turn them through engaging with them. The implication is that subjects, in fact, mold, shape, change or reproduce existing technologies of power by appropriating these in terms of various technologies of the self, which Hacking termed looping effects (Hacking, 1996). The active fashioning of stretching, expanding, or circumventing the identity of unemployed people is especially visible in my empirical material as a minority of the people I interviewed refused to identify themselves as unemployed and, in various ways, played with a self-understanding relying more on the freelancer or the entrepreneur also described in Foucault's later works (Foucault, 2008). As he notes in the following, resistance is not an oppositional reaction to a repressive power but rather, "the art of not being governed, or better, the art of not being governed like that and at that cost' (…) the art of not being governed quite so much" (Foucault & Lotringer, 2007, p. 45). To fully address the messy governing of self-management as well as the practice of the freelancers, I needed to turn to analytical categories addressing the specificities of the subjectification processes, as the governing of unemployed people through emotional and affective capacities such as self-blame and shame turned out to be of key relevance in the book.

Neoliberal Subjectification

Linked to the definition of governmentality stating that social phenomena are increasingly conceptualized in economic discourses, economic rationality becomes the principal source of legitimizing and justifying governmental technologies. This rationality is generalized to all aspects of life: not only the political domain, but social relations and individual behavior are also evaluated in terms of economic efficiency (Barry et al., 1996). Foucault identified a new configuration as 'homo economicus' who is characterized by the ability to maximize and optimize his or her human capital (Foucault, 2008) echoing the work of Stuart Mill (1874) who, already by 1836, had introduced the concept. According to Foucault, neoliberal government intervenes in the domain of the social by converting the latter into a function of the enterprise. It intervenes to promote multiplicity, differentiation, and competition of enterprises. For neoliberal social policy, the aim is to transform society into 'enterprise society' and to constitute the worker as a "kind of enterprise" (Lazzarato, 2009, p. 120). Thus, the worker is transformed into human capital in charge of his/her effort to manage this in accordance to the logic of the market (Weiskopf & Munro, 2012). The power assemblage incites and constrains everyone to become an entrepreneur of him/herself, to become 'human capital' (Burchell et al., 2003; Foucault, 2008). Human capital includes the preconditions of being employable, physically, and mentally well, and being fit for social and economic performance. This relies on certain personal traits, attitudes, and social skills. In addition to these characteristics, Foucault, and others after him elaborate on the specific features of neoliberal subjectivity (Anderson, 2012; Binkley, 2011; Brown, 2015; Read, 2009). In neoliberal states, government is based on competition, and it must ensure that the population is in a state of 'equal inequality' as Foucault expressed it, because this fosters and perpetuates a mobilizing uncertainty (Foucault, 2008). Policies that support this equal inequality mobilize insecurity, instability, uncertainty and, in many fields, both economic and also existential precariousness. Lazzarato (2009, p. 120) illustratively calls it micro-politics of little fears with inspiration from Deleuze & Guattari's (1987, p. 216) concept a 'permanent molecular insecurity'. Individualizing social policies do not aim to ensure individuals against risk but instead make up an economic space and encourage people to individually take upon themselves the responsibility to confront and manage personal risks. For unemployed people, the micro-political dynamics of 'little fears' are evident in the accounts as many of the interview participants fear sanctions faced with the suspicion of fraud and they also fear never finding a job. The 'little fears' associated with the DNA of the precariat are evident among the freelancers in the study, as most of them fear getting caught and thus losing their livelihood and they fear having to pay pack money to the welfare state.

Affective Subjectification

To fully integrate the specific ways that governmental technologies work through emotions, I needed to turn to perspectives that have elaborated on these affective issues. In addition to a deterministic reception, the reception of Foucault in the social sciences has been dominated by a linguistic interpretation (D'Aoust, 2014; Foucault et al., 2013; Raffnsøe et al., 2016). D'Aoust (2014) notes that there has been a tendency to overvalue the role of reason and rationality at the expense of emotions and affects. Recent governmentality studies have demonstrated that there is a need for affective vocabularies to sufficiently conceptualize workings of contemporary powers. The idea to integrate this dimension in the book is primarily empirically motivated to make sense of the data but it is also theoretically justified. Greco and Stenner (2013, p. 12) pinpoint the gap in the governmentality literature considering affective capacities:

> But it also reflects a typical assumption, in the literature on governmentality, that the subject at the centre of neoliberal governmentality is a subject defined by its capacities for calculation, rationality, and autonomy. Affectivity, emotion and desire do not feature in this characterization.

Greco and Stenner (2013) have begun filling this gap as have affect scholars (Anderson, 2012; Juelskjær & Staunæs, 2016; Juelskjær et al., 2013) and I seek here to contribute to that development. Even though Foucault does not explicitly develop an affective vocabulary, I argue that inherent in his writings, there is indeed an attention toward physical bodies and materiality, especially in his meticulous descriptions of how spatio-material arrangements affect the body in Discipline & Punish (Foucault, 1995). Inherent in the notion of power as fundamentally productive, there are also offshoots of material effects as power shapes particular subjectivities. These are not limited to being linguistic in nature, as implied in the following quote, "it [power] doesn't only weigh on us a force that says no; it also traverses and produces things, it induces pleasure, forms knowledge, produces discourse" (Foucault, 2003, p. 307). I argue that the affective level is implicitly present in Foucault's own writing; however, in some receptions, this aspect disappears, and Foucault never fully develops this analytical scope.

Rose (1996) contributes similar offshoots, especially in his work on further developing Foucault's thoughts on subjectivity in neoliberal states. Here, Rose conceptualizes neoliberal governmentality as being particularly prescriptive for people to conduct themselves as enterprising selves and he does so in energetic and affective terms: "to conduct themselves with boldness, and vigour, to calculate for their own advantage, to drive themselves hard in the pursuit of goals' (…) while displaying energy, initiative, ambition, calculation, and personal responsibility" (Rose, 1996, p. 154). This affective perspective remains in the periphery of Rose's thinking and, to qualify the governmentality studies approach in relation to dynamics involving affective and emotion capacities, many scholars have turned toward affect researchers (Brown & Stenner, 2009; Spinoza & Elwes, 1677; Deleuze & Guattari, 1987; Deleuze, 1992).

The 'affective turn' is broadly described as a pluralist movement drawing attention to affectivity understood as emotional and affective circulation described as energies, intensities, and potentialities and thus fundamentally involve a different set of research objects (Brown & Stenner, 2009; Clough, 2008; D'Aoust, 2014; Leys, 2011; Massumi, 2002; Staunæs & Juelskjær, 2016; Staunæs & Kofoed, 2015). Deleuze (1994, p. 136) helps explain this shift in terms of moving toward sensing encounters: "this something is not an object of recognition but of fundamental encounter. It may be grasped in a range of affective tones ... In whichevertone, its primary characteristic is that it can only be sensed."

The complex phenomena of emotions, feelings, and affects share the common feature that they are not reducible to biology, or to language (Cromby, 2012, 2015; Massumi, 2002). The affective turn (also) tries to overcome the classical dualism between mind and body by drawing attention to issues of matter, materiality and a pre-conceivable layer of meaning (Clough, 2008). Staunæs (2011) notes that the affective turn should be seen as adding to the linguistic turn rather than replacing or opposing it. Sedgwick's work (such as Sedgwick, 2003) especially paves the way for such integration between language and affects through the concept of performativity. Affect is an elusive concept due to the DNA of the concept as processual, in a state of becoming and hence notoriously difficult to pinpoint (Seigworth & Gregg, 2010). Affect are conceived on the basic premise of human beings' capacity "to affect and be affected" and thus the relational character of social life is at the center of analysis (Massumi, 2002).

Inspired by Brøgger and Staunæs (2016), I understand the concept of affect as a broader term encompassing mood, atmospheres, tensions, and sensations. However, I also agree with Burkitt (2014, p. 12), who ultimately defines affect as a "material process created by body-selves acting in relational concert". Consequently, Burkitt refrains from categorically defining affects as existing outside the conscious realm. Wetherell (2012) stresses that we need to specify how we define affects as "everything is not always circulated" (p. 142) and in acknowledgment of that point, I view affective circulation as embedded in situated practices and linked with subjects' embodied capacity to affect and be affected (Wetherell, 2012, 2015). Oftentimes the term affect is used to describe a prelinguistic layer, emotion as the social display and feeling as the inner experience of emotional qualities. Here, I use the terms more interchangeably, referring to affects and emotions both when addressing incidences of indeterminate and more determinate emotional qualities. The term feeling is used to describe people's inner experiences.

Brøgger and Staunæs (2016) also note "it is not simply a question of having feelings and affects but of exchanging, saving, spending, cultivating and capitalizing affects". In an organizational context, self-management has been analyzed from an affective perspective by Staunæs and Bjerg (2014) and they write 'affects and affectivity are not simply by-products or something to be overcome, but the core matter to be managed by and through' (Staunæs & Bjerg, 2014, p. 1). In their view, affects are not merely an afterthought to governmental technologies, but they are at the core by which subjects are governed. The quote resembles and draws on a similar point from Foucault noting that governmentality does not go against the will, but rather through it.

To further specify the concept of affects, I join Brøgger and Staunæs (2016) when they distinguish between indeterminate and determinate affects. 'Determinate affects' belong to or play at positive registers (excitement, thrill) or negative registers (shame, despair, disgust) (Brøgger & Staunæs, 2016). 'Indeterminate affects', on the other hand, are more challenging to conceptualize and they can give rise to determinate affects but do not necessarily do so. They attune and affect matter in situated places that are characterized by certain atmospheres, for instance affecting people by a "good vibe" or "bad vibe".

Anderson (2012) uses the fruitful concept of 'atmosphere' to address the fuzzy and diffuse attunement that supplements linguistic subjectification processes which are more visible in nature. Here, I define 'atmosphere' as a coordinated event between various contributors. Atmosphere is not the property of a single individual; in contrast, it is relational and, as such, is an intersubjective generator providing a layer of yet unknown indeterminate compounds of affect, energy, or intensity that has a significant effect on the subjectification processes. An atmosphere is thus a complex collective construction that leaves particular and singular tracks in the subject with the potential for manifesting itself as feelings or moods. In the empirical material, I observed how the unemployment fund works by attempting to create certain atmospheres as part of an empowerment technology. Empowerment is pushed based on "good vibes" and I refer to this as an affective governmental technology, primarily working by and through affective capacities.

The unemployment fund is decorated as a hotel where you can sit down and have a latté and meeting rooms are named after famous cities from around the world. You are encouraged to feel at ease, comfortable and attuned as a world citizen. Introduction seminars often take place in the Buenos Aires room on the second floor (see Chap. 4). Despite the unemployment fund's strategy to empower their members, it became clear that these technologies did not work in a uniform fashion affecting and attuning people similarly. In fact, the empowerment technology intersected with a more general attunement of unemployed people; that is tied to the negative representation of unemployed people in society. In addition to the latte and lounge vibe, being gathered with other unemployed people also activated and played at the negative affective registers. One of my participants illustrates this point by saying that coming to meeting with other unemployed people felt like going to an 'AA meeting' and being in a 'club of losers'. The specific ways that unemployed people were affectively subjectified influenced their unemployment experiences quite vastly and hence attuning my concepts toward affective dimensions were empirically motivated. Governing people not against their will but through it aligns well with the workings of affective technologies as these mold and shape desires and wishes.

Affective Economies and 'Sticky' Categories

What is at play when gathering unemployed people seems to affect or attune people in a negative fashion? Affect scholar Ahmed (2014a), provides useful concepts to address how emotions take place and circulate and imbue on political life in her work on the cultural politics of emotions. Ahmed conceives of emotions not as psychological states per se, but rather as cultural practices with political implications and as sites of government, despite not engaging actively with governmentality studies literature. Bodies are valorized in what she calls the 'affective economy', charging objects either positively or negatively in relation to ideology and political landscape. Emotions work by sticking to bodies and it is thus a feature linked to the embodied capacity to affect and be affected mentioned before.

In this perspective, unemployment is associated with such 'stickiness'; that is, people are affected negatively by becoming unemployed. The identity or representation of unemployment in part emerges as an effect of these concrete politics of emotions, aligning bodies in the work force and 'othering' bodies outside it. Ahmed describes, "how we become invested in social norms" (Ahmed, 2014a, p. 12) and how this is orchestrated in the affective economy by the workings of emotions as illustrated here with shame: "shame can also be experienced as the affective costs of not following the script of normative existence" (Ahmed, 2014a, p. 107). Even though unemployment is increasingly common, it does not follow the socially desirable script and as such, it is negatively charged and 'sticky'.

Affective economies are defined as economic systems that work somewhat similarly to capitalist monetary systems but are based on emotional currencies other than monetary. Ahmed (2014b, p. 45) elaborates:

> That is, emotions work as a form of capital: affect does not reside positively in the sign or commodity, but is produced only as an effect of its circulation. I am using 'the economic' to suggest that emotions circulate and are distributed across a social as well as psychic field borrowing from the Marxian critique of the logic of capital.

Ahmed further exemplifies the workings of sticky emotions in an affective economy by showing how the asylum seeker is made similar to the terrorist and thus he or she becomes an object to fear: "The slide of metonymy works to generate or make likeness: the asylum seeker is "like" the terrorist, an agent of fear who may destroy "our home"" (2004, p. 136). In a similar fashion, the unemployed person is constituted through shame and this is directly linked to being a burden on the welfare state.

Emotional Labor and Affective Economies in Networking

In addition to offering an analytical tool investigating the stickiness of unemployment, the importance of investigating such non-monetary currencies also becomes particularly salient when exploring networking practices and the emotional labor (EL) among unemployed people. Here, energy, positivity, and intensity are unfolded as key currencies in contemporary labor markets valorizing passion and dedication rather than merely objective professional skills. Affective subjectification plays a key role in psychologizing the unemployment issue.

Literature on emotional labor and the affective economy is another great source of inspiration that has been useful in terms of being able to engage with the affective and emotional sides of governmental practices.[1] At its core, networking involves an embodied and emotional-laden interpersonal interaction which requires "emotion work": the production of certain emotions in oneself or others (Hochschild, 1983; Hardt & Negri, 2001). Hochschild's (1983) seminal study, and the line of studies that follow, show how the labor process in service work commodifies this production of emotions in "emotional labor" (Hochschild, 1983; Oksala, 2016). The field of EL was originally developed in the context of the service industry identifying emotions and the production of emotions in customers as the prime work task among flight attendants and debt collectors, however by now the framework has been applied in a broad variety of workplaces such as Disneyland (Van

---

[1] See Pultz and Dupret (2023) for an earlier version.

Maanen, 1991), universities (Ogbonna & Harris, 2004), paralegals (Lively, 2002), and nursing (Gabriel, 2009; Lopez, 2006). From the outset, it was particularly the EL of frontend service workers that was scrutinized but increasingly backstage professionals have entered the empirical stage (O'Brien & Linehan, 2014, O'Brien & Linehan, 2018; Rivers, 2019; Theodosius, 2008) and here, I show that emotional labor is not only conducted in relation to paid labor but is also involved in practices of the unemployed people.

According to Hochschild (1983), emotions are not intra-psychological entities that float around people's brains. Emotions are first and foremost social. They are also distributed across different cultures and situations and are constituted in relation to special feeling rules that guide how we should feel in a given situation (Hochschild, 1983).

Different contexts are characterized by different "feeling rules," or "social guidelines that direct how we want to try to feel" (Hochschild, 1983, p. 563). Feeling rules are shared socially and provide a basis for how we can compare our own emotional experiences with an often idealized expectation of how something should be or feel. We also try to work on having an appropriate feeling, although this to some extent does not have to be visible to anyone but oneself. Emotional work is something we do on our own, but the dynamics are more complex than that. Hochschild writes, "Emotion work can be done by the self upon the self, by the self upon others, and by others upon oneself." (Hochschild, 1979, s. 526). Hochschild distinguishes between emotion work and emotional labor with the latter referring to the emotion management conducted in paid employment. Hence, Hochschild fully recognized that EL is wider than putting on a smile for commercial gains. In relation to customers, the commercialized emotional labor is characterized by being directed toward others for example colleagues inside an organization. Here, the purpose is to try to promote or produce a special feeling in another human constituting relational work. Hochschild elaborates on what different expressions emotion work can have: "By emotion work I refer to the act of trying to change in degree or quality an emotion or feeling. To 'work on' an emotion or feeling is, for our purpose, the same as 'to manage' an emotion or to do 'deep acting'". There are various ways of doing emotional work, where the overall ambition is to create an appropriate feeling for a given situation; one can show a feeling one does not sincerely feel (termed "evocation", p. 561); one can hide feelings sincerely felt (termed "suppression", p. 561). Furthermore, there is a difference between trying to change the expression of a feeling ("surface acting" p. 558) and to actually try to transform the underlying emotions ("deep acting", p. 558). While Hochschild has uncovered important distinctions or aspects with the concepts surface and deep acting, I agree with Theodosius (2008) who points out, that the distinction between surface and deep acting does not do justice to the wide range and complexity of emotions that people experience at work. Emotional labor, in my view, is not 'faking it' but far more complex: one side to it is the display of insincere emotion but another integral side to it is that emotional labor actually shapes subjectivity.

As Hochschild explains, it is not only about the emotional laborer seeming to be but also about his or her coming to be; the work requires not just the use but the production of subjectivity (Hochschild, 1983, p. 240). This understanding is more aligned with the Foucauldian understanding of subjectivity and thus it enables me to connect EL to the affective economy (Ahmed, 2014a). The language of the affective economy and relatedly affective currencies is useful for describing and analyzing the complex web of emotional labors involved in for instance networking. Examining emotions and affects as social and as structurally rooted allows exploring networking practices in a novel way and makes visible how particular affects are valorized in specific institutional contexts.

In feminist literature similar topics to EL has been raised as affective labor (Hardt & Negri, 2001). According to this perspective, how one feels and displays emotion is infiltrated with power relations and doing the "right" EL matters in terms of converting a casualized position to a tenured through the use of appropriate affective currencies in light of existing feeling rules (Pultz & Dupret, 2023). People with casual contracts have to perform a particular piece of EL, suppressing worries and demonstrating passion and dedication to be eligible for permanent positions (Pultz & Dupret, 2023). In unfolding the relationship between politics and emotions, Ahmed (2014b) describes how the "private will" must conform to the "general will", and that "willful subjects" do not fit in if "they will too much, or too little or in the wrong way" (Ahmed,

2014b, p. 3). The affective subjectification of casualized workers and unemployed people includes shaping how they feel and how they display their feelings in job searching. Adding an economic perspective and conceptualizing affective currencies allow us to think more openly about what kind of currencies are demanded, cultivated, and mobilized in different ways for people in precarious positions on the labor market either currently outside the labor market or in and out of casualized employments.

Summing Up

Governmentality studies offer a useful analytical approach and provide me with the tools and concepts to shed light on the link between technologies of power and those of the self in accordance with key attentions in social psychology addressing the problematic relationship between the individual and the society (Asplund, 1983; Mørch, 1994). A more comprehensive analysis of, in particular, the technologies of the self at a micro-political level allows for a better understanding of how young unemployed people handle the challenges they meet as unemployed and ensures an analysis that goes beyond the governance level by also encompassing how they deal with, and relate to, the technologies, how they are administered at the front level as well as more broadly in their everyday life.

An enlargement of the micro-political level thus serves to develop a theoretical lens aimed at sensitizing the subjectification analyses to everyday social practices and making visible the concrete struggles of subjectivity. Affective and emotional capacities are identified as key mediators in the subjectification of the unemployed person, albeit not in a homogeneous and monolithic way.

Insights from governmentality studies are used as a steppingstone to inquiry as they do not provide us with a "carefully established map to be followed" (D'Aoust, 2014). They serve as reminders to cultivate the necessary sensitivity to explore the messy affective subjectification processes affecting how unemployed people govern themselves in an affective economy, managing being emotionally indebted, self-blaming, and shameful.

References

Ahmed, S. (2004). Affective economies. *Social Text, 22*(2 79). https://doi.org/10.1215/01642472-22-2_79-117
Ahmed, S. (2014a). *The cultural politics of emotion*. Edinburgh University Press.
Ahmed, S. (2014b). *Willful subjects*. Duke University Press.
Andersen, H., & Mørch, H. (2000). Socialpsykologiens verdener. *Psyke & Logos, 21*(1), 383–415.
Andersen, H., & Mørch, S. (2005). Individualization and the challenged subject. *Identity, 5*(3), 261–285. https://doi.org/10.1207/s1532706xid0503_3
Anderson, B. (2012). Affect and biopower: Towards a politics of life. *Transactions of the Institute of British Geographers, 37*(1), 28–43. https://doi.org/10.1111/j.1475-5661.2011.00441.x
Asplund, J. (1983). *Tid, rum, individ och kollektiv*. LiberForlag.
Ball, S. J. (Ed.). (1990). *Foucault and education*. Routledge.
Bank, M. (2016). Enacting (post)psychological standards in social work: From regimes of visibility to user-driven standards and affective subjectification. *Theory & Psychology, 26*(2), 202–222. https://doi.org/10.1177/0959354316634216
Barratt, E. (2008). The later Foucault in organization and management studies. *Human Relations, 61*(4), 515.
Barry, A., Osborne, T., & Rose, N. S. (1996). *Foucault and political reason, liberalism, neo-liberalism and rationalities of government*. UCL Press.
Besley, T. (2005). Foucault, truth telling and technologies of the self in schools. *The Journal of Educational Enquiry, 6*(1), 76–89.
Binkley, S. (2011). Psychological life as enterprise: Social practice and the government of neo-liberal interiority. *History of the Human Sciences, 24*(3), 83.
Blackman, L. (2013). *Immaterial bodies, affect, embodiment, mediation*. Sage.
Brodkin, E. Z., & Marston, G. (2013). *Work and the welfare state, street-level organizations and workfare politics*. Georgetown University Press.
Brøgger, K., & Staunæs, D. (2016). Standards and (self)implosion: How the circulation of affects accelerates the spread of standards and intensifies the embodiment of colliding, temporal ontologies. *Theory & Psychology, 26*(2), 223–242. https://doi.org/10.1177/0959354316635889
Brown, W. (2015). *Undoing the demos, neoliberalism's stealth revolution*. The MIT Press.
Brown, S. D., & Stenner, P. (2009). *Psychology without foundations, history, philosophy and psychosocial theory*. Sage.

Burchell, G., Miller, P., & Gordon, C. (2003). *The Foucault effect, studies in governmentality, with two lectures by and an interview with Michel Foucault* ([Reprint.]). University of Chicago Press.
Burkitt, I. (2014). *Emotions and social relations*. SAGE Publications.
Butler, J. (1997). *The psychic life of power: Essays in subjection*. Stanford University Press.
Butler, J. (2007). *Gender trouble, feminism and the subversion of identity* (2nd ed., reprint ed.). Routledge.
Clarke, J. (2005). New labour's citizens: Activated, empowered, responsibilized, abandoned? *Critical Social Policy, 25*(4), 447–463.
Clarke, J. (2008). Governing the local? A response to Kevin Stenson. *Social Work and Society[online], 6*(1), 15–20.
Clough, P. T. (2008). The affective turn political economy, biomedia and bodies. *Theory, Culture & Society, 25*(1), 1–22. https://doi.org/10.1177/0263276407085156
Cromby, J. (2012). Feeling the way: Qualitative clinical research and the affective turn. *Qualitative Research in Psychology, 9*(1), 88–98. https://doi.org/10.1080/14780887.2012.63083
Cromby, J. (2015). *Feeling bodies: Embodying psychology*. Palgrave Macmillan.
Cruikshank, B. (1994). The will to empower: Technologies of citizenship and the war on poverty. *Socialist Review, 23*(4), 29–55.
Cruikshank, B. (1999). *The will to empower: Democratic citizens and other subjects*. Cornell University Press.
D'Aoust, A.-M. (2014). Ties that bind? Engaging emotions, governmentality and neoliberalism: Introduction to the special issue. *Global Society, 28*(3), 267–276. https://doi.org/10.1080/13600826.2014.900743
Davies, B. (2006). Subjectification: The relevance of Butler's analysis for education. *British Journal of Sociology of Education, 27*(4), 425–438. https://doi.org/10.1080/01425690600802029
Dean, M. (1995). Governing the unemployed self in an active society. *Economy and Society, 24*(4), 559–583. https://doi.org/10.1080/03085149500000025
Dean, M. (2007). *Governing societies, political perspectives on domestic and international rule*. Open University Press.
Dean, M. (2010). *Governmentality, power and rule in modern society* (2nd ed.). SAGE.
Deleuze, G. (1992). Postscript on the societies of control. *October, 59*, 3.
Deleuze, G. (1994). *Difference and repetition* (P. Patton, Trans.). Columbia University Press.

Deleuze, G., & Guattari, F. (1987). *A thousand plateaus: Capitalism and Schizophrenia* (B. Massumi, Trans.) (1st ed.). University of Minnesota Press.

Dwyer, P. (2004). Creeping conditionality in the UK: From welfare rights to conditional entitlements? *Canadian Journal of Sociology/Cahiers canadiens de sociologie, 29*(2), 265–287.

Elias, N. (1997). *The civilizing process, the history of manners and state formation and civilization* (Reprinted). Blackwell.

Foucault, M. (1978). *The history of sexuality*. Pantheon.

Foucault, M. (1982). The subject and power. *Critical Inquiry, 8*(4), 777–795.

Foucault, M. (1993). About the beginning of the hermeneutics of the self: Two lectures at Dartmouth. *Political Theory, 21*(2), 198–227.

Foucault, M. (1995). *Discipline & punish: The birth of the prison* (A. Sheridan, Trans.) (2nd ed.). Vintage Books.

Foucault, M. (1988). Technologies of the self. In *Technologies of the self: A seminar with Michel Foucault* (Vol. 18, p. 170).

Foucault, M. (2003). Truth and power. In P. Rabinow & N. Rose (Eds.), *The essential Foucault: Selections from essential works of Foucault* (pp. 1954–1984). The New Press.

Foucault, M. (2007). *Security, territory, population: Lectures at the Collège de France, 1977–78*. Springer.

Foucault, M. (2008). *The birth of biopolitics, lectures at the College de France, 1978–1979*. Palgrave Macmillan.

Foucault, M. (2010). *The government of self and others, lectures at the Collège de France 1982–1983*. Palgrave Macmillan.

Foucault, M., & Lotringer, S. (2007). *The politics of truth*. Semiotexte.

Foucault, M., Martin, L. H., Gutman, H., & Hutton, P. H. (1988). *Technologies of the self, a seminar with Michel Foucault*. Tavistock.

Foucault, M., Senellart, M., Ewald, F., & Fontana, A. (2007). *Security, territory, population*. Palgrave Macmillan.

Foucault, M., Davidson, A. I., & Burchell, G. (2013). *Lectures on the will to know*. Palgrave Macmillan.

Gabriel, Y. (2009). Emotional labour in health care. *Organization Studies, 30*(6), 676–681. https://doi.org/10.1177/01708406090300060502

Garland, D. (1999). 'Governmentality' and the problem of crime. In R. Smandych (Ed.), *Governable places: Readings on governmentality and crime control* (pp. 15–45). Ashgate.

Giddens, A. (1992). *Modernity and self-identity, self and society in the late modern age* (Reprinted). Polity.

Goffman, E. (1968). *Stigma, notes on the management of spoiled identity (1963).* Penguin.
Greco, M., & Stenner, P. (2013). Happiness and the art of life: Diagnosing the psychopolitics of wellbeing. *Health, Culture and Society, 5*(1). https://doi.org/10.5195/hcs.2013.147
Hacking, I. (1996). *The looping effects of human kinds.* Oxford University Press.
Hacking, I. (2004). Between Michel Foucault and Erving Goffman: Between discourse in the abstract and face-to-face interaction. *Economy and Society, 33*(3), 277–302. https://doi.org/10.1080/0308514042000225671
Haraway, D. (1988). Situated knowledges: The science question in feminism and the privilege of partial perspective. *Feminist Studies, 14*(3), 575–599. https://doi.org/10.2307/3178066
Haraway, D. (2000). There are always more things going on than you thought! Methodologies as thinking technologies. Interview af Nina Lykke, Randi Markussen and Finn Olesen. Kvinder, Køn & Forskning, 4, 52–61.
Hardt, M., & Negri, A. (2001). *Empire* (Paperback ed., 4. printing). Harvard University Press.
Hochschild, A. R. (1979). Emotion work, feeling rules, and social structure. *American Journal of Sociology, 85*(3), 551–575. https://doi.org/10.1086/227049
Hochschild, A. R. (1983). *The Managed Heart: Commercialization of Human Feeling.* University of California Press.
Juelskjær, M., & Staunæs, D. (2016). Designing leadership chairs, reconceptualizing educational research. *Methodology, 7*(2), 35–51.
Juelskjær, M., Staunæs, D., & Ratner, H. (2013). The return of the Freudian couch®: Managing affectivity through technologies of comfort. *International Journal of Qualitative Studies in Education, 26*(9), 1132–1152. https://doi.org/10.1080/09518398.2013.816885
Katarzyna, K., & McKernan, J. F. (2011). From care of the self to care for the other: Neglected aspects of Foucault's late work. *Accounting, Auditing & Accountability Journal, 24*(3), 377–402. https://doi.org/10.1108/09513571111124054
Kristensen, O. S., Oberman, M.-L., & Dolmer, A. (2007). *Notat om forskellen mellem social integration og social inklusion.* European Commission.
Latour, B. (2005). *Reassembling the social, an introduction to actor-network-theory.* Oxford University Press.
Lazzarato, M. (2009). Neoliberalism in action inequality, insecurity and the reconstitution of the social. *Theory, Culture & Society, 26*(6), 109–133. https://doi.org/10.1177/0263276409350283

Lemke, T. (2001). The birth of bio-politics: Michael Foucault's lectures at the College de France on neoliberal governmentality. *Economy and Society, 30*(2), 190–207.

Leys, R. (2011). The turn to affect: A critique. *Critical Inquiry, 37*(3), 434–472. https://doi.org/10.1086/659353

Lively, K. J. (2002). Client contact and emotional labor: Upsetting the balance and evening the field. *Work and Occupations, 29*(2), 198–225.

Lopez, S. H. (2006). Emotional Labor and Organized Emotional Care: Conceptualizing Nursing Home Care Work. *Work and Occupations 33*(2), 133–160.

Lopdrup-Hjorth, T., Copenhagen Business School, D. S. of O. and M. S., Copenhagen Business School, P. S. of E. and M., Copenhagen Business School, P. d S. L., & Copenhagen Business School. (2013). *'Let's go outside': The value of co-creation* (1st ed. 1. oplag). PhD School of Economics and Management.

Lorenzini, D. (2016). From counter-conduct to critical attitude: Michel Foucault and the art of not being governed quite so much. *Foucault Studies, 0*(0), 7–21.

Mackenzie, E., & McKinlay, A. (2021). Hope labour and the psychic life of cultural work. *Human Relations, 74*(11), 1841–1863.

Marston, G., & McDonald, C. (2006). *Analysing social policy: A governmental approach*. Edward Elgar Publishing.

Massumi, B. (2002). *Parables for the virtual, movement, affect, sensation*. Duke University Press.

McDonald, C., & Marston, G. (2005). Workfare as welfare: Governing unemployment in the advanced liberal state. *Critical Social Policy, 25*(3), 374–401.

Mckee, K. (2009). Post-Foucauldian governmentality: What does it offer critical social policy analysis? *Critical Social Policy, 29*(3), 465–486. https://doi.org/10.1177/0261018309105180

Mik-Meyer, N., & Villadsen, K. (2013). *Power and welfare, understanding citizens' encounters with state welfare*. Routledge.

Mill, J. S. (1874). *Essays on some unsettled questions of political economy*. IndyPublish.com.

Miller, P., & Rose, N. (1995). Production, identity, and democracy. *Theory and Society, 24*(3), 427–467. https://doi.org/10.1007/BF00993353

Mørch, S. (1994): Handlingsteorien. En ny fællesnævner for socialpsykologien? Udkast nr. 1 (ISSN: 0105–2691). 45s./225.

O'Brien, E., & C. Linehan. (2014). A Balancing Act: Emotional Challenges in the HR Role. *Journal of Management Studies 51*(8), 1257–1285.

O'Brien, E., & Linehan, C. (2018). The last taboo?: Surfacing and supporting emotional labour in HR work. *The International Journal of Human Resource Management, 29*(4), 683–709. https://doi.org/10.1080/09585192.2016.1184178

Ogbonna, E., & Harris, L. C. (2004). Work intensification and emotional labour among UK University lecturers: An exploratory study. *Organization Studies, 25*(7), 1185–1203. https://doi.org/10.1177/0170840604046315

Oksala, J. (2016). Affective labor and feminist politics. *Signs: Journal of Women in Culture and Society, 41*(2), 281–303.

Parsons, T. (1956). *Family, socialization and interaction process*. Routledge and Kegan Paul Ltd.

Pedersen, O. K. (2011). *Konkurrencestaten*. Hans Reitzel.

Pultz, S., & Dupret, K. (2023). Emotional status and emotional labour: Exploring the emotional labour among casualised and tenured knowledge workers. *Culture and Organization, Latest articles*. https://doi.org/10.1080/14759551.2023.2258433

Raffnsoe, S., Gudmand-Hoyer, M., & Thaning, M. S. (2014). Foucault's dispositive: The perspicacity of dispositive analytics in organizational research. *Organization*, 1350508414549885. https://doi.org/10.1177/1350508414549885

Raffnsøe, S., Gudmand-Høyer, M. T., & Thaning, M. (2016). *Michel Foucault: A research companion*. Palgrave Macmillan.

Read, J. (2009). A genealogy of homo-economicus: Neoliberalism and the production of subjectivity. *Foucault Studies, 0*(0), 25–36.

Rivers, E. (2019). Navigating Emotion in HR Work: Caring for Ourselves? *Personnel Review 48*(6), 1565–1579. https://doi-org.ep.fjernadgang.kb.dk/10.1108/PR-07-2018-0244

Rose, N. (1996). *Inventing our selves, psychology, power, and personhood*. Cambridge University Press.

Rose, N. S. (1999). *Powers of freedom, reframing political thought*. Cambridge University Press.

Rose, N., & Miller, P. (2010). Political power beyond the state: Problematics of government. *British Journal of Sociology, 61*, 271–303. https://doi.org/10.1111/j.1468-4446.2009.01247.x

Rose, N., O'Malley, P., & Valverde, M. (2006). Governmentality. *Annual Review of Law and Social Science, 2*, 83–104.

Rutherford, S. (2007). Green governmentality: Insights and opportunities in the study of nature's rule. *Progress in Human Geography, 31*(3), 291–307. https://doi.org/10.1177/0309132507077080

Sedgwick, E. K. (2003). *Touching feeling: Affect, pedagogy, performativity*. Duke University Press.
Seigworth, G. J., & Gregg, M. (2010). *The affect theory reader*. Duke.
Søndergaard, D. M. (2002). Poststructuralist approaches to empirical analysis. *International Journal of Qualitative Studies in Education, 15*(2), 187–204. https://doi.org/10.1080/09518390110111910
Søndergaard, D. M. (2006). *Tegnet på kroppen : køn: koder og konstruktioner blandt unge voksne i Akademia* (3. oplag (uændret genoptryk).). Museum Tusculanum.
Spinoza, B. de, & Elwes, R. H. M. (1677). *Ethics, ethica ordine geometrico demonstrata*. Floating Press.
Staunæs, D. (2011). Governing the potentials of life itself? Interrogating the promises in affective educational leadership. *Journal of Educational Administration and History, 43*(3), 227–247. https://doi.org/10.1080/00220620.2011.586454
Staunæs, D., & Bjerg, H. (2014). Self-management through shame—Uniting governmentality studies and the 'affective turn' | ephemera. *Ephemera, 14*(14).
Staunæs, D., & Juelskjær, M. (2016). Orchestrating intensities and rhythms. *Theory & Psychology, 26*(2), 182–201.
Staunæs, D., & Kofoed, J. (2015). Producing curious affects: Visual methodology as an affecting and conflictual wunderkammer. *International Journal of Qualitative Studies in Education, 28*(10), 1229–1248. https://doi.org/10.1080/09518398.2014.975296
Staunæs, D., & Pors, J. G.(2015). Thinking educational policy and management through (frictional) concepts of affects. In K. N. Gulson, M. Clarke, & E. B. Petersen (red.), Education policy and contemporary theory (pp. 99–109). Routledge.
Staunæs, D., & Søndergaard, D. M. (2006). Corporate fictions. *Norsk Tidsskrift for Kjønnsforskning, 3*, 69–93.
Staunæs, D., & Søndergaard, D. M. (2008). Who are ready for results?: Reflections on the Multivoicedness of useful research. *International Journal of Qualitative Studies in Education, 21*(1), 3–18.
Stenson, K. (2005). Sovereignty, biopolitics and the local government of crime in Britain. *Theoretical Criminology, 9*, 265–287.
Stenson, K. (2008). Governing the local: Sovereignty, social governance and community safety. *Social Work & Society, 6*(1), 2–14.
Theodosius, C. (2008). *Emotional labour in health care: The unmanaged heart of nursing*, 1–232. https://doi.org/10.4324/9780203894958.

Thomas, R., & Davies, A. (2005). Theorizing the micro-politics of resistance: New public management and managerial identities in the UK public services. *Organization Studies, 26*(5), 683–706.

Triantafillou, P., & Nielsen, M. R. (2001). Policing empowerment: The making of capable subjects. *History of the Human Sciences, 14*(2), 63–86.

Valsiner, J. (1997). *Culture and the development of children's action, a theory of human development* (2nd ed.). John Wiley & Sons.

Van Maanen, J. (1991). The smile factory: Work at Disneyland. In *Organizational culture*. Sage.

Van Oorschot, W. (2006). Making the difference in social Europe: deservingness perceptions among citizens of European welfare states. *Journal of European social policy, 16*(1), 23–42.

Weiskopf, R., & Munro, I. (2012). Management of human capital: Discipline, security and controlled circulation in HRM. *The Organ, 19*(6), 685–702. https://doi.org/10.1177/1350508411416536

Wetherell, M. (2012). *Affect and emotion, a new social science understanding*. SAGE.

Wetherell, M. (2015). Trends in the turn to affect: A social psychological critique. *Body & Society, 21*(2), 139–166.

Whelan, J. (2021). *Welfare, deservingness and the logic of poverty: Who deserves?* Cambridge Scholars Publishing.

3

Setting the Scene

Framing the Policy-Level and Situating the Danish Case

The state-recognized unemployment funds are an integral part of what is known as the 'Danish model' founded on the so-called September settlement from 1899, according to which the various labor market partners should respect each other, cooperate and negotiate (Pedersen, 2011). The Danish labor market is often characterized as offering 'flexicurity', which combines high levels of welfare security—as described above—together with labor market flexibility and high levels of worker turn-over with approximately 20% of the workforce changing jobs each year (Bengtsson et al., 2015). The flexicurity system is based on three features: a collective bargaining system and labor laws, an economic safety net, and active employment policies (Pedersen, 2011).

The laws and policies are designed to govern and administer the unemployed people in a way that reduces unemployment and increases labor market integration ensuring growth and global competition (Esping-Andersen et al., 2002). One way the existing literature conceptualizes differences among welfare states is to consider different countries' levels of labor 'de-commodification', which Esping-Andersen (1990, pp. 21–22) defines as the degree to which a "person can maintain a livelihood without reliance on the market". Although Denmark's welfare state has retrenched in recent decades (Bengtsson et al., 2015), in a comparative context Denmark remains on the high end of de-commodification. Schröder (2013, p. 6) finds that Denmark, along with Sweden, "are the purest embodiments" of a regime of "de-commodification of workers" with "reduced market dependency", and a commitment to "comprehensive risk coverage, generous benefits levels, and egalitarianism". In a recent comparison of six advanced economies which includes both Denmark, Kalleberg (2018, p. 38) finds that Denmark "'is the clearest example among the six countries of an inclusive regime characterized by high levels of social protections for all citizens". Going further Kalleberg (2018, p. 55) characterizes Denmark as "Europe's most generous welfare state overall". In every category of unemployment benefits examined by Wildeboer Schut et al. (2001, p. 38) for 11 countries, including duration of insurance and net replacement of income, Denmark was among the most generous. Similarly, using a composite measure of unemployment insurance generosity, Kalleberg (2018) also finds that Denmark's system is the most generous among the six countries studied. Denmark's unemployment assistance replaces up to 90% of prior earnings for low wage workers and approximately 70% of the prior earnings of an average production worker's wages (Schröder, 2013, pp. 149–150).[1] Danish benefit recipients are thus relatively generously compensated, with a degree of remuneration of two-thirds of prior income, which is high compared internationally for low wage earners but, for middle and for high wage earners, but the compensation is at the same level as other OECD countries and, in fact, lower than other Northern European countries, except Sweden (Dagpengekommisionen, 2015).

---

[1] Currently in 2023, unemployed benefit recipients with full-time work experience receive 2.646 Euros per month (corresponding to 19.728 kroner) and 1.764,47 euros per month for part-time insured (corresponding to 13.152). For graduates, below the age of 30, the rate is 1.301 euros per month (corresponding to 9.700 kr). And 1.643 Euros per month if you are more than 30 years old (corresponding to 12.253 kr). During the first three months, however, you receive 1.892 euros (corresponding to 14.106 kr.) The rates for social assistance is 1.602 euros (corresponding to 11,944 kr) if you are above 30 years and 1.032 euros (corresponding to 7699 kr) if you are between 25–29 years old. The rates are without taking into account extra money you receive if you provide for children.

Denmark is typically grouped within the social democratic welfare regimes, as opposed to corporatist such as France and liberal welfare regimes such as the US respectively (Esping-Andersen, 1990). Compared to other European nations, such as France and Spain, Denmark offers relatively modest employment protections (Schröder, 2013), and employers have "great flexibility in hiring and firing workers" (Kalleberg, 2018, p. 39). Pedersen (2011) has argued that various reforms mark a move away from the traditional Nordic welfare state to a more competitive state termed the 'competition state' that, to some degree, resembles liberal societies, what he calls "competition societies" as in the UK and the USA while still remaining distinct in comparison with these (see also Lindsay & Daguerre, 2009).

Typically, policies are divided into three paradigms: Keynesian, Neoliberal, and Social investment paradigm (Morel & Palier, 2011). In the Danish PES we see elements of all the above. Inspired by Keynesian perspective, the Danish PES includes social protection with the aim of promoting and sustaining demand. Inspired by a neoliberal paradigm during the recent decades we have witnessed attempts to reduce expenses. Last, we social investment technologies are defined employment policies that are based on a social investment logic defined by a focus of preparing (rather than repairing) as well as an investing in human capital with the intention of gaining a return in the future, whether this is economic or social (getting people into employment or improving their general wellbeing) (Cantillon, 2011; Hemerijck, 2018). This entails focusing not on problems but rather on resources among unemployed people even in cases where there seems to be little reason for optimism (Nielsen, 2021).

Overall, the Danish public employment service can be characterized as a "hybrid" or a "mix" as the active labor market policies are both linked to the neoliberal paradigm focusing on the supply side and the social investment paradigm with the goal of improving human capital (Bekker & Mailand, 2019; Hansen, 2019).

Activation at Street-Level PES

Supranational actors such as the Organisation for Economic Cooperation and Development (OECD) have played an important role in the historical shift in how unemployment is governed. The OECD focuses on supply solutions for unemployment rather than demand solutions and it highlights the active society by placing more of an emphasis on active rather than passive measures (Fryer & Stambe, 2014; Immervoll, 2012). The policies are largely aimed at reintegrating the unemployed person into the workforce by ways of making the unemployed person **active,** through constructing the active jobseeker (Bengtsson et al., 2015).

Placing more emphasis on active measures means guiding, motivating, and up-qualifying unemployed people or maintaining their skills, while passive measures include the payment of unemployment benefit. Receiving unemployment benefit has thus been made conditional on participating in these specific activities. In addition to these, receiving benefits is also conditional on the demand of availability, that is, being available to the labor market in working hours. Overall, this is referred to as the "activation paradigm" (Lindsay & Daguerre, 2009).

The active labor market policy goes back to the 1970s; however, since the 1990s, the activation policies have been expanded and the grip on the unemployed has, overall, been tightened (Jørgensen & Thomsen, 2016). Active labor market policies are employed with the purpose of getting working-age people off benefits and into work, for instance by assistance in searching for work, training, public sector job creation and subsidized employment in the private sector (Weishaupt, 2011). The political background for activation policies includes a prior system that supported unemployed people passively without making any demands or having expectations in terms of how they should handle their unwanted situation of being unemployed. This system relying on passive labor market policies evokes critical analyses suggesting that society left unemployed people to swim in their own sea rather than being helping them properly.

The case of Denmark is not unique since most OECD countries have been exposed to similar reforms restructuring welfare state institutions around the aim of labor market integration by introducing "activation" reforms (Peck, 2001; Aurich, 2011; Bonoli, 2013). These reforms are aimed toward making the unemployed active and aimed toward ensuring that the street-level bureaucrats and bureaucracies activate the unemployed. Although Denmark is not unique in this regard, it stands out as one of the countries in which the active turn has been the most far-reaching. Not only does the country rank high in terms of expenditure on active labor market policies, but it is also ranking high regarding conditionality, that is the use of control mechanisms and sanctions (Hansen & Leschke, 2022). Inherent in the activation reforms is an understanding that unemployed people are only eligible for unemployment benefit or social assistance if they comply with conditions.

The aim of these policies is twofold: (1) active behavior of the unemployed leads to a job and (2) receiving money from the state implies testing the unemployed person who must prove themselves worthy of receiving benefits. Both aims, that in practice are deeply entangled, are saturated with moral questions of worth (Hansen, 2019). In the first aim, it is a matter of bringing the unemployed to a state of worthiness (paying taxes, self-supporting, self-realizing), while in the second aim, it is a matter of evaluating the current state of worthiness of the unemployed (willingness to work, flexibility, outreaching, investing). In this way, the instruments and activities of PES have the double purpose of changing the behavior of the unemployed and testing whether the unemployed in fact change their behavior. This "moral economy of activation" (Hansen, 2019) relies on multiple orders of worth conceptualizing the unemployed in different ways—as people responding to economic incentives, as potentially lazy and incompetent and thus in need of discipline and control, as lacking skills and thus in need of investment in human capital (Hansen, 2019).

In 1993, the period in which unemployment benefit in Denmark could be received was cut from an unlimited duration to seven years. From then on, gradual further cuts have been made up until the present, where the unemployment benefit period is two years, with one year's retaining period and only one year's unemployment period for graduates (Harsløf & Ulmestig, 2013). The current Danish system is administered by governmental job centers and unemployment funds. The job centers provide social assistance to people who are unemployed. The unemployment funds administer the rules and guide members on their rights and responsibilities. Some rules apply to all unemployment funds, although the demands for job searching differ between the various unemployment funds. After the welfare reform in 2006, the unemployment funds do not only administer payments to members, but they are also required to check upon their unemployed members by, for instance, obligatory meetings about availability every third month, and by logging on to the employment website job.net.dk and confirming their active job search. The unemployment fund has the power to reduce or terminate benefits if an individual receiving them fails to undertake required activities such as attending retraining seminars, career guidance, or seeking new employment.

Concretely, the rules of activity imply active job searching as well as documenting these job search efforts. It entails participating in mandatory courses and conversations with job consultants. According to the rules of availability, unemployed people must be available in relation to the labor market, meaning that they can only be engaged in either volunteer work to a certain extent and they are not officially allowed to take on caring activities during working hours. They must be able to take on a full-time job the following day, including three hours of commuting, in order to be eligible for receiving money. Failing to live up to either of these demands can lead to economic sanctions.

On the other hand, the activities in PES are justified as "personalized", based on the idea that unemployed persons are a diverse group with multiple factors that explain their situation. A key instrument to ensure at least a formal personalization is the individual plan which is agreed by both counselor and the unemployed person at the initial meeting, and subsequently evaluated and revised. In the digitalized Danish system, the unemployed person can visit "My Plan" which provides them with "an overview of everything that needs to happen, forward-looking, in the employment effort". Thus, activation and creation of the active job seeker is enacted ensuring that the "citizen no longer experiences the plan as the administrative paper of the system but as a real plan he or she contributes to and has ownership of" as it is stated on the website informing unemployed people about what to do. Personalization has also paved the way for instruments that can distinguish and categorize unemployed people in groups which has resulted in the proliferation of profiling tools that does exactly that, categorizing the unemployed people in terms of their low, medium, or high risk for becoming long-term unemployed (Desiere et al., 2019). At the time of the second wave of data, the unemployment fund developed and relied upon a screening instrument to govern their unemployed members. The screening tool predicts an unemployed person's probability of becoming long-term unemployed based upon certain demographic risk factors such as for example age, profession, and marital status. On those grounds, the unemployed person is characterized as low, medium, or high risk and interventions are decided accordingly. For instance, if a person's likelihood of becoming long-term unemployed is estimated to be high, they must engage in PES activities more frequently (Pultz, 2016). In the next chapter, I elaborate on the specificities of the profiling tool that I came across, its effects as well as its built-in understanding of the unemployed subject.

Temporary Suspension of ALMPs during Covid-19

The first wave of the Covid-19 pandemic in Denmark in 2020 was a period with sense of deep crisis, both in terms of public health and economically.[2] In Denmark, there are indicators of this shift in policy goals in the financing of Covid-19 expenses through loan-taking and through massive investments in job maintenance resulting in rather modest increases in unemployment suggesting a return of Keynesian demand-side policies replacing neoliberal austerity. Like in many other countries, the government's intervention in the economy has been justified by a strong discourse of solidarity and collective responsibility for mitigating the socio-economic consequences of the pandemic.

In parallel with economic compensation for businesses, the government thus decided to suspend activation from March 12, 2020, including the obligations related to job searching and interviews as well as the countdown of the entitlement period for unemployment insurance. The suspension was justified by the minister of employment as "only fair"

---

[2] See an earlier version of this Pultz et al. (2021).

since the lockdown was "obviously making it harder to find a job" (Beskæftigelsesministeriet, 2020). However, activation was only suspended temporarily. Since the end of May, when the lockdown was repealed, the picture became more blurred. Some obligations have returned (e.g., having to search for a job) while others continued to be suspended (e.g., physical interviews at the employment office) until 2021. Nonetheless, the suspension showed the possibility of thinking differently about unemployment and thus, perhaps, also the possibility of a different experience of unemployment, with less self-blaming and stigma and perhaps with another approach to the quest of finding a job. The new discourse and the temporary exemption of obligations provided some room and perspective to reflect on the situation and role of PES, but it also put the unemployed in a highly ambiguous situation with increased freedom but a future ever more uncertain.

The COVID pandemic initiated a temporary paradigmatic discursive shift from internalizing to recognition of external causes of unemployment making unemployed feel less self-blaming and more dignified (Bækgaard et al., 2021; Pultz et al., 2021). This suspension period provided the unemployed interviewees who had become unemployed before the pandemic onset with a comparative perspective enabling them to reflect on how they experienced activation policies such as obligations to job search activities, attend meetings, and enroll in activation schemes (Pultz et al., 2021). The pandemic gave rise to a distinguishing between people who became unemployed during the pandemic;—the legitimate unemployed people—, and those who were unemployed before whose moral constitution could be challenged (Pultz et al., 2021) leading to less self-blame compared to before (Pultz & Hansen, 2021). The pandemic provided an interesting insight into the dynamic between the technologies of power and those of the self. Suspending activation policies gave rise to a different set of unemployment experiences and these are pursued in Chap. 8.

Summing Up

The Danish case is in many ways an extreme case to look into the dynamics between technologies of the self and those of the self in terms of understanding unemployment experience. The Danish welfare state and public employment services constitute an example of "the active turn" par excellence. Constructing of the active jobseeker involves developing various measures that makes the unemployed person aware, or remind the unemployed person of the responsibility to become economically self-reliable and hence not a burden to the state. This machinery is key in terms of developing fertile ground for subjectifying unemployed people as emotionally indebted. Viewed from a social psychological perspective this machinery comes with intended as well as unintended consequences and it is necessary to apply a relative broad analytical scope to grasp the many ways that these policies and the ways they are administered affect and influence the lived experiences of the unemployed people.

References

Aurich, P. (2011). Activating the unemployed—directions and divisions in Europe. *European Journal of Social Security, 13*(3), 294–316.

Bækgaard, M., Mikkelsen, K. S., Madsen, J. K., & Christensen, J. (2021). Reducing compliance demands in government benefit programs improves the psychological well-being of target group members. *Journal of Public Administration Research and Theory, 31*(4), 806–821.

Bekker, S., & Mailand, M. (2019). The European flexicurity concept and the Dutch and Danish flexicurity models: How have they managed the Great Recession? *Soc Policy Admin., 53*, 142–155. https://doi.org/10.1111/spol.12441

Bengtsson, T. T., Frederiksen, M., & Larsen, J. E. (2015). *The Danish welfare state, a sociological investigation*. Palgrave Macmillan.

Beskæftigelsesministeriet. (2020, April 6). Bredt flertal sætter timekrav for folk på kontanthjælp på pause. Retrieved April 6, 2020, from https://bm.dk/nyheder-presse/nyheder/2020/04/bredt-flertal-saetter-timekrav-for-folk-paa-kontanthjaelp-paa-pause/

Bonoli, G. (2013). *The origins of active social policy: Labour market and childcare policies in a comparative perspective*. Oxford University Press, USA.

Cantillon, B. (2011). The paradox of the social investment state: Growth, employment and poverty in the Lisbon era. *Journal of European Social Policy, 21*(5), 432–449.

Dagpengekommisionen. (2015). Beskæftigelsesministeriet.

Desiere, S., Langenbucher, K., & Struyven, L. (2019). Statistical profiling in public employment services: An international comparison. OECD Social, Employment and Migration Working Papers, 224, 1–29. https://doi.org/10.1787/b5e5f16e-en

Esping-Andersen, G. (1990). *The three worlds of welfare capitalism*. Princeton University Press.

Esping-Andersen, G., Gallie, D., Hemerijck, A., & Myles, J. (2002). *Why we need a new welfare state*. Oxford University Press.

Fryer, D., & Stambe, R. (2014). Neoliberal austerity and unemployment. *Psychologist, 27*(4), 244–248.

Hansen, M. P. (2019). *The moral economy of activation: Ideas, politics and policies*. Policy Press.

Hansen, M. P., & Leschke, J. (2022). Reforming the Ideal (ised) Model (s) of Danish Labour Market Policies. In *Public Governance in Denmark* (pp. 39–56). Emerald Publishing Limited.

Harsløf, I., & Ulmestig, R. (Eds.). (2013). *Changing social risks and social policy responses in the Nordic welfare states*. Springer.

Hemerijck, A. (2018). Social investment as a policy paradigm. *Journal of European Public Policy, 25*(6), 810–827.

Immervoll, H. (2012). Activation policies in OECD countries: An overview of current approaches (Social Protection and Labor Policy and Technical Notes No. 71903). The World Bank.

Jørgensen, M. B., & Thomsen, T. L. (2016). Deservingness in the Danish context: Welfare chauvinism in times of crisis. *Critical Social Policy, 36*(3), 330–351.

Kalleberg, A. L. (2018). *Precarious lives: Job insecurity and well-being in rich democracies*. New York, NY: Polity Press.

Lindsay, C., & Daguerre, A. (2009). Active labour market policies and welfare reform: Europe and the US in comparative perspective. *Journal of Social Policy, 38*, 180–182. https://doi.org/10.1017/S0047279408002638

Morel, N., & Palier, B. (Eds.). (2011). *Towards a social investment welfare state?: ideas, policies and challenges*. Policy Press.

Nielsen, M. H. (2021). Money, competences or behaviour? On the many worths of the unemployed. *European Journal of Cultural and Political Sociology (Print), 8*(2), 124–150. https://doi.org/10.1080/23254823.2020.1860785

Peck, J. (2001). *Workfare states*. Guilford Press.

Pedersen, O. K. (2011). *Konkurrencestaten*. Hans Reitzel.

Pultz, S. (2016). Governing homo economicus: Risk management among young unemployed people in the Danish welfare state. *Health, Risk & Society, 18*(3–4), 168–187.

Pultz, S. (2017). *It's not you, it's me: Governing the unemployed self in the Danish welfare state*. Copenhagen University.

Pultz, S., & Hansen, M. P. (2021). Arbejdsløs i en (corona)krisetid: et opgør med selvansvaret? *Tidsskrift for Arbejdsliv, 23*(3), 9–25. https://doi.org/10.7146/tfa.v23i3.129426

Pultz, S., Hansen, M. P., & Jepsen, H. (2021). Planning for a job: The trying experience of unemployment during the Covid-19 crisis in Denmark. *International Perspectives in Psychology: Research, Practice, Consultation, 10*(4), 228–242. https://doi.org/10.1027/2157-3891/a000028

Schröder, M. (2013). *Integrating varieties of capitalism and welfare state research: A unified typology of capitalisms*. Basingstoke: Palgrave Macmillan.

Weishaupt, J. T. (2011). From the manpower revolution to the activation paradigm: Explaining institutional continuity and change in an integrating Europe.

Wildeboer Schut, J. M., Vrooman, J. C., & de Beer, P. T. (2001). *On worlds of welfare. Institutions and their effects in eleven welfare states*. The Hague: Social and Cultural Planning Office.

4

Governing the Active Jobseeker

Answering the question, 'What do you do?' is painful for many young unemployed people and often they refrain from social encounters, simply to avoid answering the question (Sharone, 2013). Being unemployed is often experienced as a personal failure and unemployed people frequently look for personal shortcomings or deficits to explain how they have found themselves in the situation and why they have so far not been successful at getting out of it (Newman, 1988). Studies have documented how unemployment is increasingly privatized and perceived in individualized terms (Beck, 2008; Engelbreth Larsen, 2013; Pultz, 2016).

The increased responsibility is documented in the literature across various neoliberal (welfare) states (Brown, 2015; Furlong & Cartmel, 1997; Mascini et al., 2013). The individual's life course is no longer predetermined by institutions, families, or traditions (Furlong & Cartmel, 1997; Mørch et al., 2014). People in late modernity are portrayed as immensely individualized and shaped by powerful discourses of freedom of choices or as Giddens sarcastically puts it—people are forced to be free. They also

---

This chapter contains earlier version from Pultz, Governing homo economicus: Risk management among young unemployed people in the Danish welfare state. *Health, Risk & Society, 18*(3–4), 168–187, 2016 and Pultz and Hviid, Imagining a better future: Young unemployed people and the polyphonic choir. *Culture & Psychology, 24*(1), 3–25, 2018.

© The Author(s), under exclusive license to Springer Nature Switzerland AG 2024
S. Pultz, *Emotionally Indebted*, https://doi.org/10.1007/978-3-031-57156-5_4

have to deal with the responsibility that comes along with it (Giddens, 2001; Beck, 1992). Furlong and Cartmel (1997) have put forward the hypothesis of epistemological fallacy meaning that people take responsibility of events that they cannot control themselves. Freedom is a double-edged sword in the sense that whether one succeeds or fails it falls back on themselves. Responsibility of the self is identified as characteristic of neo-liberal societies. However, it has not been thoroughly investigated what this responsibility really means and how it is experienced by unemployed people. In this chapter I identify the machinery behind self-responsibilization and individualization that lay the groundwork for psychologization first of all, and secondly, for emotional debt.[1]

Psychologizing Unemployment: Governing Through Empowerment and Motivation

Individualization is not a new phenomenon; however, it is still a central backdrop for being emotionally indebted. Individualizing and activation of the responsibility of the self is bolstered or supported by more affective technologies; that is empowerment and motivation. The waiting hall of the unemployment fund is reminiscent of a lounge furnished with couches and there is an upmarket coffee machine offering espressos and café lattes. The meeting rooms are named after significant cities around the world; there is a Buenos Aires room, a New York room, etc. When people arrive at the introduction meeting for unemployed members they usually have to go to the Buenos Aires room on the first floor. There, one can choose between course titles such as 'Persuade others to say yes', 'Personal Branding', and 'Learn to network'. A consultant at a seminar, Susan, advocates that people find their passion: 'Find your passion and everything will be solved.' (Field Notes, October 2014). In the online communication from the unemployment fund to its members, there was an emphasis on the ways in which the fund could create an empowering technology: "Unfortunately, we cannot hire our own unemployed members, but we can fill them with inspiration, knowledge and energy that makes them ready for the labor market". Thus, the unemployment fund aspires to "inspire and energize" its members. The

---

[1] This chapter contains earlier versions from Pultz (2016) and Pultz and Hviid (2018).

unemployment fund does not only target the unemployed people's ability to make rational cost–benefit analyses but also to stimulate the softer sides of unemployed people by producing inspiration and energy. This form of government is thus aimed at capacities beyond rational calculation, namely affective registers. The conceptualization of the unemployed as suffering psychological consequences, has paved the way for motivation and coaching as a widespread approach to dealing with the challenge which is also represented in the amount of scholarly work on the subject (Vinokur et al., 2000; Wanberg et al., 1999).

Those working for the unemployment fund accepted the view that high-risk individuals needed to change, and they identified motivation as the key to change. Søren, the unemployment fund manager described the importance of motivation in the following way:

> We experience people who come with enough self-confidence and self-esteem. And as we meet them in here and time passes, they very openly show that their self-esteem, self-confidence, motivation, personality, and all that drops. We can see it visually. It's sort of a picture … that's why we spend a lot of time on motivation. Both courses and conversations to keep up the spirit and make people see the light at the end of the tunnel. We are not psychologists. We all have a coach education of some kind and in that sense, we have knowledge about motivation. We don't use the word 'therapy'. Because it is not what we do. But we either consult or coach. There are also people who have specialized in motivation. To coach motivation. And others have an education in dealing with stress.

Thus, for Søren the vulnerability and negative psychological effects of unemployment were inscribed on people's bodies, and it was part of unemployment fund workers' expertise to recognize and address these signs. In the discussion of motivation, Søren uses terminology derived from various psy-sciences (self-confidence, self-esteem, motivation, coaching, psychologists, therapy, consulting, and stress) (Rose, 1996). He thinks of the employees at the unemployment fund as skilled technicians who could recognize the signs (of low motivation and other psychological deterioration) from changes in behavior and body language and take action by working on enhancing motivation. He also used the phrase 'specialized in motivation'. This emphasis on motivation effectively makes unemployment a problem of the individual, a problem in the psyche of the individual weaponizing psychological narratives to turn the arrow inward. Governing the unemployed people is clearly not delimited to job search activities as they openly evaluate, judge and interpret wellbeing or lack thereof as part of the services offered. While caring for the unemployed people as people in the system is not necessarily a bad idea or normatively bad, it is crucial to be aware of what such practices imply and not least, how these technologies are experienced by the people who are the target of this care. As we shall see the caring welfare state involves turning up and weaponizing psychological constructs, narratives and understanding living alongside more bureaucratic ways of governing.

Internalizing Motivation Technologies

This conceptualization of unemployment as an individual psychological problem tended to be internalized and used by the unemployed people as well. Associated with the question of responsibility of the self, is the pressing challenge to keep up spirits in the face of adversity for unemployed people. Subjectifying unemployed people by working on their motivational levels involves making the personal or intimate aspects of their personalities an object of knowledge and intervention. In line with the calculus of biopolitics (Foucault, 2008), the construction of 'intimacy' anchored in the private, becomes instrumentalized as a measure of one's worth to the state. As Anderson (2012) has shown, motivation has become the focus of intervention and change in social work in general. The work of the Norwegian psychologist Revstedt on manifest and latent motivation inspired by humanist psychology motivational work has played a central role in this development (Revstedt, 2001). Other commentators (e.g., Villadsen, 2011) have pointed out that motivation is a prototypical example of how psy-standards are used to enact, individualize, and psychologize complex social problems by locating both the problems and the site for change in the individual. Motivation can serve as the explanation of a success (motivation) or failure (lack of manifest motivation). The emphasis on motivation serves the function of putting the focus on the individual level and to highlighting the affective or emotional aspects of challenging activities such as job searching. It involves an institutional risk management that shifts the focus to the individual and tends to conceal other relevant dimensions such as structural factors or labor market dynamics.

In the interviews, young unemployed people tended to see keeping up motivation in the face of rejections and adversity as one of the most challenging aspects of unemployment. Motivation seemed to play a key role in the governing of the self and the young people were constantly fostering and modulating their own motivational levels. Sophie, 27, who had graduated in Digital Communication seven months before the interview but had still not found a job at the time of her interview, described the challenges of motivation in the following way: "It [being unemployed] demands that you can pick yourself up every time something doesn't work, right? And that you believe that at some point it will turn around even though it goes up and down, right?". The management of energy levels requires individual belief or hope in the wake of the defeats that are part of the everyday life as an unemployed person. Mobilizing an orientation toward the future that enables more hope than worry is a key emotional challenge for unemployed people.

The ability to keep up spirits in the wake of rejections was affected by the fear of staying unemployed that most of the young unemployed people described. There was an atmosphere of uncertainty, and this sometimes manifested in feelings of fear and anxiety. This experience of insecurity is weaved into what Norris (2016) terms a culture of insecurity which also has an impact of people's sense of identity. The unemployed people are not only afraid of not being chosen for a specific job; being unemployed raises the more fundamental fear—will I ever be chosen for a job? As Lowe (in press) argues it is immensely important not only to measure and explore insecurity in terms of a specific job, but also take into account what he terms labor market insecurity referring to the individual's sense of labor market chances more broadly. While labor market statistics can easily map probabilities for different profiles, this part of the analysis shows the importance of understanding how these objective structural conditions are filtered through people's understanding of them. The same objective conditions can give riser to very different subjective experiences. Thinking about the future involves varying degrees of positive and negative attunement. Actively managing these levels of motivation is often described as a key task among unemployed people and it requires explicit emotional labor.

From the viewpoint of the unemployed people themselves, they do often describe a lack of energy and discouragement. For many, the uncertainty about the future imposes itself on the present. Motivation is oriented toward an indeterminate future and works in ways of animating, charging, or mobilizing the individual's capacity to act. Unemployed people are governed through their capacity to feel responsible, empowered, and motivated in their quest for a job. Inherent in the applied technologies, there is an intensification of governing through affective registers. The work on motivation and energy levels serves the purpose of casting the unemployed person not only as a self-responsible and self-blaming individual but simultaneously as an empowered, active citizen able to find a job. Such discursive, governmental, and material subjectification places specific demands on the individual: the job seeker is promoted to engage in self-work in the sense of working on motivational levels and on developing professional and social competencies.

The Many Faces of Self-Blame

The empirical material shows that activating the responsibility of the self is not only linked to becoming active but also by influencing more emotional experiences such as feeling blame for being in this situation. This blame has many faces and it is far from a 'single story'.

Dominating neoliberal and self-blaming trend push unemployed people to look for answers within their own subjective trajectory. There is a pressure to understand the situation as unemployed as self-inflicted, as something that could have been prevented by making other choices earlier at bifurcations points in one's trajectory. Morten attributes his unemployment primarily to the aftermath of the financial crisis of 2008, but he also balances his own responsibility and demonstrates an awareness of the pressure to blame oneself: "In some sense I feel like it has something to do with me, I can't honestly say that I am free of that." The promotion of attributing unemployment to oneself is very influential and in the quote,

Morten not only acknowledges the discourse of self-blame, but he also reveals his vulnerability in relation to it. Morten attempts to hold this individualizing narrative at bay, yet it takes up resources to resist the pressure to blame himself, he explains. He reasons that understanding societal dynamics has a somewhat relieving effect, and he imagines how being unemployed must affect other people without such frame of thought: "I think about people who don't think that it is a crisis in the system and stuff like that, and they must—if I am having a hard time—I think, other people are having a really, really, really, really hard time." Morten's analytical reflections emphasizing structural factors serve as a buffer for him and they allow him to be "governed a little less and not at that cost". Sophie describes how the duration of unemployment makes you more vulnerable to the self-blame as time passes:

> Of course, the longer you're in this you will probably think 'Oh no, I will never get a job'. I think I will think that way and be more and more worried. On the other hand, you probably also develop your job application skills. But, I think it will only become easier to blame yourself the further down the road you get.

Sophie also experiences a social pressure to blame herself for unemployment. She has not been unemployed very long, and it seems she can mobilize some resistance in relation to the self-blame pressure, but she also imagines becoming less resilient as time passes.

Most of the interview participants engage in self-blaming thoughts about what they could have done differently. For example, Stefan, who was 31 years when I interviewed him, had been unemployed for a couple of months but he had a prior record of long-term unemployment. He accepted responsibility for his unemployment, "it's in the zeitgeist that it is my fault that I don't have a job". He also draws attention to the fact that self-responsibility was not invented by the unemployment fund but exists as a discursive repertoire in society ("zeitgeist"). Stefan did not consider wider social factors as causes for his situation noting: "that I have not applied sufficiently broadly, that I haven't made myself sufficiently attractive to the labor market". Stefan's precise words, that is, "making myself attractive to the labor market" implies that he views his inadequacy as caused by some internal defect as lack of interpersonal or social competencies rather than by lack of education or skills. Networking is pivotal in order to get a job implying that job searching requires softer skills or immaterial labor rather than merely objective specs (which is the focus of Chap. 8). Thus, for both those providing benefits and support and for the unemployed, making oneself attractive to potential employers or to intermediaries is a key element in mitigating the risk of unemployment and promoting a return to the labor market.

Another face of self-blame takes on a different form. One of the influential figures and representations of the unemployed person is a lazy slacker. Negotiating one's self-understanding as unemployed for many involves being in some sort of dialogue with a laziness or moral incapacity. Morten explains the fear of being a "slacker" and elaborates on everyday drinking: "I do it [everyday drinking, ed.] sometimes, but you get another relationship to yourself when you do it. You are harder on yourself, or you blame yourself more I think." Demonstrating productivity constitutes a defense in relation to the representation of the unemployed as lazy and in that sense the image of the lazy unemployed person works as a counter-image; an image that has to be proven wrong. Morten's experience reveals an intimate dialogue with the discourse of laziness: "If you don't get up in the morning then you easily feel lazy or you begin to feel that thing about not being a decent citizen or whatever it is called". To Morten, one needs to be persistent in knowing that one is not "some sort of a careless dude, a wife-beater with drool all over". Generally, he describes being harder on himself as unemployed. Julia also mentions that her boyfriend jokes about lying on the couch the entire day. The joke confirms the existence of the stereotype, and even though it is said in a humorous voice, Julia still responds to the portraying of the unemployed as lazy indirectly, by elaborating on how busy she actually is. Sophie also positions herself in relation to the imagination of unemployed people as lazy by saying that she plans her time and fills it out with exercise and social arrangements "So I don't just wind up not doing shit all day long." Thus, the voice of laziness is identified as influential even though none of them actually consider themselves as lazy—the fear of being seen as lazy invades their personal narratives and they feel obliged to defend themselves against the subtle accusation embedded in the social representation of an unemployed person.

Another face of self-blame relates to issues of identity. Especially for graduates, identity issues come up and the participants describe a lack of identity asking the question; who am I now? Going against the societally paved route is often experienced as challenging. Being "out of time" and especially "falling behind" is not only structurally challenging, but it also challenges the person's understanding of him or herself (Hviid, 2008; Neugarten, 1996). Understanding oneself is at least partly channeled through societal expectations of specific and culturally guided norms. In this case study, especially for the graduate Sophie, being out of work leaves her with an experience of "falling behind" especially in comparison with her employed peers. As Sophie notes, previously she subscribed to an identity as a student. This structured her everyday life in the community of fellow students and pointed toward certain promises about the future. But the category of "unemployed" does not provide a desirable identity:

Sophie: A month and a half ago I was under the protection of saying that I was a student.
Interviewer: Protection?
Sophie: Yeah, in the sense that I didn't have to—and it's not because you necessarily have to be, but—justify why I don't have a job, and I have to do that a little bit now, because in some way it's a little … It's not a taboo but it's not the dream scenario to graduate and not have a job. It's much nicer to say, 'Well, I have a job and I have started right away'. Before you were still a student, and it's also that you're an adult now and you have to have your first adult job and find out 'Well now I have graduated as Master of Law. But who am I as an adult?'

In the quote, we see how Sophie travels in time to make sense of her current situation. She compares currently being unemployed to what was recently familiar to her. Being unemployed interferes fundamentally with her identity work, more specifically with her emerging adult identity. Sophie is experiencing a lack of desirable identity and the promises for the future that go with it. She has not yet developed her professional identity but has lost the identity she knows from being a student associated also with the youth category. She does not have the opportunity to employ the strategy of sustaining (Norris, in press) that help unemployed people hold on to their professional identity, as this is not very developed for graduates with limited work experience and hence have less to fall back on as unemployed.

In accordance with this observation, Morten reflects on the detrimental effects of unemployment on his experience of belonging, of being part of society: "You begin to feel more rusty (…) You begin to question your … worth in some ways … I mean, (you question, ed.) that you are ever gonna find your shelf, where there is room for you … so much identity is tied to work." Becoming unemployed, for Morten and Sophie, attacks their fundamental feeling of being able to contribute to society and thus challenges their experience of being a worthy citizen. Morten elaborates on how these thoughts interfere with the ways he relates to and governs himself when it comes to more quotidian self-evaluations. He and Sophie both feel attacked on their fundamental sense of being of value, of being a dignified member of society.

Competitive Infrastructures

Most of the individuals I interviewed told me that they needed to work on their emotions to maintain their motivation when their job applications were rejected. Mette, a newly qualified graduate engineer who had been unemployed for six weeks at the time of her interview, noted the motivational impact of competition for jobs in the following way:

> I think it does require a lot. But it is a pressure I put on myself. There is a demand that you have to make that many applications each month, but it's more when I find out that the others have got jobs. Then you put yourself under a greater pressure. Come on, Mette, now you really have to find something in the next month, hopefully not longer than that. Yeah, it's more the pressure you put on yourself.

While the activation policies are closely linked to making the individual responsible of being unemployed, it is notable, that Mette describes it as a pressure coming mainly from within as well as she experiences the pressure to be fueled by a comparison with peers rather than by the demands embedded in the activation policies. The experience of the 'real' pressure as coming from within is common among many of the young unemployed people.

The pressure and competitive infrastructures are cultivated in society but from a first-hand perspective, it is experienced as private, indicating a close link between the technologies of power and technologies of the self. Mette describes the comparison with peers as even more productive than the requirements embedded in the system. As an unemployed person and jobseeker, you are painfully aware that the people you share the situation with are in fact also your competition. Being unemployed is a situation in which many people evaluate their worth and it is common to look sideward to your peers in order to judge how you are doing.

In accordance with Foucault and his ideas on neoliberal governmentality (Foucault et al., 2007), Lazzarato (2009) points out that the installation of competition is the dominating principle in the social domain. Competition is constantly nourished and maintained by inequality in neoliberal states and the competition with one's peers as unemployed is a concrete example of this and how it works at a micropolitical level. The unemployed people manage risk by comparing themselves to unemployed peers. Their position in this ongoing competition affects them either by empowering them or by discouraging them. Thus, they do not only act in a competitive field, but they also reproduce competition as an organizing principle in the way they relate to themselves. In his work on neoliberalism, Foucault challenges the view that neoliberalism equals a lack of government; indeed, producing a market organized by competition demands a competent government (Foucault et al., 2007; Oksala, 2016). He observed that: "Neoliberalism should not therefore be identified with laissez-faire, but rather with permanent vigilance, activity, and intervention" (Foucault et al., 2007, p. 131). The tendency to compete should continuously be fostered and enhanced. Likewise, the competition and comparative infrastructures do not just naturally arise; rather they are orchestrated and enacted in specific practices and technologies and from there, they seep down and affect the ways people relate to themselves and others.

What Alleviates the Self-Blame?

The self-blaming narrative is not nearly as pervasive or detrimental among interview participants who work in professional domains characterized by a precarious market such as the cultural industry (Pultz & Dupret, 2023) or academia (Gleerup et al., 2018) in which periods of unemployment are almost impossible to avoid. A possible explanation is that being in and out of employment is more normalized. Another possible explanation is that it is less obvious whether you have a job or not.

I talked to Julia who just finished her PhD and she reasoned that her period of unemployment is a predictable and natural part of her career. She feels capable of finding a good job, whether she chooses to stay in academia or transit to the private sector.

Some participants have volunteer jobs, and they all describe how ideas for jobs originate in encounters with others, facilitated by events at these workplaces. Volunteer work provides structure and a network, and Sophie says that she does volunteer work to keep herself active and to "work on herself", in terms of improving her profile in the competition for a job. In the literature on neoliberalism, this process is conceptualized as an optimization of human capital in the competitive labor markets. To some extent, both Morten and Julia have a hard time defining the exact difference between their situations now and when they had a job. They work on some the same things, and concretely they go to the same workplaces where they used to get paid. They know that the limit between work and non-work is there, but it is increasingly blurred. As Julia says, "we give lectures on the brain and that is with former colleagues, so yes, I think that other people still need me". Building on the seminal work of Jahoda (1982), belonging to a meaningful community, sharing goals and being needed are some of the characteristics of having a job. From the present study, we can conclude that new contours of what it means to work in a precarious and flexible labor market appears. For some people, this means that being unemployed is not necessarily associated with the same deprivations of latent functions (time structure, common goals, activity, social contact, and social status) as before. Activities, both in terms of work experience in the past and current volunteer work while being unemployed, inspire imaginatory work about present and future selves for the young people and thus work as a resource. As Norris (in press) argues, sustaining a sense of a professional identity can serve as a buffer against some of the feelings of being vulnerable and less worthy. This perspective will be elaborated on in Chaps. 6 and 7.

Technologies of Fear and Risk Management

Fear and anxiety were also engendered in the social practices in the unemployment fund itself. For example, at a welcoming meeting, the new young unemployed people were shown a statistical survival curve that indicated that individuals who were still unemployed after four months have a much lower probability of finding a job than individuals who had been out of work for less than four months (field notes, October 2014). This type of information is targeted homo economicus characterized by the ability to make cost and benefit analyses that direct behavior based on these analyses. Mentioning this piece of statistic is not viewed as a neutral conveying of objective information; rather it is understood as a practice with the aim of providing unemployed people with an incentive to engage in active job search from the beginning as the probability of finding a job later on drops. This sort of knowledge about risk and risk management has a particular emotional and affective side to it. Most of the participants worried about the future and information like this contributed to such feeling of insecurity. Lars, a theology graduate who had been unemployed for five months at the time of interview says:

> Hey, it never ends. When am I going back to work or to study? When will I ever do something again? I don't know. (…) My frustrations and my fundamental anxiety and insecurity about the future rubs off on me and puts me in a foul mood, makes me frustrated,and quick to anger.

The aim of the governmental technologies is to act as a stimulant to action, however governing of affective registers such as fear, there are no guaranties that the technologies will actually provide an incentive for action or in fact have quite the opposite effect. As mentioned, the technologies do not work in a monolithic fashion and thus some interview participants describe feeling powerless in the face of receiving such pieces of information from the very beginning of their unemployment period. These technologies are designed to work rationally, for example, providing individuals with information that the shorter the period of their unemployment, the higher the probability of finding a job constituting an incentive to take immediate action. The technologies, however, are also designed to work on affects and the same information that incentivizes action can stimulate fear and anxiety.

Showing such a graph is a way of outsourcing a threat of becoming long-termed unemployed by presenting a seemingly neutral piece of information. However, noting what specific numbers and statistics are communicated at PES is important, as the numbers are not just neutral or randomly selected. They are selected with a particular goal in mind and attending to the concrete methods of communicating the message of the necessity to be pro-active from the very get go and also quickly adapt or downgrade from a dream job toward something more feasible. That process involves invoking a sense of unease, insecurity, and even fear of being one of the people mentioned in the statistics presented because such statistics have overlooked affective dimensions as well.

Another side of the story about self-blame is the various ways that unemployed people take on the risk management and as such rely very little on getting qualified help from PES. The unemployment fund referred to the laws and rules in the area as a 'jungle of rules', and many participants describe a latent fear of doing something wrong and getting caught. Thomas compared how it was receiving educational benefits as a student to receiving unemployment benefits and he noted that as an unemployment benefit claimant: "You feel a lot more surveillance".

Handling unemployment and the risk of unemployment for the unemployed people entailed dealing with the unemployment fund. It was not uncommon for people to cheat in that they fabricated activities in order to live up to the requirement to be an active job seeker. Julie, who had been unemployed for a couple of months, said: "I have written down jobs that I didn't apply for in order to fill out that goddamn list. In a way, I keep a creative book."

Case workers evaluate each case and determine to some extent the number of activities that the unemployed person had to participate in, and thus the interpersonal relation between the case worker and the unemployed person was central to issues of risk management. Julie noted:

> I don't expect anything from the unemployment fund, they don't understand my situation. I know what they want to hear so I tell them that story. Luckily, I am gifted with the ability to laugh at the right times and to be serious. Then I go out from there and I feel dirty because I conned her. It serves the purpose of providing me with ease for three months. It's terrible. I can't use the unemployment fund, the job centre or any other agency for anything. All contact should be minimized.

Not only is Julie aware of the rules she has to live up to, but she was also conscious of the unwritten norms embedded in the technologies applied by the unemployment fund valuing empowerment and self-responsibility. Julie describes deciphering what it takes to be evaluated as a competent and self-reliant job seeker and she plays that role in order to avoid being required to attend meetings and seminars. In that sense, part of her risk management entails dealing with the unemployment fund in a way that involves intellectual analysis, but she also noted the non-intellectual or affective work involved in the contact with the caseworker.

Both in terms of analyzing what the unemployment fund wants to hear and then perform that version even though it entails lying and 'feeling dirty' as Julie says. A key role of the unemployment fund is to monitor and ensure that their members comply with the requirement of active job searching and to sanction them if they fail to do so. The unemployed people view the role of institution as control, and they do not expect that the mandatory activities will get them closer to a job. Morten says: "I just think that there is very little about who you are and where you were at (…) I got totally turned off by that. You say the right things to live up to the demands so they write 'check', but that won't get you closer to the labor market." Morten describes managing the system in a strategic way by telling them what they want to hear—or what is necessary in order to receive unemployment benefits. He, and the others, quickly decode the language and comply with it officially. Making sense of the demand of activity becomes, for Morten, an isolated challenge dissociated from the overall goal of finding a job. He problematizes that the demands are not synchronized with what it takes to get a job in contemporary labor markets, which supports the idea of the unemployment fund as an institution of control rather than one that brings unemployed people closer to jobs. Laughing at the right times and being serious at others involve applying more sensitive capacities and these are deemed important in relation to dealing with PES and unemployment. The unemployed people feel monitored and respond to some degree with fear, but they also manage the technology of surveillance with the resources available to them, including putting in the necessary affective and emotional labor to be governed a little less or not at that cost.

Managing Risk Through Future Selves

Imagining possible futures plays an important role when it comes to the continuous repair of one's self-image or identity as unemployed (Norris, 2016). A vivid subjective imagination of what the future might bring serves as a psychological buffer against the uncertainty characterizing the experience of unemployment and the unwanted permanent identity as "an unemployed person". Imagining a far-sighted plan has the effect of making the immediate present better. Such a far-sighted plan creates bifurcation points in the future: "I have said to myself that if I do not find a job within a year then I have to take a job that I am overqualified for, just to do something." Morten is imagining what to do in the future. He constructs the choice of either getting a job he wants or taking on a job that he is overqualified for, which shows the malleability and creativity involved in the generativity of imagination and goals. By nuancing the ultimate bifurcation point—getting a job or staying unemployed—he gains a sense of agency. It allows him to take control over potential events in the future. While he succeeds in living up to taking on the responsibility of unemployment, the drawback is a reproduction of an individualization of unemployment. When asked what it means for him to have made this plan, he replies: "A sort of ease I guess (…) then you know what you have to do. It's all this about finding meaning in the things you do." For Morten, imagining the future and making actual plans keeps him aligned with who he is, and it gives him a better sense of what he wants. However, the idea of lowering the ambitions with regard to targeted jobs is not Morten's alone as the term "good enough job" is often promoted in the system to avoid the steep decline in probability of finding a job as time passes.

Governing Through Algorithms: Job Suggestions and Profiling

The unemployment system also tries to take into account projected future scenarios through predictions and algorithms. Digital technologies such as job suggestions and profiling impact unemployment experiences and especially the way they are encouraged to manage risk.

Developing employment technologies relying on data and algorithms in PES both are used both as profiling tools and to generate suggestions for jobs. But how is this experienced by the unemployed people? Governing through probability is central to Danish PES as described in Chap. 3 and is part of an international trend incorporating big data in the technologies (Desiere et al., 2019). The suggestions for available positions are generated automatically. However, the suggestions are not always relevant according to the unemployed participants. Having to deal with suggestions that feel irrelevant causes frustration. As Taus describes here reflecting on the demands required at PES:

> It makes a lot of sense that you have to apply for two jobs a week because, I mean, how would you ever get a job if you didn't apply, right? On the other hand, I'm really tired of that rule that requires me to look at the job suggestions that Jobnet automatically generates for me. I've been penalized for not doing it several times because I simply forgot. I also find that there

are a lot of jobs that are completely insane for me and my profile. I have a long education, I live in Frederiksberg, and I have a partial paralysis. So, I get penalized because I don't check if I want to be a waiter in Aalborg, for example. What kind of algorithms are finding these kinds of jobs or waitressing positions in Næstved? Maybe I should think outside the box, but I have a disability. But the algorithm can't see that, and it's because I don't check those types of jobs that I get penalized for unemployment benefits. I've experienced this many times. And it's only for a day because I realize it and sign up immediately, but the principle of it, that I can be financially penalized for not checking those lousy jobs that are auto-generated for me, is frustrating.

The algorithms are not necessarily able to take into account important aspects of life, such as a disability. To Taus, it is frustrating that he sometimes loses money because he forgets to deal with the meaningless suggestions generated by the system. He describes feeling frustrated and also critical toward generating a system by which he can be penalized for not checking irrelevant job openings. Accepting meaninglessness in fact challenges a fundamental part of feeling like dignified citizen. The digital technologies are not neutral but partake the shaping the unemployment experience and for the time being they do not seem to enable a sense of agency among the unemployed people. Taus cannot choose *not* to look at the suggestions. The constraints on not being governed quite so much become very visible.

Another example using big data and algorithms within PES is the use of a profiling system employed in many European countries (Desiere et al., 2019). The purpose of this profiling tool is to identify those who are likely to become long-term unemployed so that resources can be more effectively allocated to the people who need them.

In the unemplouyment fund the tool was designed to identify individuals in a high-risk category and also identify interventions that would mitigate this risk. The unemployment fund justified screening as cost effective and as a way of targeting resources at 'high-risk' individuals by 'individualizing counselling of job seekers' and so ensuring the 'optimal distribution of resources'. The statistical model was based on a combination of data from the membership register and information about unemployed members, background information and job outcomes gathered in

2009–2011 by the unemployment fund. Statistical consultants were hired to develop a statistical model that could identify risk factors predicting unemployment. Using multiple linear regressions, a statistical model was developed and on that basis, a survey consisting of 16 items was constructed as a screening tool.

The risk factors identified were:

Language: not speaking Danish as a first language;
Residence: making more than five changes of address during membership had a significant effect and making three to four changes in the same period also had an effect.
Age: being 50 years or older.
Length of Employment: working for more than 5 years in the last job,
Certain occupations: such as electrical construction engineer.

The consultants also found some factors that reduced the probability that an individual would be unemployed.
These protective factors were:

Education: graduating within the rated time frame and performing at A or A+ level in exams;
Earnings: more than 6704 euros a month in the last job;
Student work: in relevant field of work;
Type of occupation: such as marine engineering.
Trade union: not being a member of a union;
Participating in courses: on how to write CVs offered at the unemployment fund;
Partner: living with a partner.

There does not seem to be an overarching logic or an obvious link between the different variables identified by the statistical analysis. Furthermore, most of these factors are not amenable to change or intervention by the unemployment fund managers, nor by the unemployed people themselves. If a claimant is aged 50 or over, this cannot be altered. Since the analysis is based on a specific data set, some factors are more visible and prominent than others such as those relating to the person's social and work background registered in the membership database. However, other factors such as motivation are not measured and are outside the scope of the model. Despite these limitations, at the time of the study all new unemployed people were assessed by the screening tool and categorized as high, medium, or low risk.

The screening tool contributed to knowledge about unemployed people in the sense that it made it possible to measure and compare them on specific parameters. Thus, screening made it possible to collect information about a specific individual and in the context of the model, to make predictions about that individual and plan interventions to improve those predictions. The screening relied on the application of probabilistic models to a large database enabling the targeting of resources to mitigate the risk of unemployment. The existence and accessibility of data on unemployed people served as the basis for the development of the screening tool in the sense that the technology was available and the widespread practice of gathering and storing data makes it very easy to engage in statistical analysis. In his interview, Søren, a manager in the unemployment fund, discussed the possibilities that the analysis of the large-scale database provided and how these could be used in the following way:

> We have known data. We know where people live. We know their education and we know how old they are. These pieces of information are a part of being a member of an unemployment fund (…). And then we started to be more systematic about these things because some colleagues, employees in the team and I, had tons of experience with this and we could say something about what was relevant. But we didn't actually know. We didn't have evidence. We just thought.

In this extract, Søren was suggesting that there was a hierarchy of knowledge. He considered that experience was valuable, but inferior to systematic knowledge created by the structured statistical analysis of a large database. The screening tool is thus a form of power; it is created by technical experts and used by agents of the unemployment fund to identify who should be subject to greater surveillance and intervention. An internal document of the unemployment fund described the aim of screening as ensuring a 'targeted effort from first contact'. For example, the case worker responsible for making decisions about specific unemployed people received and read a case file that included a risk profile before they met the individual. The screening tool and associated risk categorization thus provided the starting point. The actual process of screening a specific candidate was covert and the unemployed members filled in a survey as a part of signing on as unemployed. The members were at this point in time not informed that the data would be used to create a risk profile and that this profile determined how much they would have to participate in meetings and courses at the unemployment fund. As Søren observed:

> We invite all members to a welcoming meeting when they become unemployed. And at the same time we offer members different things based on their profile. You have the same rights. Everybody's entitled to the same help from us (…) If you are in Group Y [high risk] then we recommend some things. We write: 'Others like you have participated in the workshop about networking or in the course about personal branding'.

The unemployment fund tended not to draw attention to screening and risk profiling but did provide some hints that the unemployment fund response to their members was based on knowledge they collected about them. In making references to 'others like you' in the communication to its members, the unemployment fund was signaling that it had a mechanism for making comparisons but was not transparent about how this was done. This implied that to some extent the unemployed people were informed that they are being watched and monitored, but without disclosing to them precisely how.

The young unemployed people I interviewed were aware that the unemployment fund did categorize them and that such categorization formed the basis for the way they were treated. For example, Camilla, a 28-year-old unemployed biologist, observed that the unemployment fund had been relatively relaxed about her and that:

> I haven't got those warnings. They are pretty relaxed with me (…). At least I am in a group that they expect is able to find jobs. Then they have another group that they don't expect will find a job. I am under the impression that they divide us.

While the individuals I interviewed had not been formally told in which category they had been placed, most of them were aware that the activities which the unemployment fund asked them to engage in reflected how the unemployment fund categorized them. As Camilla noted, the unemployment fund did not pay her that much attention as she had been placed 'in a group that they expect is able to find jobs'. Camilla clearly accepted this categorization and accepted that she was better off than many of her unemployed peers as she was likely to find a job relatively quickly. By accepting that she was in a group that is better off, she gained some sort of empowering capacity enabling her to initiate activities and take on the responsibility of the self. Her individual risk management entailed navigating in this terrain of inequality or difference by means of 'sensing' or as she said 'being under the impression'. Thus the categorization had an affective dimension; it enabled the low-risk group to be identified as such, even though it is not explicitly out in the open and thus reproduced or produced the assumed differences between the groups.

The basis of the screening model is solely statistical and not reliant on research-based knowledge or coherent theoretical frameworks. In this context, those who deviate from the established norms are identified as weak and a danger that needs to be identified, prioritized, and managed. The screening practice is not highly visible as it uses already existing data; however, it affects the production of subjectivity, and it is also reflected in how the unemployed people view and conduct themselves. People who are in the 'low risk group' thus feel empowered by sensing that they are placed in this category. While the screening tool is yet another administrative system, the analysis shows the importance of exploring the built-in understandings and the potential harm such systems can do reproducing and exacerbating existing inequalities among unemployed people. These systems rarely survive in PES practices across Europe; they struggle both with legal impasses as they discriminate citizens on illegal grounds (Eubanks, 2018) and at the street-level the validity of their predictions are also not only supported by counselors who meet unemployed people and witness their complexity (Griffin et al., 2021). Despite the fact that profiling system have a hard time surviving in practice, there is still political interest and prioritization in developing instruments based on big data and algorithms as the main goal is to digitalize PES. The persuasive power of "objectivity" and "data-driven" should be balanced against the research uncovering how these tools work in practice; in both the intended and unintended ways.

Summing Up

The unemployed people blame themselves for not having made the right decisions and for not being 'attractive' enough on the labor market. They engage in self-work in the pursuit of optimizing their human capital in the competitive field. They work on motivation and fight off depression in the wake of numerous rejections. They are not governed just as rational actors—homo economicus—responding to economic incentives making cost-benefit calculations. They are also governed through emotional and affective registers and these emotional and affective capacities are economized and capitalized in new and unforeseen ways in the governing of young unemployed people.

Private aspects of their personalities become the object of intervention and thus the explanation of unemployment is limited to an individual or interpersonal context and the field is to some extent depoliticized. Unemployed people working on optimizing their human capital are locked in competition in a neoliberal labor market with great implications for dealing with risk at both an institutional and an individual level.

Increasingly, ideas and imaginations about the future are mobilized in the way unemployed people govern themselves. In various ways, the negotiate a balance thinking about the future with worry and hope. Also at a system level, big data and algorithms have increasingly introduced the use of predictions as a way to govern unemployed people. These projected selves made by people themselves and machines affect the lived experience of unemployment.

References

Anderson, B. (2012). Affect and biopower: Towards a politics of life. *Transactions of the Institute of British Geographers, 37*(1), 28–43. https://doi.org/10.1111/j.1475-5661.2011.00441.x

Beck, U. (1992). *Risk society: Towards a new modernity.* Sage.

Beck, U. (2008). *World at risk. Polity.*

Brown, W. (2015). *Undoing the demos: Neoliberalism's stealth revolution.* Mit Press.

Desiere, S., Langenbucher, K., & Struyven, L. (2019). Statistical profiling in public employment services: An international comparison. *OECD Social, Employment and Migration Working Papers, 224,* 1–29. https://doi.org/10.1787/b5e5f16e-en

Engelbreth Larsen, R. (2013). *Ledighed og ledighad : kritisk analyse af et politisk normskred.* (1. udgave.). Dana.

Eubanks, V. (2018). *Automating inequality: How high-tech tools profile, police, and punish the poor.* St. Martin's Press.

Foucault, M. (2008). *The birth of biopolitics, lectures at the College de France, 1978–1979.* Palgrave Macmillan.

Foucault, M., Senellart, M., Ewald, F., & Fontana, A. (2007). *Security, territory, population.* Palgrave Macmillan.

Furlong, A., & Cartmel, F. (1997). *Young people and social change, individualization and risk in late modernity.* Open University Press.

Giddens, A. (2001). *Modernity and self-identity, self and society in the late modern age* (Reprint.). Polity.

Gleerup, J., Nielsen, B. S., Olsén, P., & Warring, N. (2018). Prekarisering og akademisk arbejde. *Tidsskrift for Arbejdsliv, 20*(1), 9–29.

Griffin et al. (2021). Report - Ethical, Social, Theological, Technical Review Of 1st Generation PES Algorithms And Data Use. *HECAT, Project Deliverable, Number D1.3,* online, Available from: http://hecat.eu/wpcontent/uploads/2021/01/D1.3_Ethical-social-theological-technical-review-of-1st-generation-algorithms-and-datause.pdf

Hviid, P. (2008). Interviewing using a cultural-historical approach. *Studying Children: A Cultural-Historical Approach,* 139–156.

Jahoda, M. (1982). *Employment and unemployment.* Cambridge Books.

Lazzarato, M. (2009). Neoliberalism in action inequality, insecurity and the reconstitution of the social. *Theory, Culture & Society, 26*(6), 109–133. https://doi.org/10.1177/0263276409350283

Lowe, T. (in press). Seeking shelter from the storm. In V. Chen, S. Pultz, & O. Sharone (Eds.), *Handbook of unemployment and society.* Edward Elgar Publishing.

Mascini, P., Achterberg, P., & Houtman, D. (2013). Neoliberalism and work-related risks: Individual or collective responsibilization? *Journal of Risk Research, 16*(10), 1209–1224.

Mørch, S., Pultz, S., & Stroebæk, P. (2018). Strategic self-management: The new youth challenge. *Journal of Youth Studies, 21*(4), 422–438. https://doi.org/10.1080/13676261.2017.1385747

Newman, K. S. (1988). *Falling from grace, the experience of downward mobility in the American middle class.* The Free Press.

Norris, D. R. (2016). *Job loss, identity, and mental health.* Rutgers University Press.

Norris, D. R. (in press). Unemployment counseling: An identity-based perspective. In O. Sharone, V. Chen, & S. Pultz (red.), *Handbook on unemployment and society.* Edward Elgar Publishing.

Oksala, J. (2016). Affective labor and feminist politics. *Signs: Journal of Women in Culture and Society, 41*(2), 281–303.

Pultz, S. (2016). Governing homo economicus: Risk management among young unemployed people in the Danish welfare state. *Health, Risk & Society, 18*(3–4), 168–187.

Pultz, S., & Dupret, K. (2023). Emotional status and emotional labour: Exploring the emotional labour among casualised and tenured knowledge workers. *Culture and Organization, Latest articles.* https://doi.org/10.1080/14759551.2023.2258433

Pultz, S., & Hviid, P. (2018). Imagining a better future: Young unemployed people and the polyphonic choir. *Culture & Psychology, 24*(1), 3–25. https://doi.org/10.1177/1354067X16660853

Revstedt, P. (2001). *Motivationsarbejde.* Hans Reitzel.

Rose, N. (1996). *Inventing our selves, psychology, power, and personhood.* Cambridge University Press.

Sharone, O. (2013). *Flawed system/flawed self: Job searching and unemployment experiences.* University of Chicago Press.

Villadsen, K. (2011). Modern welfare and 'good old' philanthropy: A forgotten or a troubling trajectory? *Public Management Review, 13*(8), 1057–1075. https://doi.org/10.1080/14719037.2011.622675

Vinokur, A. D., Schul, Y., Vuori, J., & Price, R. H. (2000). Two years after a job loss: Long-term impact of the JOBS program on reemployment and mental health. *Journal of Occupational Health Psychology, 5*(1), 32.

Wanberg, C. R., Kanfer, R., & Rotundo, M. (1999). Unemployed individuals: Motives, job-search competencies, and job-search constraints as predictors of job seeking and reemployment. *Journal of Applied Psychology, 84*(6), 897–910. https://doi.org/10.1037/0021-9010.84.6.897

5

The Sticky Shame and What to Do with It

Unemployed people are not only governed through definitions of appropriate behavior. They are also governed in what Ahmed (2004) calls the "affective economy," loosely defining appropriate ways of feeling; about the situation; about the labor market and not least; about how one feels about oneself. The workings of shame are key to understanding the emotional debt that unemployed people find themselves in.

While guilt refers to the negative feeling of having done something wrong, shame refers to the fundamental experience of being wrong (Brown, 2006a). In that sense, shame excels at making unemployment a sensitive and private problem that should be hidden from others.

In the previous chapter, it became clear that when meeting the system, there are particular emotional demands such as demonstrating enough motivation and empowerment as well as taking responsibility for the risk profile you are. Further exploring the affective sides of subjectification of unemployed people, I foreground how it impacts unemployed people that the representation of the unemployed person is a general questioning of one's moral worth. By analyzing the empirical material through affectivity perspectives on shame and affective economy, I identify how the people make contortions to avoid identifying themselves as unemployed. The unemployment label affects them negatively. To a greater extent, young unemployed people draw on the configuration of the 'entrepreneurial subject' or the 'freelancer' to establish a meaningful everyday life (Bröckling, 2015). Developing the theoretical apparatus and hence conceptualizing how unemployed people are governed through their feelings is crucial to understanding why unemployed people often struggle to feel worthy as citizens—a question that is deeply related to agency and to the question of how people can take action.

Elias (1997) characterizes shame, embarrassment, and humiliation as some of the dominant emotions in modern societies as they form the basis for morality. Furthermore, he understands these emotions as taboo that not only have to remain hidden from others but also from oneself. Scheff (2000) has also taken up the topic of shame and, in accordance with Elias (1997) and Sennett (1980), notes that an individual who feels ashamed tends not to conform to prescribed codes of behavior and that shame thus serves a socializing or disciplining function. Self-conscious emotional experiences such as shame or pride have been shown to play an important role in conducting behavior (Goffman, 1968; Scheff, 1990, 2000; Gibson, 2016), and specifically shame has been identified as a mechanism to induce compliance to social norms (Combs et al., 2010). Studies show that people struggling with poverty tend to feel ashamed or humiliated (Nussbaum, 2004). Inspired by Foucault's concept of productive power as effects emerging from social relations, Creed et al. (2014) construct a framework of shame. Here, what they term 'systematic shame' is of relevance. Systematic shame is defined as comprising shared understandings of the conditions that give rise to what they illustratively term 'felt shame'. Institutions develop shared rules defining what is appropriate and inappropriate behavior and the authors note that these boundaries between appropriateness and inappropriateness are often taken for granted and perceived as objective and natural (Creed et al., 2014). In their view, people can assess any given situation in terms of shame, and they perceive themselves and others in accordance with these assessments. This intersubjective surveillance underpins how people regulate themselves to avoid shame (Gibson, 2016).

The Duality of Shame and Passion, Affective Economy, and 'Sticky Categories'

In order to develop a more nuanced theoretical approach when focusing on shame, I turn to Tomkins' seminal work on duality of shame and passion. Tomkins argues that, without interest, there cannot be shame (Tomkins, 2008). In accordance with Tomkins, Probyn defines shame as, "the body calling out its interest" (Probyn, 2004, p. 28). Interest and intention is the prerequisite of shame as it is only possible to feel ashamed of something that is of value to the individual. Shame is the self-reflexive and self-conscious affect par excellence (Brøgger & Staunæs, 2016). Ahmed observes that what is valued is linked to social norms and an attached affective economy: "shame can also be experienced as the affective costs of not following the script of normative existence" (Ahmed, 2014b, p. 107). While people may not personally abide to the idea that is only through paid labor we have access to a sense of worthiness in a capitalist society, the underlying values in society still affect the way people relate to themselves from a marginalized position in the labor market.

Shame is also inherently relational and the way we see ourselves through shame lenses is intimately connected to the way we imagine that other people see us or evaluate us. These imaginations or evaluation are often based on embodied experiences of being met by other people. Clinical work on trauma suggests that if we have experience being treated as having little or no value to people around us, and naturally in particular if these experiences are with family members such as parents, it can distort or severely affect our experience of being worthy and make us prone to feeling ashamed in various life circumstances, such as unemployment, but also other events such as the experience of loss and divorce.

In the psychological literature there has long been a tradition of distinguishing between self-worth and self-esteem, where the latter is closely related to performance and the former is more related to a fundamental experience of having value as human being—as Kant expresses it; being of value as a goal in itself, not as a means (Kant, 2020). This book does not focus on the life historical and personal trajectories that precede unemployment experiences. For now, alluding to this psychological work serves the purpose of identifying one out of many possible explanations that shame does not affect us in a uniform fashion. We are not equally prone to feel shame, however, this is not centered here.

What is interesting here is the fact that even though we might have political views that challenge a purely capitalist notion or protestant work ethics, the social value of paid work as a generous source of both dignity, money and status in western societies affect citizens socialized in most western societies (Elias, 1997; Lamont, 2023; Tomkins, 2008). Shame is a socializing complex emotion that serves a civilizing purpose, and a shameless society is not necessarily the end goal.

Interestingly, people who are prone to feel ashamed of being unemployed, might not necessarily share or explicitly agree with the underlying value system. As an example, I have talked to people whose self-worth take a dive during their unemployment period, many of them would not evaluate their unemployed friends the same way. They would not question other people's worth on the basis of their employment status but simultaneously it is not easy for them to get rid of the stickiness on their own behalf. In a parallel vein, work on intersectionality, race and gender has taught us the last couple of decades, dominant value systems such as white supremacy or patriarchy can be far away from over political attitudes, but they might still pull a few strings behind the curtains (Crenshaw, 2017; Hancock, 2016; Rosette et al., 2018).

A large proportion of unemployed people report feeling ashamed of their status as measured in survey studies such as Rantakeisu et al. (1999) and Pultz and Teasdale (2017). From literature on shame, it is noteworthy that shame does not only work in the explicit but might in fact affect more people than the ones who self-report feeling ashamed. At this point, this is purely a speculative suggestion; however, I will briefly dwell on the challenging methodological questions relating to shame issues.

With inspiration from clinical psychological work such as Jørgensen (2023) and Asper (1992), there are underlying thought patterns and ways of relating to oneself that reveal the workings of shame behind the curtains. The literature on trauma and shame also shows that a response to feeling ashamed often involves making oneself either as small as possible or in the worst-case scenario making oneself disappear.

5 The Sticky Shame and What to Do with It

Even though unemployment is increasingly common, it does not follow the socially desirable script. Shame must be handled somehow and, on this point, Probyn writes, "through our public statements, we want to distance ourselves from this uncomfortable proximity. In uttering the phrase, we call upon others to witness our pulling away" (Probyn in Ahmed, 2014a, p. 95). Shame feels uncomfortable and thus people seek to escape it, as also noted by Creed et al. (2014).

I have lost track of how many times interview participants have mentioned that they find it morally appalling that people who use the system as scroungers. That way of 'distancing oneself from this uncomfortable proximity' thus involves reproducing the negative representation of unemployed people. How else can they try to control the moral judgment they feel is happening as soon as you say you are unemployed? The immediate response is a defense rather than resisting the moral test to begin with and the premise it is built on.

What follows is an exploration of shame and its workings with a particular emphasis on the various dynamics that give rise to shame and encourage us to be shameful. While the clinical psychological literature is abundant, only recently, the more sociological and social psychological literature is catching up. The seminal work of Tyler (2020) plays a fundamental role here, while smaller more field specific contributions also have their merit in adding nuance to the unemployment literature (Creed et al., 2014; Pultz, 2018; Peterie et al., 2019; Boland & Griffin, 2021).

In accordance with this, Ahmed notes that shame does not adhere to the intra-psychological domain but is rather orchestrated by the political and societal affective economy in which having a job and being self-sufficient are valorized. Subjectifying unemployed people as a burden to the state and problematizing unemployment as a moral issue serves the goal of ensuring people try to avoid unemployment, as this is too costly for the state. I supplement Tomkin with Ahmed (2014b) and her useful concepts of an 'affective economy' and 'sticky emotions'. Ahmed conceives of emotions not as psychological states per se but rather as cultural practices with political implications and as sites of government.

Bodies are valorized in what Ahmed calls the 'affective economy', charging objects either positively or negatively in relation to ideology and political landscape. Stickiness is a feature linked to the embodied capacity to affect and be affected. From this perspective, unemployment is associated with such 'stickiness'; that is, people are affected negatively by becoming unemployed. The concept of stickiness enables me to analyze shame from a strictly contextual and relational perspective even though Ahmed's work in the context of cultural studies does not engage with phenomenological experience of first-hand accounts, which comprises the main empirical material here. Again, I do a little retooling as I try to get closer to the situated perspectives and experiences. The purpose is not to develop a strictly psychological perspective but to clarify the intricate interactions between the political and institutional perspective and the intimate and psychological one.

Recoding Unemployment: Passion as a Prerequisite

As mentioned, we are only ashamed of something that is of importance to us. If we feel indifferent about something, we will not react with shame. Exactly, that is also the vulnerability evident in shame—we show up as ourselves in shame. In order to understand the workings of shame, we therefore need to take a step back and further explore what needs to be present or what logics, understandings and technologies that mature the ground and make unemployed people prone to shame. Holding it as a value that having a job is important is a widespread attitude in a Christian country in which protestant work ethic is potent. In the previous chapter, I demonstrated how both activation policies inspired from both neoliberalism and social investment paradigm encourage unemployed people to pursue the good enough job rather than solely aiming for their dream job. The unemployed people are not only governed in a way that require them to engage actively in job search, they are also affectively governed to feel empowered and motivated to conduct themselves as passionate jobseekers. This affective dimension in the technologies in the employment system is not detached from the workings of shame; rather empowerment and reminding people of the importance of the underlying values in society create emotional hooks that enable subtle shaming dynamics. The empowerment technologies and the encouragement to act as a passionate jobseeker in fact prepare the ground for feeling ashamed if you do not get the job.

During a mandatory course, a consultant says, "Find your passion and everything will be solved". The context is a mandatory course called "Persuade other to say yes" with the purpose of teaching unemployed people to convince potential employers about their competences in the job search. Passion is referred to as a capacity that can be extremely powerful in face-to-face interactions, but it is also a capacity that can be disseminated in writing. Job applications should also contain an affective undercurrent convincing the reader about that candidate's passion. In that sense, the ability to display passion is used as a measure to distinguish between candidates in the competitive infrastructures of job search.

In most interviews, people talk about passion as being the inner force that may potentially move them into a job, and they identify the importance of passion in different stages of job search. Instead of focusing on how to optimize objective skills at the seminars, the unemployed people are encouraged to 'sell' themselves as passionate and interesting people. Thirty-two-year-old Elisabeth, who has been unemployed for five months, reflects on what it takes for her to find a job. It is the step before getting a job, she reasons—it is the condition of being able to find a job. However, she is not yet capable of enacting this passion. Assistance is needed. She explains:

> Personally, I need some clarification. I have to find out where to put my energy. One of my bosses told me that I have a lot of drive, but that I need to find out where my passion is, so they run in the same direction, then I would be okay, or kick even more ass. Even though he is a dickhead, it was correct and spot on.

According to Elisabeth, 'drive' is essential in order to be employable and thereby get a job. However, drive, as the direction of a movement, cannot make it alone: drive must be underscored by passion, enthusiasm, interest, and strong feelings. Elisabeth speaks of passion as a sincere and deep interest in a specific work field. According to her boss, the 'dickhead', she must find and enact this passion in order to be employable. However, it seems difficult for her to find and feel this passion. What she needs is a kind of clarification, an analysis of where the passion is and what it consists of so she can spend her energy effectively and 'kick some more ass'. In that sense, passion also must be found and cultivated to be used as fuel in self-management. It thereby moves from an inner state of mind and body to an external and manageable (out)side that can be scrutinized, governed, and put into action. However, as the quote illustrates, it is not enough to feel passionately engaged. One must showcase and perform one's passion, make it heard and seen and affect others. Staging passions is central in the job search process and presumably the ability to communicate and convince others, for instance, potential employers, of one's passion. Hence, there is an inner component cultivating the affective capacities within as well as an outer component making them visible to others, both potential employers and PES through emotional labor.

Selling Oneself in the Competitive Labor Market

Many of the participants use the metaphor of 'selling oneself' on the labor market and this metaphor is also reinforced at the unemployment fund, for instance at courses promoting 'Personal Branding' as part of job search. However, what does sell oneself mean? As mentioned the interview participants are aware that they are competing with other candidates and thus look sideways in the competitive infrastructures to know more about how they are positioned in this competition. Getting closer to the micropolitics of how this is done in everyday life, we see here how unemployed people reflect about lying and exaggerating in job search. As one of the interviewees Morten notes, you must take into account the fact that the people one is competing with (also) lie and exaggerate:

> There is a balance between telling enough lies or these white lies and still being able to do it. Perhaps I will experience having sold myself at 100% but only being able to do 50%. I know how to do many things ... also things I do not do 100%. However, it is a difficult balance between selling oneself and not lying too much. It is difficult. Perhaps the ones you are competing with are lying 40%, and if you only lie 20% then there is a difference—you might be just as good.

Morten identifies several dilemmas in relation to lying and competing for jobs related to the theme about comparing with peers in competitive infrastructures. One dilemma relates to the issue of not 'over-selling' oneself, lying so much in the recruitment process that it would be a problem to actually do the job. Another but related issue has to do with thoughts about competing with others who are also encouraged to sell themselves. Morten's practice is to some extent mediated by his ideas and expectations of what other people do and how much they lie in the process. As Morten indicates, it is important to strike a certain balance between telling the truth and inventing lies; however, this line between true selves and untrue selves may be quite thin and negotiable because, as Morten points out in the following quote, things, circumstances, and assignments do have the potential to get him hooked even though he might not at a given point in time be passionate about the specific work tasks: "Yeah, you have to say it is exciting and interesting. In my world, everything is exciting; everything can be exciting, if you do it every day, it will get exciting." What Morten finds interesting and exciting is constantly emerging. Morten relies on an affective capacity—to be affected—as an integral part in the competition to find a job. In the quote, he indicates that interest and excitement circulate with the hope that he can convert these capacities into a job that will pay in monetary currency. He views his ability to get excited as an asset in the recruitment process as well as more broadly as an asset of a professional in today's labor market and affective economy.

Not Only Good Feelings

To many it is challenging to mobilize passion while simultaneously dealing with the feelings linked to being outside the normative script, including the sticky shame that comes with it. But how does the shame manifest itself? Covertly unemployed people describe a feeling of losing status, but there are also very subtle dynamics at play. Unemployed people refrain from social encounters simply to avoid conversations involving their employment status. The data include manifold stories of how being labeled unemployed is often experienced as a personal failure and how unemployed people look for personal shortcomings or deficits to explain why they are in this situation. The unemployed young people will go a long way to avoid using the term 'unemployed'.

As a parallel, and probably intertwined paradox, the word 'unemployed' has, as mentioned earlier, almost disappeared from the vocabulary in the unemployment system. Andreas, aged 27 years, has been receiving benefits for five months, and he reflects on his appropriation of the discourse of being a job seeker rather than the unemployed category:

> I have learned to call myself a job seeker. It is probably because my wife is a social worker. She doesn't think I should call myself unemployed because I am an active job seeker. In my head, I am unemployed. I mean, you have—I have—the feeling of belonging to a group of losers, if I can put it like that. That was the first feeling I had joining one of those meetings (with other unemployed people). But, I have reached the conclusion now that is just the conditions when you are unemployed. It has changed during the last month and a half in a positive direction.

Andreas initially felt that he belongs to a group of 'losers' and this was especially salient to him when he was at meetings with other unemployed people. Several times during the interview Andreas mentions his wife who works as a social worker with a group of unemployed people who receive social assistance.

The distinction between social assistance recipients and the unemployment benefit recipients plays an important role in the construction of the active job seeker as it enables associating the stigma of unemployment with a group that is 'further down the social ladder' in Danish society. Andreas underlines that he should identify with being an active job seeker, but he also claims, "in my head, I am unemployed" reflecting that initially he did not feel empowered and active; he felt like a 'loser'. The dissonance between how Andreas felt and how he was supposed to feel mediated by the technologies and subjectifying capacities creates tensions and a sense of ambivalence.

These small cracks and fissures reveal the becoming of a multiplicity of possible identities and experiences. Andreas experiences his transforming into an active job seeker and from this transformation, he begins to feel more empowered and able to conduct himself as an active job seeker. That shift in identification is enabled by his ability to distance himself from the 'club of losers'.

Categories such as 'unemployed' and 'job seeker' are labels; however, labels serve a purpose. They are performative; they bring energy, activity, and direction. As Andreas notes, by familiarizing himself with, and using, his wife's terminology, he reflects on the process of becoming an active jobseeker. The active job seeker contrasts with someone who has simply lost a job or has never had one. He becomes a person not only seeking pre-given opportunities but also enquiring, looking for and creating new ones, in line with the entrepreneur or homo economicus. This figure is obviously more attractive on the labor market and to PES compared to a passive individual defeated by the circumstances of life. Taking initiatives while training and transforming oneself is thus crucial and closely linked to both responsibilization and empowerment technologies. The analysis of this empirical material reveals that labels actively draw us in and out of certain communities and activate feelings of belonging creating hierarchies between these groups.

Shame and Its Workings

The pressure to live up to social norms seems to impact differently or perhaps harder, when one has stepped outside the path of normativity, as is the case for the unemployed. Most of the interview participants describe feeling ashamed of receiving money from the state. This is related to a general sense of feeling under suspicion for conducting fraud. Even though unemployed people might rationally know that their family, partner, or friend does not judge them, they still feel as if they are under suspicion of not doing enough to find employment. This dynamic is familiar to almost all participants in the study. The idea of the unemployed as lazy and/or incompetent is insidious and participants are affected by this in all social interactions. Ditte, unemployed for five months, tentatively explains how this suspicion is constantly present in her everyday life:

> Sometimes you can just sense; 'does she really do enough'… I think. I don't know. It's just something you feel that everybody is thinking, that you have to explain all the time. It's just there all the time; are you sure you're doing everything you can? All the time, it's like that. You feel that way even though that might not be the case.

The little hunches and hints, the 'senses', and ideas relating to what the other person might think affects Ditte's self-understanding negatively. The idea of not being sufficiently active imposes itself on her and she describes it as present all the time even though she knows "that it is not true". From the quote, it is evident that Ditte is ambivalent and doubting whether people around her really have these implicit accusations. The suspicion might originate neither in Ditte nor in her specific conversation partner, but the idea or representation of the inactive unemployed person is somehow a culturally understandable figure present in the discourse as well as embedded in activation policies (see Chap. 3). The lazy figure is in fact so present that she feels she needs to defend herself when talking to others about her situation; at the same time, she feels ambivalent about that strategy because she also knows that she shouldn't need to defend herself. Dealing with the tension and ambivalence is a demanding piece of continuous emotional labor.

Almost all the interview participants mention that their interpersonal relations are strained because people enquire how the job search is going. Encounters could also be strained if close ones refrain from asking about job search. You damned if you ask about it, and damned if you don't.

The unemployed people sense that they are under suspicion for not doing enough to get a job. Communicating and showing diligence thus becomes a form of defense against this presumed accusation. The orchestration of the specific interpersonal interaction between an unemployed person and another human being, whether this other is a stranger, a friend, a partner, or a family member, thus reaches beyond the specific interaction between those specific two people. In the conversation, social representation and attached affects partake and shape what is possible to say and think. Even though there are no explicit questions with regard to activity level ("is she doing enough"), the unemployed person often feels in a defensive position having to wave off the questioning of morals and competence that is linked to the negative representation of unemployed people. In the concrete conversation between two people, it is not only what is said and how this is responded to. There is a choir contributing with various perspectives carrying diffuse questions such as are you a worthy citizen? Are you trying your hardest to find a job? Are you lazy and entitled? The questions are nurtured by the indeterminate silence that often arises in conversations where stigma and taboos are present. They might easily be overlooked when exploring the unemployment experience. Staying with the trouble (Haraway, 2010) and sorting out why it is there and what it means is crucial in terms of understanding the unemployment experience and the emotional debt.

What happens is affected or tuned by discourses outside the specific context. Jonas, also unemployed for five months, concurs: "If you think that they see you as lazy, it hurts. Maybe you are under a lot of pressure, so you perceive good intentions differently". The mechanism of suspicion penetrates the intimate social sphere and shape already strained social interactions and conversations. For both Ditte and Jonas, it implies a doubt and an insecurity in interpersonal perceptions. In that sense, unemployment indirectly affects social relations pervasively and adds additional strain to the private and social life of unemployed people. Below, Sandra struggles feeling useless that, in Ahmed's terms, sticks to her body and affects her in a negative way, and how it is paradoxically tied to passion:

> My entire emotional life is screaming that I am useless. You'd better drop that and apply for retirement. It's really extreme, but my sense is telling me

that I chose an education that I think is so much fun and that I really like (…). Of course, I can get a job, because I really think that I have the best education. I really think that it is the best thing in the whole world to do PR strategies. I almost laugh when I do it. There has to be somebody who wants to hire somebody who enjoys it that much. (…) My rationality knows that I have learned stuff and developed competencies. I have just temporarily forgotten that in this process. I can't feel it, but I know it. It's extremely important for me to hold on to the fact that my feelings shouldn't determine it. Because my feelings are not doing me any good right now.

Sandra describes a general sense of feeling useless indicating that she cannot provide any value on the labor market and therefore might as well give up and go straight to retirement. The negative affects manifest as a burgeoning lack of confidence in skills and competences. While sharing these negative self-appraisals with me, she also remarks that she seeks to ignore these feelings as they "are not doing me any good right now". However, these feelings "keep popping up" even though she is trying to control them.

At the same time, she recognizes, as I have identified, that, paradoxically, her feelings, her joy and passion for her professional field doing PR, also constitute a key currency and an asset in the job search; "there has to be somebody who wants to hire somebody who enjoys it that much". She also mentions professional competencies and experience as being important in the labor market, but enjoyment and passion are in the foreground of her argument reflecting an understanding of a particular affective economy valorizing the ability to underscore objective skills with a passionate undercurrent.

Another claimant, Nina, portrays this internal oscillation between different versions of herself as a dialogue between the former self with a job and the new self as unemployed with the amount of stickiness and negative affects that the label brings with it. She compares being unemployed with postpartum depression:

> Do you remember those surveys you had to fill out when you were on maternity leave about postpartum depression? (…) You are sitting there crying because it is quarter to four and he [the husband, ed.] gets home at four. My old me is thinking: 'get a grip'. But the new me (making a sobbing sound). It's the same now. If you look at yourself from the outside, you go;

'Come on'. But from the inside (making a sobbing sound). Total paranoia. It's not coming from the outside. It comes from the inside to be worried about those things.

Nina feels that being unemployed brings out a fragile sense of herself who is sincerely and utterly worried about never finding a job. She draws a parallel to when she felt depressed as a new mother and experienced an emotional toll that made her feel unable to deal with 15 minutes more alone with her child. Fifteen minutes should be doable to cope with on her own, but they are not. It should be easy, or easier, but it is not. The intense vulnerability she felt at the time is parallel to how she feels as unemployed. Nina describes a sense of powerlessness, which is also a symptom of postpartum depression. Rather than invoking agency, powerlessness is linked to giving up altogether. The fear of never getting into the labor market again is familiar to most of the unemployed people interviewed. Notably, Nina also takes on the responsibility for feeling this way—it comes from within, as she says. This notion echoes feeling the pressure of self-blame also as coming from within (see also Chap. 4). The extract is a specific example of how the discourse representing unemployed people as failures is internalized and experienced as originating from the private and intimate aspects of their personalities. It is an example of a pattern identified across the data. In the interviews, the participants often distinguish between a pressure coming from within and a pressure coming from outside. The configuration of pressure coming from within is dominating in terms of how the unemployed people experience and put into words how they experience the struggles echoing the psychologization of the unemployment issue. Feeling the pressure from within makes it more probable to direct critique toward oneself, rather than outwards which is characteristic feature of the psychologization. Psychologization provides the fertile ground for feeling emotionally indebted.

Not Me: Then Who?

The cultivation of shame and also self-blame is intensified and developed as part of the responsibilization and personification of the unemployment problem. As it is intimately interrelated with the subjectification of a responsible citizen valorizing self-reliance and not being a burden to society, it is complicated to reject or disengage from the shame-producing relation.

The interaction between the individual and society is at the heart at the neoliberal governmentality. Andreas, who had then been unemployed for five months, further elaborates his experience of the depressing effects of participating in seminars with other unemployed people:

> The first time I went to one of the meetings I felt like I was at an AA meeting. Nothing negative about that, but the feeling of sitting with a lot of people and it is sort of a club for the outcasts. This is a club for losers. It's no fun being around other unemployed people (…). It differs according to which group you are in. I was at a three-day course at Niels Brock (a business school, ed.) and that was an entirely different segment. Everybody was looking for a job, but it was another group and motivation. It was interesting, instead of these standard groups with a lot of middle-aged women and men who got fired because they simply aren't good enough. Perhaps they are good, but I feel that this is the club for people who aren't good enough at what they do. I comfort myself saying that we are graduates. I was sitting next to a girl, she was also a graduate, and we could see it was the same feelings—it was weird being there. You sit and listen to a woman in her 40 s who is talking about the ethical problems about using her network. I mean—I really don't need that.

It is hard to escape the 'unemployed label' at meetings at the unemployment fund or job center, as being formally unemployed is the very condition for being there. There are limits to what a positive recoding can achieve. Andreas experiences feeling like a 'loser' and viewed from a strictly individual psychological perspective, we might investigate personality traits, socio-economic background, emotional disposition, and track record of psychological or perhaps even psychiatric experience. However, turning to the affective subjectification with inspiration from Anderson (2009), I investigate atmospheres to grasp how people are affected or 'tuned' in specific ways, depending on the context. According to Andreas, the atmosphere at the unemployment fund leaves the participants with a vague sense of a common tuning in a negative direction, and this attunement can manifest as shame, and is dealt with differently. This negative attunement happens alongside the empowerment technologies.

By portraying middle-aged men and women who "'got fired' simply because they weren't good enough", Andreas reproduces a negative representation of unemployed people as incompetent. He thus re-introduces the idea that unemployment is caused by shortcomings or deficits of the individual.

By sharing this negative appraisal of the middle-aged people who had been dismissed, Andreas and the other graduate distance themselves to the 'sticky' object, the sad unemployed person. In the quote, Andreas is clearly ambivalent on the matter questioning his own statement saying, "perhaps they are good". He thus oscillates between 'kicking downwards' and sensing a double standard subscribing to this perception. If he judges his unemployed peers as incompetent, what does that make him?

Andreas thus feels 'othered' by belonging to the category of unemployment represented by the expressions club of losers, AA meeting etc., and he manages this othering by distinguishing internally in the unemployment group. This allows him to attach the sticky shame to a different group of people and thus releases himself from some of the discomfort associated with the negative representation and associated affective subjectification.

In the extract from Andreas, we also see another interesting feature, namely that the attunement is context-dependent in the sense that it differs according to the activity at hand. He describes that it is entirely different to participate in a seminar at a business school with other 'motivated job seekers' in comparison to being with the heterogeneous group of unemployed people meeting in the unemployment fund. It does make sense that there would be a selection bias in that a particular segment chooses to go to the business school. However, it might also play a significant role whether unemployed people are gathered around activities concerned with being unemployed or whether the focus revolves around something different, in this case around project management. It is also noteworthy that he in fact uses a psychological construct such as motivation to make the distinction between the two groups of unemployed people.

John, unemployed for five months, similarly addresses the depressing atmosphere that is created in a gathering of so many unemployed people: "If you gather unemployed people in one place you have a lot of people who lack social competencies and who are tired of being unemployed (…). You don't want to see the people next time; you want to get a job and hope they'll do that as well". The individualization of unemployment has resulted in a need to identify personal shortcomings or deficits in the unemployed person and the lack of social competencies is one of these explanations. In John's words:

> Generally, I do feel that it's a taboo to be outside the labor market, to be one of those who receive unemployment benefit, but it does not affect me personally. Generally, if I see one of those programs on television with people who are on unemployment where you see pitiable examples of unemployed, then I am the first to say—that's not me—even though we receive the same income, I don't identify with him.

John rejects the stickiness of the shame associated with being unemployed. To deal with it he deflects it from himself and projects it onto others. This move, although not necessarily intentional or deliberate, makes it possible for him to escape the detrimental effects associated with it. John is an example of how handling otherness is performed by subcategorizing the unemployed group and, on that basis, othering the 'real' unemployed. The quote is also a good example of the widespread management strategy to defend oneself against the diffuse sense of people being suspicious toward unemployed people as 'pitiable examples'.

In that sense, two othering processes are active at the same time—one othering process distinguishing between people who have a job and unemployed people but also internally between different types of unemployed people. We have encountered this here, where Andreas distinguish between motivated and unmotivated unemployed people, and we have also seen how unemployed people mention the scrounger in order to distance themselves and stick the shame to someone else below in the social hierarchy.

Escaping Shame: The Freelancer and the Affective Economy

So far, by reading the material through governmentality and affective categories, I have highlighted how unemployed people are attuned and affectively subjectified in different ways. Being unemployed not only brings into play feelings of passion, interest, and empowerment, but also blame and shame. I have identified various ways in which the young unemployed people manage or deal with shame. Some deflect it away from themselves and onto other unemployed people, seemingly refusing to identify with the category of being unemployed. However, what categories of identification are available to assist in this way of constructing and conducting oneself as something else than the typical unemployed person? What comes in handy when unemployed people are not governed quite so much or at that cost?

During the recruitment phase of the second wave of data collection which was my doctoral studies, I came across an interesting experience. I received a list of randomized unemployed members from a large unemployment fund, and when I started to call around and invite people to participate in interviews, I got this answer or some variation of it: "I do not think you want to talk to me; I am not a traditional unemployed person". I did not get that answer once, but along the lines of one third of the people I called. Luckily, I insisted that I would still like to invite them. Talking to this group has contributed to the discovery of a relatively widespread practice among unemployed people made possible by some of the labor market changes discussed in the previous chapters such as precarization.

Approximately one third of my interview participants, indeed engaged independently with an alternative construction of being unemployed by understanding and conducting themselves as freelancers. The term freelancer means working as self-employed and usually working for several companies rather than only one as a traditional employee. One of the useful aspects of this is that it is hard for other people to know about one's level of activity and employment status. The term freelancer thus offers a way out in terms of concealing if you in fact receive money from the state. Among my interview participants, being a freelancer while receiving benefits means being hired for small projects or doing voluntary work outside the permitted activation schemes enforced as active measures by the unemployment fund and job center. The freelancers among my interview participants here work in a wide range of professions such as artists, graphic designers, researchers, journalists, psychologists, consultants etc.

Governing oneself as a freelancer not only entails rejecting the label of unemployment but also of not identifying or ever describing oneself as an unemployed person. Scratching the surface of this way of conducting oneself has made visible that, to many, this practice involves a positive attitude toward seizing new opportunities and embracing networking possibilities often associated with working for very little or no money.

Here, Anne Kathrine explains what this practice entails, "It demands that you tend to your network. (…) I am not promising anything, but I see where it's taking me. That's my deal; I'm using all the opportunities that somehow arise". By opportunities, she means taking on small assignments: teaching, writing, providing feedback for others. She does not perceive labor as defined by wage but instead by being needed to solve pressing assignments. She is open to new connections and becomes involved at every networking occasion that appears, and interestingly, this paves the way for cutting the connection to the unemployment identity.

One of the interview participants, Philip, has taken leave after submitting his bachelor's thesis. He uses the unemployment period strategically to work voluntarily as a freelancer and thus establish a network sufficient to improve his chances of finding a job when he graduates after his master's degree. For Philip, who has been formally unemployed for six months, in the choice of using unemployment benefit as support, the cost seems rather small, almost non-existent.

> I now have the network and I can keep track of the projects based in these networks and that will help me a lot faster after my master's. I know what they put weight on at job interviews—through my network—so it only takes interest and courage to do it.

Philip sees this as being a strategic move in terms of improving his chances of finding a job after his education. Stepping outside the paved educational track, and establishing network, however, does demand interest and courage as he sees it. These capacities again resonate well with the affective economy, not only valorizing objective skills but increasingly also calling for emotional capacities. Making choices in the here and now to increase possibilities in the foreseeable future can also be referred to as 'potentialization', however this strategy is also beneficial in the present as it counteracts what could have been fear of not finding a job after his master's. Developing aspiration and hope while paving the way to realize these aspirations have a positive effect on his subjective wellbeing.

Even though practice is relatively widespread, the unemployment fund still has the duty to financially sanction a member who fails to comply with the laws and rules defined at a political level. The ability to sanction is also often mentioned in the system thereby governing the unemployed people through fear as mentioned in Chap. 4. For some, the freelancer practice comes at a cost, as there are many rules that counteract the possibility of using the system for something other than intended. The individual must handle these tensions. Julie explains her fear of being caught:

> I am shit-scared that the unemployment calls me up and says that I have failed to do something. When they called, I was petrified. I was horrified. There are a lot of things. Can I blog? I am not paid to do it. Can I write on my LinkedIn that I am a freelancer, even though I am unemployed? I am too afraid to ask those questions, because I am afraid of getting a no. I think that those things bring me closer to a job. But I am not sure the unemployment fund feels the same way (…). When I am offered these small freelance jobs and the whole finding out how it works with the unemployment benefit; it's a strange feeling. That of constantly being in the system.

The redefining of the unemployed person as a freelancer for Julie does not allow her to fully escape the ever-present feeling that she is 'in the system'. Somebody else has the authority to provide her with money, and they also have the power to take it away from her again.

There is an obvious dissonance between the construction of the active job seeker that is promoted in the system who is conceptualized as an employee searching for jobs through formal routes on the one hand and the freelancer on the other. The freelancer is also promoted in the governmental practices and technologies drawing on branding, enterprise vocabularies and entrepreneurial values associated with neoliberal government (Bröckling, 2015) but the PES is designed to govern traditional employees leaving the freelancers in a pickle. The freelancer frequently does things that are not allowed, such as working on projects that prevent them from meeting the availability requirement. These unemployed people are thus negotiating new categories and practices and in that, they must deal with both the opportunities (they actually get money to live on) and the worries (the practice is contrary to the rules and laws): "The structure in this unemployment fund is designed for you to find a job, and not create your own job. Of course, everybody shouldn't be allowed to spend half a year; (…)—'I don't want do anything!' under cover of being an entrepreneur." There is an ambivalence at a personal level; it is one thing to conduct oneself in accordance with the juridical and disciplinary dos and don'ts and it is another—and also ambivalent, tense and contradictory—to conduct oneself in accordance with the technologies of enterprise constructing oneself as a freelancer. Being a freelancer while being supported by unemployment benefit is, in fact, illegal and this brings with it feelings of insecurity and fear, often associated with austerity and precarious living. Escaping the shame by being a freelancer involves managing the self in terms of fear and insecurity. Conducting oneself as a freelancer also raises political and moral issues, in that Julie problematizes if 'everybody' were to use the unemployment benefit system in this strategic way and thus this practice also involves a degree of shaming. In one sense, they avoid the stickiness of shame and sometimes stick it on to others, and they cultivate aspirations and hope that improve their wellbeing in the moment by generating future selves that indeed make it on the labor market despite the disadvantageous working conditions for many professions such as art and cultural work.

Summing Up

This chapter has drawn attention to new practices of governing young unemployed people through the duality of shame and passion in times of neoliberalism. Passion, motivation, and energy were cultivated and economized in unforeseen ways in the unemployment system. Questions of unemployment were previously associated with lack of skillsets or of objective merits but currently, in the context of the Danish welfare state, the problem of unemployment for well-educated young people has shifted to new, more personalized foci encompassing the new imperative to passionately feel and display feelings of desire in contemporary labor markets. This poses a particular challenge for unemployed people who must deal with the stickiness of unemployment at the same time.

The joint venture between governmentality studies and affect studies seems promising in getting closer to understanding subjectivities without losing sight of the (affective) politics and management of today indeed governing with "affects as the core capacity to be managed by and through" (Staunæs & Bjerg, 2014, p. 1). The category of unemployment seems to be a particularly fertile ground for researching the affective sides and entanglements of subjectivities and self-management. If people agree that a paid job should be the only gateway to a sense of feeling like a dignified citizen they should indeed feel ashamed as unemployed. However, if they disagree or want to mold or alter that underlying value system giving rise to the current distribution of dignity, becoming aware of it, and relating to it critically, is the first step.

A substantial group dis-identifies with the unemployment label and instead they present themselves as freelancers. This finding stresses the importance of maintaining empirical sensitivity in unemployment research, as unemployed people are by no means a heterogeneous group. In the next chapter, I dig a little deeper in terms of understanding what this practice has to do with shame and getting rid at it.

References

Ahmed, S. (2004). Affective economies. *Social Text, 22*(2 79). https://doi.org/10.1215/01642472-22-2_79-117

Ahmed, S. (2014a). *The cultural politics of emotion*. Edinburgh University Press.

Ahmed, S. (2014b). *Willful subjects*. Duke University Press.

Anderson, B. (2009). Affective atmospheres. *Emotion, Space and Society, 2*(2), 77–81.

Asper. (1992). Ravnen i glasbjerget: følelsesmæssig forladthed og ny terapi (4. opl.). Gyldendal.

Boland, T., & Griffin, R. (2021). *The reformation of welfare: The new faith of the labour market*. Policy Press.

Bröckling, U. (2015). *The entrepreneurial self: Fabricating a new type of subject*.

Brøgger, K., & Staunæs, D. (2016). Standards and (self) implosion: How the circulation of affects accelerates the spread of standards and intensifies the embodiment of colliding, temporal ontologies. *Theory & Psychology, 26*, 223–242.

Brown, B. (2006a). Shame resilience theory: A grounded theory study on women and shame. *Families in Society, 87*(1), 43–52.

Combs, D. J., Campbell, G., Jackson, M., & Smith, R. H. (2010). Exploring the consequences of humiliating a moral transgressor. *Basic and Applied Social Psychology, 32*(2), 128–143.

Creed, W. E. D., Hudson, B. A., Okhuysen, G. A., & Smith-Crowe, K. (2014). Swimming in a sea of shame: Incorporating emotion into explanations of institutional reproduction and change. *Academy of Management Review, 39*(3), 275–301.

Crenshaw, K. W. (2017). *On intersectionality: Essential writings*. The New Press.

Danneris, S. (2018). Ready to work (yet)? Unemployment trajectories among vulnerable welfare recipients. *Qualitative Social Work, 17*(3), 355–372.

Elias, N. (1997). *The civilizing process, the history of manners and state formation and civilization* (Reprinted). Blackwell.

Gibson, M. (2016). Constructing pride, shame, and humiliation as a mechanism of control: A case study of an English local authority child protection service. *Children and Youth Services Review, 70*, 120–128.

Goffman E. (1968). *Stigma: Notes on the management of spoiled identity*. Penguin. (Original work published 1963)

Hancock, A. M. (2016). *Intersectionality: An intellectual history*. Oxford University Press.

Haraway, D. (2010). When species meet: Staying with the trouble. *Environment and Planning D: Society and Space, 28*(1), 53–55.

Jørgensen, C. R. (2023). *Skam—i spændingsfeltet mellem moralsk kompas og psykisk lidelse* (1. udgave.). Hans Reitzel.

Kant, I. (2020). *Groundwork of the metaphysic of morals* (pp. 17–98). Routledge.

Lamont, M. (2023). *Seeing others: How recognition works—and how it can heal a divided world*. Atria/One Signal Publishers.

Nussbaum, M. (2004). Emotions as judgments of value and importance. *Thinking About Feeling: Contemporary Philosophers on Emotions*, 183–199.

Peterie, M., Ramia, G., Marston, G., & Patulny, R. (2019). Emotional compliance and emotion as resistance: Shame and anger among the long-term unemployed. *Work, Employment and Society, 33*(5), 794–811.

Probyn, E. (2004). Everyday shame. *Cultural Studies, 18*(2–3), 328–349.

Pultz, S. (2018). Shame and passion: The affective governing of young unemployed people. *Theory & Psychology, 28*(3), 358–381. https://doi.org/10.1177/0959354318759608

Pultz, S., & Teasdale, T. W. (2017). Unemployment and subjective well-being: Comparing younger and older job seekers. *Scandinavian Journal of Work and Organizational Psychology, 2*(1).

Rantakeisu, U., Starrin, B., & Hagquist, C. (1999). Financial hardship and shame: A tentative model to understand the social and health effects of unemployment. *British Journal of Social Work, 29*(6), 877–901.

Rosette, A. S., de Leon, R. P., Koval, C. Z., & Harrison, D. A. (2018). Intersectionality: Connecting experiences of gender with race at work. *Research in Organizational Behavior, 38*, 1–22.

Scheff T. J. (1990). *Microsociology: Discourse, emotion, and social structure*. University of Chicago Press.

Scheff T. J. (2000). Shame and the social bond: A sociological theory. *Sociological Theory, 18*(1), 84–99.

Sennett, R. (1980). Authority and freedom. *The Kenyon Review, 2*(2), 81–110.

Staunæs, D., & Bjerg, H. (2014). Self-management through shame—Uniting governmentality studies and the 'affective turn' | ephemera. *Ephemera, 14*(14).

Tomkins, S. S. (2008). *Affect imagery consciousness, the complete edition*. Springer Pub.

Tyler, I. (2020). *Stigma: The machinery of inequality*. Bloomsbury Publishing.

6

Resisting the Shame and 'Unemployed by Choice'

The Danish welfare system inadvertently provides a good opportunity for young creative people to pursue their dreams in creative fields such as art, acting, music while receiving unemployment benefits. As Michael, one of the participants, puts it, "I consider unemployment benefit entrepreneurial support". The practice can be viewed as subversive in Butler's terms, meaning that the young people seek to change the society they are part of through this practice. They openly criticize the structural conditions of producing art and culture in the Danish welfare state and in their view, this justifies using other institutional settings to engage in such creative activities.

This group reflects the contours of a new type of unemployed that so far has received very little attention in the research literature with some exceptions such as Lazzarato (2011). The group challenges the traditional representation of the unemployed and portrays themselves as innovative, competent, and able to cope with financial insecurity even though it is psychologically distressing and a risky path to go down. They use educational systems and unemployment benefit systems for something entirely different from what they are intended—they use it to create their own artistic life courses. This group is interesting to explore in itself and also because of the expanding trend of precarious work life (Fogh Jensen, 2009; Kalleberg, 2018).

The analysis is based on the first wave of data based on a pilot study conducted in 2011 in which I interviewed six creative people who were formally unemployed but who used the unemployment benefit system to pursue careers in various creative fields. Specific working conditions are associated with the cultural industry which has a long tradition for precarious work lives (Hesmondhalgh & Baker, 2008), however I also argue that these tendencies tend to spread and spill over to other industries and professions (Gleerup et al., 2018) and thus it is not limited to these professions.

These creative people use up all possible resources to pursue their dreams of becoming professional artists. Even though they are aware that their practice is technically illegal, they do not view it as such because they think of their practice as serving a larger purpose in a society that needs culture to flourish. This may be special for the creative people. However, re-conceptualizing the unemployment benefit in terms of entrepreneurial support provides them with a much more legitimate position in a contemporary neoliberal economy which values activity and productivity. The chapter underlines the necessity of empirical sensitivity as this group handles unemployment and the sticky shame in an alternative fashion. Critique both of employment policies and capitalist values in society largely impact their reasoning and justify their practice. They seek to negotiate an alternative value set placing them differently than the capitalist value system only providing dignity, respect, and recognition to paid laborers.

To give the reader a clearer picture of this group of young, creative people who I call 'unemployed by choice' the participants will briefly be introduced below.

> Nadia is a 27-year-old artist who has just graduated from a master's in fine art in London. She has recently moved back to Copenhagen and has been unemployed a little less than half a year at the time of the interview. She works part-time in a shop, but this interferes with her artistic practice.
>
> Peter, 30, graduated as primary and secondary school teacher a couple of years ago at the time of the interview. He never intended to work as a teacher but because the study was not very demanding, he had the time to

engage in other creative projects. His creative aspirations are in music, and he wants to establish new music venues.

Thomas, 33, has been on and off unemployment benefits since he graduated from the Danish Art Academy 3 years ago at the time of the interview. He has partly supported himself through his practice as an artist mainly working with installations and video-art. He experienced a psychological breakdown half a year ago, which he ascribes to the hardships of his work life including his dependence on the employment system. He works off the books as a street sweeper at a flower store and finds this humiliating. He has a wife and a child and thus has additional economic obligations in comparison with the others.

Madeleine, 34, works in theater and aspires both as an actress and as a director. She has a master in literature and has taken courses at private international theater schools. She has been unemployed for a year's time at the time of the interview, but she has been on and off unemployment many times.

Michael, 29, is a musician and he does music gigs off the books to supplement the unemployment benefits. He is into event making and political activism. He has a master in humanities and has been unemployed for around a year. He does volunteer work.

Sophie, 32, aspires a career within in music management. She has a master in communication and has worked in a wage subsidy at music venue and otherwise she has worked for very little money as a manager of bands. She has been on and off unemployment benefit the last 4 years.

Self-Responsible Creative People

Mechanisms of social inequality and reproduction of power have been hidden and replaced by an immense focus on individual power and agency leaving an enormous pressure on the single person (Furlong & Cartmel, 1997). Furlong and Cartmel (1997) calls this the epistemological fallacy: we overestimate the agency of the individual, and at the same time neglect to understand the massive impact of the reproduction of social inequality in society. The epistemological fallacy is intimately linked to individualization and a sense of personal freedom which they describe as a double-edged sword in the sense that whether you succeed or fail, it falls back on you. Across the interviews with these young, creative people it is noticeable that most of the participants emphasize that they have actively chosen their situation as unemployed which has given rises to the term "unemployed by choice" (Pultz & Mørch, 2015).

The choice derives from creative aspirations but they all state that they could have gone what they phrase the 'easy way' as many of their peers who have taking on more traditional paid jobs in more secure industries. They all point to ideas from nature and uncontrollable creative forces when asked about the origin of their creativity. In unique but also very similar ways, they say that they have always been creative and that giving up on that is impossible. Thomas expresses it this way: "It is simply how I meet the world". Echoing the neoliberal value of freedom and choice (Rose, 1999), they still identify freedom as the greatest incentive to pursue a career in which they are in the driver's seat and control their own time. Freedom is described as the right to structure one's own time but also to work in accordance with one's personal interests and hobbies. Knowing your own desires and interests is thus essential to this practice and everyday life.

The creative young people use institutionalized educational paths and the unemployment system for something else from what they are intended; they manage their life by using for example, the unemployment benefit system to support their artistic endeavors. Peter says, "It is difficult to say no to money you are entitled to". This quote illustrates the link to discussions on citizenship and how neoliberalism has shaped the concepts of right and duty in the sense that being a citizen is subjectified as a consumer of society (Dean, 2006). While the participants feel entitled to receive money from the state and are very conscious about their options, they also express thoughts about societal responsibility admitting the problematic aspect of receiving unemployment benefits out of choice, not need. Peter elaborates: "I need to justify that I am on unemployment benefit. I define a time frame and then hopefully it will lead to the creation of something sustainable. Then I will pay back". Echoing the more general need among unemployed people to defend receiving money from the state, there is perhaps an even bigger need to justify it among the people who are unemployed by choice. In Peter's case, it is not entirely clear whether he talks about paying back in monetary currency or in a different currency, such as through the production of arts and culture. Peter views unemployment benefit as an investment in his artistic practice here and now tied to a future scenario in which the investment will provide a return, whether this is of economic or social value.

The participants view their practice as a necessary response to the opposing demands of being innovative and responsible of the self in a society that does not sufficiently offer institutionalized paths for creative people who wish to contribute to society by creating art and culture. They experience receiving something from the state and hence being in a position of debt, but they imagine that they will pay back in a longer perspective. They spend time justifying how 'paying back' is not a simple monetary transaction but rather a practice involving different currencies; some of it money, but others being paying back with cultural artifacts to society and taking on responsibility for creating a culturally rich society.

The majority of the participants operate with a concept of a trial period meaning a limited period in which they pursue their dreams of establishing creative careers. If they do not succeed, then they have to give up as they phrase it and get a regular 9 am to 5 pm job. The interesting aspect of this metaphor is that the time limit is loosely defined, and Peter says, "In 2 years' time I might say that I'll give it a go for another 2 years". The trial period thus has a justifying character that does not necessarily direct future behavior. The concept supports the notion that unemployed people experience psychological distress. It also links it with the extensive responsibility of the self and the need for constructing 'buffers'.

They are aware that they might not make it but it remains their aspiration to try to get it to work. It becomes clear that it takes some compromises; especially in terms of living with economic insecurity and also postponing major life decisions about family such as having children or changing housing situation. In other words, it fundamentally affects the vision or imagination of one's future self and one's ability to plan the everyday life ahead.

Sophie describes how she worries more about pension and financial security impacting her perspective on the basis of making a family. Being young, it is possible to keep expenses down and, in many ways, represent the archetypical poor artist (Steiner & Schneider, 2013). There is absolute consensus that it is almost impossible to make it as an artist due to the structuring of the creative industries in which there is only money to gain for a selected few. The participants are indeed aware of the financially risky path they go down. The ability to postpone family and suppress worries about the future and personal finances are identified as some of the crucial competencies of this group. Thomas puts it: "You have to close your eyes so as not to see how fucking hard it is (…) and then just hope that everything will be ok." They develop certain buffering strategies to deal with the condition of being on your own and they express wishes that the unemployment system or the insurance funds were geared in relation to dealing with this group since they have different challenges compared to the more traditionally unemployed. Postponing life decisions is a deliberate consequence and only one participant has children. This might also be due to a selection bias, as people without children might be more likely to find time to participate in a research project. There is consensus, however, that having a family challenges the lifestyle typically led by these people as it places more demands on income, housing, and professional and economic stability. These young people perceive their labor market conditions in a way that these goals are not easily attainable. Their objective conditions are filtered through their experiences shaping how they conduct themselves and also largely affecting the emotional toll involved in this practice balancing an affective tension between worry and hope.

Alternative Value Systems

There is consensus among the participants that receiving money and being inactive—or even lazy—is morally problematic and also in these interviews, this is explicitly mentioned by the majority. Michael says, "You are placed in a situation as an unemployed and people feel sorry for you, and this is what I can't deal with". He continues: "It is expected of you to have a crappy life when you are unemployed". At the question who expects this, he answers, "It's in the air". There are no explicit interactions; the negative attunement works more subtly as quiet expectations or feeling rules.

Rejecting the negative representation of the unemployment identity and claiming competence is of vital importance to the participants in their negotiation of this new type of unemployed. Hard work and an industrious attitude weigh heavily in demonstrating self-responsibility and protestant work ethics serves as the moral backbone justifying their practice. The exact content of activities is less defined, but the investment of time and energy and dedication are deemed crucial. They all emphasize that being an artist means working day and night, weekends and vacation time and as such, it is closely linked to an ideal of productivity—also vital in capitalist economies.

At the same time, they challenge a traditional perspective on work, as Michael puts it: "There is this liberal work logic that people just have to have jobs. You work if you have a job. That is not the only way you can work". Besides challenging cultural idea of unemployed people, work can also be qualified in new ways according to the participants. In current debates on post work and work less movements (Aronowitz & Cutler, 2013; Weeks, 2007, 2020) the tight link between paid labor and dignity or status is systematically challenged, and these thoughts and values are closely aligned to the way this group conceptualize alternative values. The participants all agree that receiving unemployment benefits while pursuing a creative career is a widespread practice in creative communities. Within these communities, new meanings, and representations of unemployed people as competent and in charge are shared and recognized as cultural understandable identities. Michael uses Facebook to judge whether his activity is only private or if it resonates with a wider audience and it can thus be viewed as a substantial cultural input. He interprets it as recognition if his posts on Facebook are shared beyond his own immediate community. He describes it as "hitting a nerve". When money or employment status cannot be used as a guidance of success, social media fill an important role in the social domain. In some sense, it is a quantifiable measure of social capital which is easy to navigate by in a community with alternative social values. They view themselves as being outside the mainstream materialist and capitalist society and in that sense they understand themselves as critical of capitalism. The critique of capitalist and material values provides them with an argument to distance themselves from the welfare state. Rather than feeling like a citizen in the Danish welfare state, obliged to contribute to society, they are very much involved in immediate, creative communities. They invest time, energy, and effort in maintaining creative networks by contributing with art and cultural work. Participating in creative communities and networking practices are not without their own potential pitfalls, though. The interview participants describe issues in terms of managing blurry lines between defining who your friends are and who you are networking with. As has been noticed in other contexts, the division between private and professional identity is to a large extent eroded and whether you succeed in participating in projects also reflects your social and personal abilities. The participants concur that instrumentalization of friends and acquaintances is amoral and thus for example, Madeleine only network with so-called good people. These dilemmas will be explored more thoroughly in Chap. 7.

The social relations and mutual recognition strategies provide a good base for challenging the traditional views on unemployment. They do not ask each other whether or not they are supported by the state—they assume that it is a possibility and leave it at that. It is so to say a term directly related by the structuring of the creative fields with very little money. Confronted by 'outsiders' for example, at family parties, they become aware of their practice as it is formally defined. Michael says:

> I have never felt like an unemployed because I have always had long pages of to-do lists, that just keep on growing and growing. (…) I do as much as I can and then hopefully it will pay off in the long run. That's also the reason I can't identify with being unemployed as if I am missing something in order to create. That's also why I consider it entrepreneurial support. But again, off course that it just something I tell myself. According to the rules, I am unemployed, obviously.

By contraposing unemployment and activity, they redefine the traditional representation of the unemployed as inactive and use this representation to distance themselves and portray themselves as extremely hard working and industrious. This aligns well with how Gibson (2009) understands unemployed people in relation to effortfulness repertoire—if you put in enough effort as an unemployed person, you are deserving of financial support, but if you do not put in very much effort, you are undeservingly exploiting the welfare system.

What seems to be critical in defining the meaning of unemployment is the contextualization of the situation and the social category to which a person belongs. Among innovative and creative people, the notion of the competent and upcoming artist is a culturally understandable and a legitimate position in society (Butler, 1997; Søndergaard, 2006). No doubt for many of them, the end goal is to be able to live on earnings from the creative work. But because this is only possible for a tiny fraction of the creative group, unemployment does not necessarily equate to personal failure. Your financial situation is thus not determining in relation to whether you succeed or not as a creative individual. Drawing on traditional representations of the poor artist with the rich inner and social life, this group develops its own alternative norms of recognition (Honneth, 1996) and respect (Sennett, 2003). Here, paid labor is not the only source of dignity, respect, and status and thus, they challenge the pervasive social hierarchy by which underlying value systems distribute respect and dignity unequally in the population according to capitalist logics.

Through organizations of office milieus and networking at openings, members of this group acknowledge each other as artists and innovators and do not take on or identify with the traditional understanding of the category unemployed.

Turning the Arrow Toward Society

The people who are unemployed by choice implicitly draw upon these citizens' right to "get money they are entitled to" and simultaneously they distance themselves from the duty of paying tax through paid labor. The emphasis on rights and not on duties has been characterized as a typical response to neoliberal tendencies in studies of citizenship (Finkel & Moghaddam, 2005; Passini, 2011).

The participants identify structural problems as explanations for their hardships and tie these political analyses closely together with the justification of doing what they do (and also explicitly noting that it would not work if all citizens did what they do). They see it as their responsibility to create new jobs, especially in light of the economic recession at the time contributing to an increase in unemployment numbers leaving it challenging for 'regular people' to find jobs. In that sense, this group takes on an important societal function as innovators and they engage actively with the values and virtues associated with the neoliberal mindset valorizing productivity and innovation.

They criticize art schools for not preparing their students to learn how to navigate in the labor market upon graduation. They consider education an investment in their individual, creative competencies and as a waste of resources if they do not apply these competencies to their jobs. Again, we see some echoing of the social investment idea stating that a person is made up by a bundle of skills and competences, ultimately constituting a person's human capital (Morel & Palme, 2017). While still being relatively young, they have invested both education, and time and energy to build their creative trajectories and they view these investments as waste of time if they have to give up on their creative paths.

While they criticize the close link between paid labor and dignity, they also problematize the bad working conditions for artists and cultural workers. They particularly criticize the extensive use of volunteers that makes it difficult to get pay for doing anything in the creative fields. This is often described in the literature as the expectation that if you love art so much, you do not need to get paid as symbolized in the concepts labor of love (Butler & Stoyanova Russell, 2018) and hope labor (MacKenzie & McKinlay, 2021). As Sophie puts it, "There is this attitude that it is so cool to be at this festival (…). That's not where I am anymore—I am too old and experienced". She continues, "I don't consider myself a person who is just grateful to be here. I also have something to offer that's worth something". Sophie describes wanting recognition in monetary currencies and a general frustration that immaterial currencies such as coolness perhaps best translated into cultural capital could compensate for actual monetary pay. Affective currencies are no longer enough to her.

Also, recruitment and hiring processes mainly exist outside formal recruitment process. It is widely known that new opportunities arise from networking and through common activities rather than through job portals and writing applications. This generates a fundamental critique of the requirements defined by activation policies such as the demand at the time of sending out six to eight job applications a month. Living up to the demands is perhaps even more so in this group experienced as a waste of time and as activities quite detached from actually taking care of one's professional trajectory.

Late modern challenges of individuality, creativity, networking, and projects demand a certain independence and innovation by the individual. In other words, the demands of activation are neither timely, nor consistent according to their own logic. This group does indeed succeed in meeting the contrasting demands on a systemic level, but they do so by acting illegally. A critical finding in the data is that the case worker teaches the unemployed how to navigate in the system without fulfilling the increasing demands thus avoiding economic sanctions. Their practice is officially illegal, but five of six participants describe how they are guided in the system. Caseworkers at the front level go against the rules and demands embedded in the activation policies to help unemployed people. Stories about the meaninglessness of the unemployment system take up a large amount of the data material. The participants all describe lying and giving up wrong information but most of them do so under the guidance of the case workers. The entrepreneurial practice is somewhat widespread, as it is known by case workers, which also demonstrates that they accept some level of civil disobedience. Their work also requires an enormous effort to balance constricting demands and dilemmas, described by Nielsen (2022) as "balancing as a line dancer".

In that sense, the conditions are set in a way so that they can only be met by transcending them. The participants oppose the positioning of the unemployed as passive objects that can be controlled according to political initiatives. Michael says in an ironic voice imitating the state, "If we push them in certain directions, then they will go over there. But people are not like that! If they are presented with certain incentives, they will react to them in way that it is most meaningful to them." The quote demonstrates the importance of investigating how people make sense of their situation because their sense making also entails a transforming potential. When the political requirements are impossible to meet, an individualized positioning is called for. This group of people are not governed quite so much or at that cost. Importantly, however, we need to understand the scope of the cost they pay.

The inherent inconsistencies in the requirements of the unemployed justify a certain degree of cheating and lying that is supported by the silent acceptance among the case workers. This group is not solely defined negatively by what they do not have (a job) but their practice also provides them with material in how they view themselves and each other. As unemployed, they lack economic capital, but the group is strongly organized providing the members with social and cultural capital and a strong sense of purpose in their everyday life which is also spreading as an ideal in current labor markets (Pultz & Dupret, 2023; Dupret & Pultz, 2021). In the context of these innovative young unemployed, it is exactly their concrete creative and strategic ways of using systems that are of interest. Not only does that build on important information about how unemployed make sense of their situation and their future, but it also demonstrates how people affect and change society as it is. Their subversive practice contains a transformational potential and through the case workers' guidance, the phenomenon is recognized and tolerated to an extent although not made legal. It is necessary to lie and cheat to engage in this practice which all participants except one also openly tell me. More generally, their practice provides important insight in terms of how people handle the challenges of increased responsibility and individualization and indeed how they insist on agency in even the most vulnerable situation. This is in accordance with the finding of Mascini et al. (2013) who found neoliberal individualism to be strongly valued among vulnerable citizens.

This group advocates a normalization of a work life with periodic phases of unemployment—a tendency that already Beck documented but which has become more widespread today (Beck & Beck-Gernsheim, 2009; Fogh Jensen, 2009). They all describe the immense challenge of dealing with insecurity and not having anything to lean on if they fail in pursuing their creative life courses. In the light of individualization and responsibility of the self, they govern and control themselves in a way that disguises the reproduction of social inequality. Instead of mobilizing a political activation against the dominating structures that leave them financially very vulnerable, they advocate a socio-cultural change of meaning based on critique of materialistic and capitalistic values.

Summing Up

People who conduct themselves as unemployed by choice position themselves according to existing welfare systems and institutions as well as according to existing ways of understanding unemployment. They challenge the traditional view of the unemployed and emphasize their industrious work attitude, innovation, and ability to create as societally desirable. Young creative and entrepreneurial people experience unemployment differently than most others and that they subscribe to alternative understandings of work. Consequently, their practice challenges the assumption that only formal employment can provide people with latent functions (time structure, common goals, activity, social contact, and social status) and a sense of dignity sustaining well-being and through they practice they show a different set of contours of future labor market and how to navigate in them in a capitalist-critical way. The practice is not easy though.

References

Aronowitz, S., & Cutler, J. (2013). *Post-work*. Routledge.
Beck, U., & Beck-Gernsheim, E. (2009). Global generations and the trap of methodological nationalism for a cosmopolitan turn in the sociology of youth and generation. *European Sociological Review, 25*(1), 25–36.
Butler, J. (1997). *The psychic life of power: Essays in subjection*. Stanford University Press.
Butler, N., & Stoyanova Russell, D. (2018). No funny business: Precarious work and emotional labour in stand-up comedy. *Human Relations, 71*(12), 1666–1686.
Dean, M. (2006). Governmentality and powers of life and death. Analysing Social Policy: A Governmental Approach, 19–48.
Dupret, K., & Pultz, S. (2021). Hard/heart worker: Work intensification in purpose-driven organizations. *Qualitative Research in Organizations and Management, 16*(3/4), 488–508.
Finkel, N. J., & Moghaddam, F. M. (2005). *The Psychology of Rights and Duties, Empirical Contributions and Normative Commentaries*. Washington: American Psychological Association. https://doi.org/10.1037/10872-000

Fogh Jensen, A. (2009). *Projektsamfundet*. Aarhus Universitetsforlag.
Furlong, A., & Cartmel, F. (1997). *Young people and social change, individualization and risk in late modernity*. Open University Press.
Gibson, S. (2009). The Effortful Citizen: Discursive Social Psychology and Welfare Reform. *Journal of Community & Applied Social Psychology, 19*, 393–410. https://doi.org/10.1002/casp.1003
Gleerup, J., Nielsen, B. S., Olsén, P., & Warring, N. (2018). Prekarisering og akademisk arbejde. *Tidsskrift for Arbejdsliv, 20*(1), 9–29.
Hesmondhalgh, D. & Baker, S. (2008) Creative work and emotional labour in the television industry. *Theory, Culture & Society* [Online] 25 (7–8), 97–118.
Honneth, A. (1996). *The Struggle for Recognition: The Moral Grammar of Social Conflicts*. MIT press.
Kalleberg, A. L. (2018). *Precarious lives: Job insecurity and well-being in rich democracies*. John Wiley & Sons.
Lazzarato, M. (2011). The misfortunes of the 'artistic critique' and of cultural employment. In G. Raunig, G. Ray, & U. Wuggenig (Eds.), *Critique of creativity: Precarity, subjectivity and resistance in the 'creative industries'*. MayFlyBooks (pp. 119–131). [Online]. Retrieved August 21, 2012, from www.mayflybooks.org
Mackenzie, E., & McKinlay, A. (2021). Hope labour and the psychic life of cultural work. *Human Relations, 74*(11), 1841–1863.
Mascini, P., Achterberg, P., & Houtman, D. (2013). Neoliberalism and work-related risks: Individual or collective responsibilization? *Journal of Risk Research, 16*(10), 1209–1224.
Morel, N., & Palme, J. (2017). A normative foundation for the social investment approach. *The Uses of Social Investment, 13*, 150.
Nielsen, M. H. (2022). Fremtidens jobcenter bør ansætte linedansere: Man vil lave en bedre, men billigere indsats. En fri, men styret indsats. En værdig, men kontrolleret indsats. Politiken.
Passini, S. (2011). Individual Responsibilities and Moral Inclusion in an Age of Rights. *Culture and Psychology, 17*, 281–296. https://doi.org/10.1177/1354067X11408130
Pultz, S., & Dupret, K. (2023). Emotional status and emotional labour: Exploring the emotional labour among casualised and tenured knowledge workers. *Culture and Organization, Latest articles*. https://doi.org/10.1080/14759551.2023.2258433
Pultz, S., & Mørch, S. (2015). Unemployed by choice: Young creative people and the balancing of responsibilities through strategic self-management.

Journal of Youth Studies, 0(0), 1–20. https://doi.org/10.1080/1367626 1.2014.992318.

Rose, N. S. (1999). *Powers of freedom, reframing political thought*. Cambridge University Press.

Sennett, R. (2003). *Respect, the formation of character in a world of inequality*. Allen Lane.

Søndergaard, D. M. (2006). *Tegnet på Kroppen. Køn: Koder og Konstruktioner blandt unge Voksne I Akademia*. Museum Tusculanum.

Steiner, L., & Schneider, L. (2013). The happy artist: an empirical application of the work-preference model. *Journal of Cultural Economics, 37*, 225–246.

Weeks, K. (2007). Life within and against work: Affective labor, feminist critique, and post-Fordist politics. *Ephemera, 7*(1), 233–249.

Weeks, K. (2020). *The problem with work: Feminism, Marxism, antiwork politics, and postwork imaginaries*. Duke University Press.

7

The Intimate Dance of Networking

Comparing unemployment experiences across United States and Denmark is called for due to the specific combination of differences and similarities across these sites. The differences are well-known. Most scholars are aware of Denmark's expansive welfare state and generous social safety net, which includes extensive unemployment insurance provisions. By contrast, the United States is the paradigmatic neoliberal economy with the least generous welfare state among advanced economies, and not surprisingly, the United States offers much lower levels of support to unemployed workers than Denmark. But alongside these differences, the two sites Boston and Copenhagen also have important similarities. In both the United States and Denmark, employment is precarious and characterized by relatively short tenures. Consequently, workers in both sites frequently need to search for new work and engage in networking. The sites are also similar because employer hiring practices focus on interpersonal 'chemistry' and fit (Rivera, 2012; Sharone, 2013a), and prior

---

An earlier version of this chapter is Pultz and Sharone, The intimate dance of networking: A comparative study of the emotional labor of young American and Danish jobseekers. In E. H. Gorman & S. P. Vallas (Eds.), *Professional work: Knowledge, power and social inequalities (research on the sociology of work)* (Vol. 34, pp. 33–58). Emerald Group Publishing. https://doi.org/10.1108/S0277-283320200000034006, 2020.

studies suggest that hiring practices which are attentive to fit go hand in hand with particular networking practices (Sharone, 2014). Given this combination of differences and similarities, the aim is to shed light on the extent to which networking practices and experiences are broadly shared across advanced economies with similarly flexible labor markets and hiring practices focused on fit, or diverge related to country-level factors such as the breadth and generosity of the welfare state. Findings reveal cross-national similarities in networking advice discourses and in the kind of 'emotional labor' unemployed people perceive to be required for effective networking. However, there are also differences. These include the perceived need for more intense and pervasive engagement in emotional labor among American jobseekers, and greater concern about the potential of networking to involve exploitation, corruption, and pressures to conform oneself to standards of marketability, among Danish jobseekers.

The field observations are applied as lens to explore the specific ways the institutional actors encourage people to conduct themselves to handle the unemployment challenge. There are also some interesting differences as Danish jobseekers are more critical toward networking as they associate it with nepotism. This perspective was absent in the American material. The unemployed people engage in networking practices, however doing so bring out vulnerabilities as they expose more of their personalities compared to job searching in the formalized hiring systems. Interestingly, networking constitutes an alternative to the 'black hole' into which formal job applications are often considered to have disappeared, as described in qualitative unemployment research (Sharone, 2013b). While networking can mobilize hope and energy, it also takes an emotional toll and involves some exhausting emotional labor. The psychologization more specifically encourages the cultivation of certain traits such as being outgoing while at the same time problematizing, for instance, being introverted.

In recent decades, as employment relations in both the United States and Denmark have become more precarious and fluid, we see a corresponding intensification in the discourses and practices of networking. The purpose here is to explore the institutionalized discourses of networking as disseminated in public employment centers and career centers as well as the subjective experiences of young unemployed workers engaged in networking.

Using in-depth interviews and observations of unemployed people in Denmark and the United States the comparative analysis sheds new light on the varied and complex web of emotional labors required by networking interactions. Drawing on the emotional labor literature and the more recent literature on the affective economy various and affective currencies implicated in the practices and experiences of networking are explored. While the data reveal some cross-national differences more striking are the cross-national similarities in networking discourses and experiences that transcend differences in local cultures, hiring institutions, and welfare state provisions. Common across the U.S. and Denmark is the intimacy involved in the dance of networking with unemployed people in both sites frequently drawing on romantic dating as a key metaphor. While networking is at the core of how contemporary unemployed people navigate fluid and precarious labor markets, the subjective experiences of unemployed people engaged in networking, and how such experiences may vary across institutional contexts, have received scant attention from researchers.

Networking and the Unemployment Field

Since Granovetter's (1973) seminal work on the strength of weak ties a vast literature has emerged examining the relationship between strength, quality and structure of social ties, and employment outcomes (Forret & Dougherty, 2004; Mouw, 2003; Yakubovich, 2005). To generate support social ties must be activated through "networking," defined as "individual actions directed towards contacting friends, acquaintances, and other people to whom the job seeker has been referred for the main purpose of getting information, leads, or advice on getting a job" (Wanberg et al., 2000, p. 492). Studies have examined the relationship between networking and individual success (Casciaro et al., 2014; Cross & Cummings, 2004; Higgins & Kram, 2001; Wolff & Moser, 2009), as well as the amount of time job seekers devote to networking (Van Hoye et al., 2009), and how these might vary due to individual level differences in extroversion or conscientiousness (Forret & Dougherty, 2004; Kanfer et al., 2001; Van Hoye et al., 2009; Wanberg et al., 2000). The voluminous networking literature surprisingly neglects the specific discourses, processes, and experiences of networking. More specifically, although prior studies have shown that cross-national differences shape networking behavior and the efficacy or focus of strong versus weak ties (Benton et al., 2015; Bian, 1997; Sharone, 2014), these studies have not explored the extent to which networking experiences may vary cross-nationally.

Comparing between networking discourses and experiences in the U.S. and Denmark, calls for briefly outlining relevant features of the political-economic context in the American site. The U.S. labor market shares Denmark's flexibility but not its security. In recent decades, employment relations in the U.S. have become increasingly contingent and precarious (Kalleberg, 2013) while at the same time social welfare provisions from the state have diminished. With respect to unemployment insurance benefits most U.S. states have traditionally provided unemployed workers with 26 weeks of benefits, though in recent years this duration has been significantly shortened in certain states. In Massachusetts, the state in which the empirical data for this paper were gathered in 2015, unemployment benefit recipients receive up to 50% of their average weekly wage for a period of 26 weeks. The differences between the Danish and American systems are evident, however the networking technologies applied in both local context turned out not to be so different which provides a solid foundation for exploring the different possibilities of appropriating the technologies in the two settings.

Institutionalized Networking Technologies

The importance of networking is conveyed to unemployed workers in both sites through the sheer variety of trainings. In the U.S. the workshops are given straightforward names like 'introductory course' and 'networking' while in Denmark similar courses are given more striking titles including 'Persuade others to say yes', and 'Personal Branding'. These workshops broadly draw on similar discursive repertoires of career advice as well as similar conceptualizations, techniques and practices aiming to shape not only the ways job seekers engage in networking but also the ways they understand themselves in relation to such practices.

In both countries workshops introduce networking as providing entry to opportunities in the 'hidden job market' if one follows the right set of strategies. The right strategies, as presented in the introductory course on networking in Boston, are captured by the acronym 'AIR' which conveys the fundamental, if counterintuitive, rule of networking: Never ask for a job. Instead, you can ask for AIR (Advice, Information, and Referral). A trainer in Boston named Billy suggests asking networking targets for an 'informational interview'. The message is that successful networking is governed by a relational logic, which crucially requires masking the instrumental motivation underlying networking such as the need for a job. Billy explains how the informational interview label is effective at masking: "Calling it an informational meeting sort of takes that away that the purpose is to find a job".

Networking aims to encourage one's personal and professional ties to provide referrals, introductions, or information about job openings, and effective encouragement is not achieved by directly asking but by creating a connection that leads the other person to provide support.

Conveying a similar message in a seminar in Copenhagen, Kathrine uses the salesperson as a symbol of what not to do when networking. Salespeople are notorious for their use of assertive and blunt transactional tactics, which are precisely the opposite of the relationship focused approach needed for effective networking. To develop a relationship while also distinguishing yourself from the pack it is important to avoid 'bragging'. The advice is that "you have to show it, not tell it".

Because the need to mask the instrumental goal of networking might produce concerns among unemployed workers that they are manipulating or exploiting others, workshop trainers attempt to preempt such concerns by emphasizing that the relationship logic of networking involves mutuality and reciprocity. Workshops in both Boston and Copenhagen emphasize that the networking interaction should be conceived of as "two-way street" in which both parties give and take. Expressions such as "scratching each other's backs," an "exchange of value" or "mutual benefit" are often used to convey this idea. Establishing reciprocity is pivotal according to trainer Billy as networking cannot rely on the naïve idea that people just want to help without there being anything in it for them. Thus, Billy encourages "find[ing] a way to be of value to that person", and states there are limitless possibilities in this regard. He explains: "The purpose is to help others with their goals. Keep showing value to people". Even if one is not positioned to reciprocate with a referral or introduction one can "send them stuff they might be interested in", or recommend a good restaurant.

While reciprocation is critical, one must also be mindful of walking the fine line of providing value while also masking the underlying transactional logic of the interaction. Aware that unemployed job seekers may not have much to offer by way of concrete reciprocation, workshop trainers encourage job seekers to experience a sense of reciprocity from the emotional labor of inducing positive feelings in the networking target. In the affective economy of networking one important currency that unemployed workers possess is the ability to produce positive feelings in their networking partners by making him/her feel helpful. Martin in Boston explains that in networking interactions when the job seeker is asking for advice and information that other party feels needed and important: "They are loving it. They talk about themselves and share experience and expertise—everybody loves it. They are having a good time." That notion is also emphasized in the Danish context in which Karin states: "It's all about them; listen, listen, listen". She also notes that it is ok to fake it till you make it, thus implying that 'surface acting' can be sufficient to achieve the goal of the emotion work of making the network target feel positive. Networking's relationship logic means that it is not simply a matter of discussing one's skills and credentials but of bringing forward one's entire self, including intangible characteristics and passions, that may not be gleaned from a resume but are key to creating rapport and connection. Martin, a trainer in Boston, uses yoghurt as a metaphor of how job seekers should present themselves: "We have to stir it up to show the fruits. You have to put your spoon in that yoghurt and put in their mouths and say: don't I taste good? Want some more? You have to spoon feed them". The yogurt metaphor encapsulates how job seekers have to make themselves attractive to networking partners. Implicit is an understanding that all the sweet fruit pulps usually lie at the bottom and require bringing to the surface to appear convincingly delicious.

Back in Copenhagen, Kathrine, the workshop leader mentions a young woman who talked very passionately about jellyfish at an aquarium. Rhetorically she asks, "How can I talk passionately about numbers?" "You can! Something is behind accounting. If you're passionate, you'll land it!" In both contexts, passion is enacted as a general readiness to display one's professional competences in an affective vocabulary. In discussing passion for one's work Martin, the workshop leader, asks the participants to reflect on: "What makes it interesting to you? ... Why [do] you want to do it? What's the kick for you?" Networking is conceptualized in these workshops in ways that require various emotional labors, from presenting oneself as a 'tasty fruit' to making the network target feel good, to exhibiting passion. But even more fundamentally the very initiation of an interaction where one must bring forward their full self, and face the possibility of rejection, requires generating hope and confidence in the efficacy of this practice.

One way in which job seekers are encouraged to induce such feelings is to conceive of networking opportunities as limitless and potentially arising with everybody and anybody they come across. The phrase 'you never know' is frequently used and repeated by workshop leaders and participants to elevate unemployed workers' sense of hope. Martin encourages unemployed workers to network with their hairdresser: "don't be judgmental", he notes. As a response the group together bursts out, 'You never know!' The affective implication of this phrase is that it mobilizes a sense of potentiality. It also solidifies the group by ways of attuning or creating a certain vibe that for most participants manifest in feelings of belief and hope in finding work in the hidden job market.

Another consistent theme in the workshops is that effective networking requires a focus on one's physical image and body. Trainers not only advise job seekers to strategically select professional clothes that match their brand, and to attend to their 'skin and hair', but also delve into issues of body language, gestures, and behavior. A trainer in Copenhagen begins by mentioning neuroscience research and then proclaims with an air of authority: "From now on, none of you guys will ever stand with your hands in your pockets again when you are talking" as such pose sends negative signals. While the science behind such claims is highly controversial, in workshops the language of science, and particularly neuroscience, is routinely used to convey indisputable support for the trainers' advice. Martin, the trainer in Boston, similarly emphasizes the importance of body language, and particularly eye contact, in creating connection. He explains: "Make a good eye contact. Be personal. They're looking for somebody they would like to work with ... The single most important variable no matter what the context is—eye contact ... Trust me, they feel more open and receptive to you". Another trainer in Boston, Donna, provided specific advice on another bodily interaction: the handshake. Donna explains: "On a good handshake—use as much energy as it takes to use a hand knob". The Copenhagen workshops mirror those in Boston in emphasizing the importance of likeability and the link between likeability and body language. Wrapped in scientific authority trainers explain that body language speaks to the 'reptile brain' of the other as they provide advice on how to behave, talk, and charm. The focus on using one's body and body language in developing the networking relationship ultimately conveys the same core idea which underlies much of networking advice: networking practices aim to generate feelings of interpersonal connection. For this reason, workshops teach unemployed workers to focus on the human dimensions of the relationship. As the trainer Martin explains, the purpose of informational meeting is less about information and more about developing feelings of connection. Martin rhetorically asks the group in information interviews "what am I doing?" He then answers his own question: "I am becoming a person". Strikingly, Martin encourages participants to draw on a language usually considered more relevant for the intimate sphere of life using a dating analogy: "Don't waste the humanities away. We are persons. That's where the energy is ... You want them to determine that they want to go steady. I am so glad I met you. This was really interesting to me. Don't be coy. This is not a time for subtlety".

In sum, in both Boston and Copenhagen institutionalized networking advice discourses emphasize the relational logic of the interaction, which requires masking instrumental goals and developing rapport and connection. In both sites trainings assume that connection requires the emotional labor of exhibiting passion and producing positive feelings in the networking party. In both sites advice on how to achieve the needed emotional connection focuses on both verbal and body language. The underlying assumption in both sites is that one's personality and bodily expression is malleable and should be molded to maximize one's likeability and attractiveness to networking counterparts.

The Experience of Networking in the U.S. and Denmark

How do unemployed workers adopt, appropriate, transform, or contest the above advice? In this section the lived experience of networking is explored. First, the various ways in which networking experiences are similar in both sites are discussed and then the cross-national variations are discussed. The most important perceived benefit of networking, and the reason job seekers are motivated to engage in it, is increasing their chances of getting a job. Yet, mirroring the training, job seekers in both sites also perceive the need to mask this instrumental motivation. Katy refers to networking as "doing a song and a dance". She elaborates:

> If you ask people for a job, they won't take the time to talk to you. But if you ask people for advice, then they'll talk to you … It's like a song and dance. You're really asking for a job, but you have to do it, instead of saying, 'I would like a job with your organization.' You have to say, 'These are my skills. I'm not sure exactly where I would fit in.' And then they say, 'Have you thought of this job that's open here?' And you're like, 'Yes, that's why I'm here.' But instead of just being able to say that you have to go through the whole song and dance. I would leave it more up to them to figure out what might work. I know that sounds sort of counterintuitive.

Katy vividly describes the tacit rules of networking which require concealing her instrumental motivation. Moreover, she describes engaging in the emotion work of creating a positive experience for her networking contact by positioning him/her as both knowledgeable and helpful. In Hochschild's terms Katy describes "surface acting" as she experiences herself as doing a "song and a dance", implying a gap between external performance and internal experience, which can produce "emotional dissonance" (Bericat, 2016). Indeed, for many interviewees, the surface acting of a "song and dance" raises uncomfortable feelings of inauthenticity. The emotion work of creating a positive networking interaction may require the unemployed worker to not only mask their motivations but also adjust their self-presentation to fit their networking target. Josh describes his experience of modulating himself in relation to the contexts he is in:

> My wife calls me a social chameleon because I tend to play into whatever setting I'm presented with. I'll give you an example. I keep my boat down in Southie and the yacht club I keep it at is very townie. Everyone has been there for their whole life. It's not fancy, they're all construction workers. When I go in there, I bump up my Boston accent. I might still be wearing a cable knit sweater, but, "Oh yes, you guys what's up?" I play up and down. I think I'm pretty good at matching emotional intelligence. Matching the setting. But I don't really know. Maybe I think I am and then it just comes across as being inauthentic. Maybe that's why I'm not getting any jobs.

In addition to inauthenticity, workers are also concerned that in their masked interactions they are exploiting or taking advantage of others. One job seeker explained: "I wouldn't want to just leech off someone and be like, 'Hey, do this for me. I don't really have anything to give you in return." To avoid feeling exploitive some workers construct an understanding of the reciprocal nature of networking by projecting into the future and imagining that over a longer timeframe there will be situations when help will flow in both directions. As Danish Mads explains, "There are periods in which you take advantage of your network and other periods in which you are able to help out your network. It's just accepting that now you have to call around asking for help and a cup of coffee. You have to be pretty pro-active".

The most common approach in both sites to avoid feeling exploitative or inauthentic is to blur the line between market and social motivations. Evangeline, an American job seeker appropriates the language of networking by breaking down differences between the private and work sphere:

> In fact, it's just sort of making friends. So, when I reframe it in my mind as just like making friends, who might potentially one day get me a job, then it's a lot easier ... And to just think, 'I am just here with this person right now and that's all that matters' Then that really helps me focus on just chatting with them and not being super awkward. (laughing) ... I think a big

part of it is whether or not I find it interesting ... As long as the conversation itself is interesting and I feel like I've gained something from it, that's enough for me. I have to mentally make that enough because if I'm relying on every conversation to get me a job, then that's just a fool's errand.

Thinking about networking as a way of making friends enables Evangeline to feel less awkward by reducing the gap between external performance and internal experience. Unlike Katy's surface "song and dance", Evangeline's conceptualizing of networking as a social activity—"making friends"—enables deep acting in which real feelings such as enthusiasm are generated (Hochschild, 2012). To engender the emotional tones of an authentic social connection Evangeline focuses on finding or producing interest in the other person and the conversation. The emotional labor of personalizing networking relationships produces important benefits that extend beyond dealing with the discomfort of inauthenticity or exploitation from masked motives. Networking as a process of fostering affective connection can yield—as Julie put it—"psychological and social" benefits. Since unemployment is often accompanied by social isolation, networking can provide a welcomed opportunity to socially interact with others, and if the interaction is positive, it can generate feelings of being supported. As Evangeline explained: "One of the things that's been oddly encouraging about losing my job is that it made me realize how many people I have who want to see me succeed. That was incredibly encouraging. It was incredibly, I don't know if flattering is the right word, but just so heartwarming I guess."

Andreas similarly describes experiencing an emotional boost from the human interaction of networking: "Yeah, it gave a boom to send something to somebody who answered. It wasn't just that black hole." In other words, in the affective economy of networking job seekers can attain a positive emotional payoff from successful interactions. Yet, one of the central challenges of engaging in personalized networking is the typical experience of multiple networking interactions that do not produce any concrete help. Interviewees describe emotional vulnerability from attempting to obtain help from others. Emily describes it this way:

A lot of it is just the vulnerability of putting yourself out there. That's really scary, and it's hard and it's tiring. I think the biggest cost is time and energy. And also, the vulnerability of relying on other people. Basically, relying on your family and friends and colleagues and saying, 'I need something, please help me'. That's scary, that's terrifying.

Comparisons to romantic rejections are common. For example, Margaret compares the vulnerability of networking as an unemployed worker to being single because, as she explains, in both cases one must grapple with the question of "why has nobody chosen you up to this point?" To reduce their vulnerability to the pain of rejections interviewees describe several protective re-framing strategies. Much like Evangeline who limited her expectations to having an interesting social conversation, Carol explains: "I suppose some people could get frustrated about it, but I don't get frustrated. I'm trying to be realistic that not every connection is going to lead to my dream job!" Laura, another unemployed worker, grapples with the same challenge but takes a different approach. She reminds herself that she is only networking with strangers and then if something is not successful, she will not have lost anything:

> The worst thing that can happen is that you leave the event, and you don't really have a contact. So you just left the way you came. I guess it requires confidence and doing your homework before you go to the event. I guess just push yourself. If I'm in the corner, I'm like, 'Suck it up Laura. You're here for a reason.'

As the above quote suggests for Laura, as for many job seekers we interviewed, engaging in networking requires the complex task of both vulnerably exposing oneself to rejection and managing one's expectations to contain the pain of rejections.

Networking in the Affective Economy

In the affective economy of networking unemployed workers have at least three kinds of currencies at their disposal. The first currency is presenting themselves as professionally valuable and employable to the networking target, and thus in a position to reciprocate value. The other two currencies are affective in nature: generating a positive emotional experience for their networking target by making them feel powerful, helpful, or interesting, and generating an experience of affective connection by presenting themselves as socially attractive and interesting and thus enticing a 'true connection' and the experience of mutual affective investment. While all three currencies can be used to improve one's likelihood of receiving support, these currencies are not equally available.

The first currency of professional value is generally unavailable for unemployed workers because in both the U.S. and Denmark the primary means by which people display their professional value is through their current employment. Samantha describes how having a job improves one's image as valuable: "I think it just makes you look more marketable. This company already has her. They obviously like her because she's still working there." The paradox is that the very status of unemployment that leads one to need support also makes support difficult to receive. Ben explains how simply reaching out for support is itself portraying something other than success. As he puts it, "It's a little scary because there's an inclination to want to portray that you're doing well. So, asking for a job reference or recommendations is not portraying that you're doing well." As Jonathan similarly explains, having a professional identity through an attractive job provides a "cultural definition" of yourself. He explains: "Your cultural definition of yourself is tied to employment. Without that cultural definition, you are unable to network." Given the difficulty of using the first currency of networking, unemployed workers typically turn to the two other currencies. Efforts to use the second currency of representing the other person in flattering ways were previously heard in Katy's description of her "song and dance". Yet, the core of the networking advice, and a common focus of job seekers, is on the third currency: Generating a connection. Creating interpersonal connection is understood by our interviewees to require significant work on oneself to muster positivity, enthusiasm and an energetic presence. Unemployed workers in both sites discuss the absolute imperative to exhibit positivity. As Carol Ann puts it: "Something that has worked for me in my career is being positive and enthusiastic. I've been able to keep that up even in hard times. I know that works for me, I know that people like that. So that's something that I'm very mindful of when I meet people." As interviewees explained, producing a genuine connection does not just happen on its own but requires the self-work of modulating one's own emotional and physical state to one in which connecting becomes possible. For this to happen Johan describes the need to generate a state of being "on," a presence that will make him attractive. He explains what this form of self-work entails: To be able to sit and chat demands that you are fresh and rested, that you are well prepared and engaged. "You know the feeling, that if you are having some indifferent conversation, if you are not really interested, you might as well not do it. It's difficult if you are not in the right zone. It differs from day to day. You are not equally able to take initiative all days. Sometimes the body is set for assembly line work, and other days the body is adjusted or set for being 'on'". Echoing the workshop trainers focus on the importance of body language Johan recognizes that what is communicated during the interaction is not only conveyed by words but equally so by one's body and the emotions and affects one is able to produce, display and put at play in the interaction. To be effective the body must be set and ready for a social interaction with adequate intensity and engagement. Displaying one's exhaustion or indifference is not an option in this affective economy.

The Double Mask: Hiding the Emotional Toll

Networking requires job seekers to mask the instrumental goal of the interaction, however there is also second level of masking that is necessary for creating a connection: masking the emotional toll of unemployment. In both sites our data show that the experience of unemployment negatively affects how people perceive themselves and gives rise to self-doubts and feelings of anxiety. For example, Katy explains how "unemployment has shaken my confidence in a lot of different things. I don't feel like I'm good at anything." The immensely challenging emotional labor of networking for someone who is unemployed is that it requires projecting a cheerful and confident demeanor and masking the negative emotions one is experiencing. Carol explains: "Nobody wants to work with a Debby Downer … You don't want to bring a negative vibe to a new company or employer. They want somebody with a positive outlook and not somebody who could be demoralizing." Unemployed workers repeatedly explained in various ways that being open about their negative emotional toll of unemployment would undermine any hopes of successful networking. As Evangeline puts it:

> Part of the reason why I don't bring up those kinds of things [like the emotional toll] and part of the reason why other people don't bring up those kinds of things is because it's a lot harder to move past. You don't want to be, 'Man yes, networking sucks. So anyway…' You don't want to derail the conversation to only talk about how tiring everything is … There's no easy way to talk about it.

As this quote reveals, the assumption is that showing one's discouragement would 'derail' the goal of the interaction which is to mobilize support, develop rapport, and encourage affective investment in the relationship. There is no room for negativity. Anders, another Danish unemployed worker, explains how the imperative to be positive creates a growing gap between how he feels and how he is supposed to interact to develop rapport:

> It takes a lot, you have to 'be on' and not doubt your abilities so that you come off as insecure, because if you do that then it starts spiraling … and then you can sort of come to resent all that about selling oneself and all that … you have to be on, be proactive and all that and you have to call and sell yourself.

Anders' quote not only illustrates the challenge of appearing confident while one is feeling insecure but also how the discrepancy between one's feelings and the networking imperative can generate an experience of ambivalence and resentment, an experience we discuss in a later section. Relatedly, in addition to erasing negative emotions job seekers must also engage in the emotional labor of suppressing any hints of desperation. According to Carol the challenge is balancing being proactive but not to the degree that you appear too eager. She explains: "You don't want to come off as desperate." Similarly, Josh describes the necessity of convincingly performing his interest but avoiding signs of desperation: "And you try to say, 'I'm really excited about the company. I just want to get in and help however I can.' But I don't try to say, 'I need this one job and I'm not interested in other jobs.' Not seem desperate or something." Balancing between appearing interested and available but not too available is key in the affective economy of networking, and the parallel to the dating metaphor again stands out as apt.

Differences Between Unemployed Danish and American Workers: Positivity and Critique

Thus far the various ways in which the networking experiences among American and Danish unemployed people are similar have been identified. Yet the interviews also reveal important differences. The focus is on differences in networking experiences; however, our data do reveal a host of other differences in job searching behaviors that likely reflect the relatively greater level of security provided by the Danish welfare state. For example, Danish job seekers largely search for jobs that match their past work experiences and education and in their preferred geographical location, whereas our American interviewees searched for work in a wider range of fields as well as over much larger geographical areas. With respect to networking, notwithstanding the many similarities described above, data also reveal striking cross-national differences. Hiding the emotional toll of unemployment is perceived as essential for effective networking in both sites. However, the imperative to exhibit positive affect exerts a more pervasive and intense pressure on American job seekers where it is understood to require 'deep acting'. Katie, an American job seeker, explains that her positive affect "works because I believe what I am saying. But in the back of my head, I also hear all the negative things that people don't need or want to hear." In other words, for Katie's positivity to have the desired affect she has to believe it herself, requiring that she ignore those other thoughts that she believes others do not want to hear. By contrast to deep acting, a strategy reported by Danish interviewees to divert negative affects is to discuss their unemployment openly but with humor, for example, describing themselves as 'work-free', 'on vacation' or in other ways creating an ironic distance from their situation and the imperative to avoid stigma and pity. Julie explains her rationale for employing a humorous stance: "It's probably to maintain this positive side I think I just clown about it [unemployment] to avoid showing that it's not exactly the nicest situation."

There is a cross-national difference regarding the degree to which networking pervades everyday life. The American interviewees were much more likely than the Danish ones to describe tensions from the pressure to network in their personal lives. As networking erodes the boundary between professional and private spheres—an erosion which is the flipside of the previously discussed mantra 'your never know' and its encouragement to be open to the 'limitless opportunities' for networking—it simultaneously generates an ever-present pressure to be available, ready, and alert to networking opportunities. Sarah from Boston describes the tensions arising in her personal life:

> I'm at church or I'm standing on the sidewalk with someone, and I want to answer their question but there's part of me that will then start thinking, 'OK, someone is asking me what I'm looking for. Now it's time to pull out the 30 second elevator speech.' But then there's this part of me that really does not want to do it that way. I'm at church, I'm not at a job fair. I don't want to function like I'm at a job fair.

In the American context the discourse of networking as an ever-present possibility implies that there is no haven; and that all of one's social life is an arena for self-marketing performances. Sarah experiences the pressure, if not obligation to perform, even at her church. But at the same time, she acknowledges, "Sometimes I just want to be a person". We can also see the greater pervasiveness of networking's feeling rules, like the need to be positive, in the fact that many of our American interviewees, but not their Danish counterparts, report not sharing their negative feelings and thoughts with their intimate partners. Josh, an American job seeker describes his reluctance to share with his girlfriend the negative emotional toll of unemployment: "I guess there is a tendency to be not as forthcoming if I'm disappointed or something is not going well, or I'm not as excited about something as I should be. That can bring up difficulties, if that makes sense." By contrast, among the Danish job seekers there is an inclination to feel entitled to complain to one's intimate partner in order to feel supported. As Elizabeth puts it: "I am definitely more up-and-down, in a yo-yo mood, and I take that out on my husband, or not take out, but it affects our relationship … [being unemployed] puts a pressure on it. All the worries I have about being unemployed and the future, he has to listen to that." Underlying the greater willingness of Danish interviewees to share emotional hardships with intimate partners, as well as their use of humor and irony in discussing unemployment, are differences in how young unemployed workers in each site interpret their career difficulties and thus the very need to network. American job seekers are comparatively much more likely to blame themselves for their unemployment while Danish job seekers are comparatively more likely to articulate a critique of the broader structural conditions that make networking a necessary element of career success. For example, Ashley, an American job seeker, in discussing the reasons for her unemployment describes her difficulties with cold calling potential network contacts and criticizes her own inability to be proactive. As Ashley puts it:

> Yes, and it's all about me. It's something I know intellectually I need to do it more. I don't even know if I have a good reason for it. 'You should cold call people. You never know.' Intellectually I know I should be convinced of that, but emotionally I'm not, so I don't end up doing it because I'm really shy about it.

Several Danish interviewees offered a critique of broader societal conditions and problematized networking as deviating from meritocracy. This critique was articulated by a minority of the Danish interviewees—but strikingly by none of our American interviewees—is exemplified by

Emily's feelings about networking: "I don't like networking because I don't feel like it should be my contacts who gets me a job. I want to be recognized for what I am capable of." Implicit in Emily's dislike of networking is the notion that it should be one's capabilities, as opposed to one's contacts, which determine his getting a job. Stephan is more explicit is articulating these concerns when he raises the issue of nepotism in assessing the fairness of networking and feels bad even when he personally benefits:

> That's just sweet old nepotistic Denmark where everybody gets a job through friends. We are not corrupt, I know, but we are extremely nepotistic. I think it's a problem. I have a nice network. I also have an interview with somebody I got through networking next week. I just feel bad about it. I think it is the step just before corruption. But the unemployment [services] says 'network, network, network.'

Some Danish job seekers also took a critical stance toward the institutionalized pressure to reshape or modulate their personalities and styles of interaction. Whereas American job seekers found various ways to respond to their discomforts with networking by, for example, conceptualizing it as making friends or as a reciprocal relationship, a significant number of Danish job seekers problematized the institutionalized pressures for all unemployed workers to engage in networking. For example, in response to the detailed information on how to conduct herself and her body in the job search, one Danish job seeker criticized the system for patronizing her: "I actually got an email with 10 pieces of good advice on how to shake hands at a job interview. I mean, I really can't take that. I can't have people think they can tell me stuff like that." Anders, another Danish unemployed worker, describes the estranging effects of the pressure to work on the self to network:

> You have to change, it doesn't matter what you think, what views you have. You have to change yourself to get a job … When I went to a job interview at [tax company] I got to see the next one who was going to the interview. I almost died inside. He looked like me. He was the same age. He wore light grey pants, the same shoes, and we graduated from the same university.

We are little clones because we are not allowed to bring in our personalities.

Echoing the detailed advice given at networking trainings, Anders describes modulating himself to the extent that he feels like a clone. These young Danish job seekers critique and resist the institutionalized pressures to shape and modulate their personalities into more employable selves. What is being resisted here is the pressure to view oneself through an employability lens and adjust oneself to more marketable ways of being, of dressing, of conducting oneself. In Anders case the sheer resemblance between him and the other competing candidates made it obvious to him that he had succumbed to this pressure by stripping away aspects of his personality, molding himself into a more mainstream figure, but all at the cost of, as he puts it, "almost dying inside."

The cross-national differences described above are not rooted in job seekers' different assessments of the efficacy of networking—in both sites, only a minority of unemployed workers express skepticism. For example, at a seminar in Copenhagen one woman pointed to the elephant in the room by saying: "But we are not even getting job interviews! There are no jobs available and the ones that are certainly don't go to unemployed people." Similarly, a participant in Boston challenged the optimistic assumptions encouraged by the previously discussed mantra "'you never know' pointing to her experience with racism.

While in both sites a few jobseekers express skepticism about the efficacy of networking, it is only in the Danish context that critiques of networking practices were put forward rooted in concerns about the work-on-the-self that it entailed. In sum, while both young Americans and Danes engage in networking, and most think its effective, Danish job seekers often do it while maintaining a critical distance.

The analysis reveals a set of cross-national differences which are worthy of further exploration. In the U.S. context we see a relatively greater erosion of the boundaries between the professional and the personal spheres of life, with some job seekers feeling that no location is demarcated as off limits and no time demarcated as off duty. For example, American job seekers report feeling comparatively more obligated to conceal negative emotions in all interactions, while Danish job seekers more openly vent their negative thoughts with close family, friends, and partners. Another cross-national difference is the relatively greater concern expressed among Danish interviewees that networking is exploitative of the other party, or a troubling deviation from meritocracy due to nepotism. These differences suggest that the discourses and practices of networking are, now, more suspect, and less taken-for-granted in Danish context as compared to the U.S. This difference helps explain why Danish job seekers, much more than their American counterparts, employ a humorous stance to networking practices. Notwithstanding these cross-national differences, when stepping back, a more striking cross-national convergence in networking advice discourses, practices, and experiences appears. That suggests that important elements of the relational logic of networking, and the various challenges that this logic poses for unemployed workers, can transcend differences in local cultures, hiring institutions, regimes of unemployment benefits and wider welfare state provisions. While the data do reveal important cross-national differences, these differences neither alter the fundamental requirements of networking for emotional labor and work-on-the-self nor the affective economy within which networking occurs.

Common across the U.S. and Denmark is the intimacy involved in the dance of networking. Revealingly, in both sites unemployed workers frequently draw on romantic dating as a key metaphor for networking, pointing to the profound ways in which emotions are implicated in the networking interaction and in the stakes. In both dating and networking succeeding requires vulnerably putting yourself out there in ways that can pay off with positive emotional experience of connection, but it also necessarily involves the exposure to the possibility of painful rejection. In both sites a similar affective economy appears in which currencies such as producing positive feelings in the networking partner, such as helpfulness or connection, are perceived as essential to successful networking. The data reveal that across both sites the logic of networking demands multiple and interrelated dimensions of emotional labor, including the need to mask the instrumental motives underlying the interaction. Much like Bourdieu's argument that currencies in a gift exchange lose value if the gift bears a price tag (Bourdieu, 1998) the networking exchange must avoid open acknowledgment of transactional motives to set up the right conditions for putting the right affective currencies at play.

In both sites this masking generates feelings of inauthenticity and exploitation, which in turn lead unemployed workers to engage in further forms of emotional labor. While Casciaro et al. (2014) distinguish between "professional" and "personal" ties and argue that instrumental networking with professional ties makes people feel moral "dirty," the comparative study shows how unemployed workers engage in practices to breakdown the very distinction between professional and personal ties using metaphors such as "making friends." Interestingly, networking constitutes an alternative to the 'black hole' into which formal job applications are often considered to have disappeared, as described in qualitative unemployment research (Sharone, 2013a). Job seekers engage in deep acting to generate feelings of sociability partly to protect themselves from negative self-perceptions or feelings of being dirty.

The emotional labor of generating feelings of social connection is rooted in the structural condition of unemployment, which entails a scarcity of what we have called the first currency of reciprocation, that is, professional support, and leads unemployed job seekers to rely on affective currencies to reciprocate, most prominently generating feelings of social connection. In both sites the emotional labor of creating a social relationship requires generating a positive, passionate, and connecting presence, which frequently entails masking the negative emotional toll generated by the experience of unemployment. The complex web of emotional labors implicated in the practice of networking suggests new ways of analyzing the effects of networking beyond the narrow and often studied question of efficacy for finding work with its primarily focus on individual differences as explanatory variables. As the analysis shows, networking can yield certain emotional benefits, particularly to those with supportive social ties. Yet, as we show, networking also raises significant challenges, most significantly, a vulnerability to experiences of highly personalized rejections intrinsically tied to the affective economy of networking. As prior studies have shown, when job market outcomes are personalized, understood as not based on assessment of professional skills but of the self behind the skills (Sharone, 2013b), these rejections often have severe negative effects on self-perceptions. The more networking feels like romance, the more everyday efforts to find work turn into a series of heartaches. In both sites the emotional labors and affective economy of networking impose vulnerabilities and pressures on unemployed workers who are already experiencing the intense emotional toll of unemployment. Layered on top of employer rejections, the practice networking exposes unemployed workers to more personalized interactions and potential rejections.

In addition to studies showing how network-based hiring reproduces traditional stratification lines (e.g., DiTomaso, 2013), the discourses and practices of networking shape and promote a specific type of person: idealizing and valorizing the outgoing and likable personality while marginalizing any dimension of the self which could be deemed eccentric or less social. Networking discourses and practices reach beyond interaction styles and identify the body as a site for work and modulation that is pivotal to the success of networking. The detailed advice about the right eye contact, handshake, and holding one's body encourages a broad and deep self-assessment and self-conscious strategic manipulating of aspects of one's embodied self that are typically not scrutinized, evaluated, or modulated. While unemployed people looking for work can choose to ignore the rules of effective networking, given the vulnerability of unemployed workers who are looking for any edge in their pursuit of work the networking advice likely creates a force for homogeneity of selves, bodies, and interactions. The upshot of networking is to open realms that at earlier eras might have been perceived as belonging to the private or intimate sphere and to target these as sites of scrutiny and change in the name of effective networking, marketability, and career success.

Summing Up

As unemployed people in more and more societies operate in neoliberal institutional contexts which discursively encourage—and materially demand—proactive networking as a condition to finding employment, we are likely to witness the institutionalization of ways of understanding and relating to oneself and others. At core networking demands emotional laborers to convince and seduce others to believing in one's worth, attractiveness and likeability. As the empirical material suggests regimes of networking involve the intensification of the self-evaluating gaze, and the modulating of oneself in alignment with the kinds of selves valorized in the labor market. As such it becomes yet another way of encouraging unemployed people to critically assess and evaluate themselves. In Anders' case, we see how the resultant self-molding into a marketable subject produces the experience of "almost dying inside". A deepened understanding of the implications of networking may contribute to efforts to counteract the difficult challenges the practice of networking generates for our sense of self and social relations. The encouragement to network involves the cultivation and display of affective currencies necessary to create rapport with possible gatekeepers in the gray economy. Engaging in networking also produces a sense of hope as well as it feeds off hope to begin with. The emotional labor involved in networking adds to the complexity and cross-over of emotional demands for unemployed people. Paying back money is not a possibility, however, engaging relentlessly and without any boundaries between private and professional domains become one way of alleviating some of the emotional debt. Paying back in proactive networking behavior again centers the personality and social skills, investing psychological capabilities in the quest for a job.

References

Benton, R. A., Mcdonald, S., Manzoni, A., & Warner, O. D. F. (2015). The recruitment paradox: Network recruitment, structural position, and East German Market Transition. *Social Forces, 93*(3), 905–932. https://doi.org/10.1093/sf/sou100

Bericat, E. (2016). The sociology of emotions: Four decades of progress. *Current Sociology, 64*(3), 491–513. https://doi.org/10.1177/0011392115588355

Bian, Y. (1997). Bringing strong ties back in: Indirect ties, network bridges, and job searches in China. *American Sociological Review*, 366–385.

Bourdieu, P. (1998). *Practical reason, on the theory of action.* Polity.

Casciaro, T., Gino, F., & Kouchaki, O. M. (2014). The contaminating effects of building instrumental ties: How networking can make us feel dirty. *Harvard Business School NOM Unit Working Paper No.* 14–108. https://doi.org/10.2139/ssrn.2430174

Cross, R., & Cummings, J. N. (2004). Tie and network correlates of individual performance in knowledge-intensive work. *Academy of Management Journal, 47*(6), 928–937.

DiTomaso, N. (2013). *The American non-dilemma, racial inequality without racism*. Russell Sage Foundation.

Forret, M. L., & Dougherty, O. T. W. (2004). Networking behaviors and career outcomes: Differences for men and women? *Journal of Organizational Behavior, 25*(3), 419–437. https://doi.org/10.1002/job.253

Granovetter, M. (1973). The strength of weak ties. *American Journal of Sociology, 78*(1), 1360.

Higgins, M. C., & Kram, K. E. (2001). Reconceptualizing mentoring at work: A developmental network perspective. *Academy of Management Review, 26*(2), 264–288.

Hochschild, A. R. (2012). *The managed heart: Commercialization of human feeling* (3rd ed., Updated with a New Preface edition). Berkeley, CA: University of California Press.

Kalleberg, A. L. (2013). *Good jobs, bad jobs* | Russell Sage Foundation. https://www.russellsage.org/publications/good-jobs-bad-jobs

Mouw, T. (2003). Social capital and finding a job: Do contacts matter?. *American Sociological Review, 68*(6), 868–898.

Rivera, L. A. (2012). Hiring as cultural matching: The case of elite professional service firms. *American Sociological Review, 77*(6), 999–1022.

Sharone, O. (2013a). *Flawed system/flawed self: Job searching and unemployment experiences*. University of Chicago Press.

Sharone, O. (2013b). Why do unemployed Americans blame themselves while Israelis blame the system? *Social Forces, 91*(4), 1429–1450. https://doi.org/10.1093/sf/sot050

Sharone, O. (2014). Social capital activation and job searching: Embedding the use of weak ties in the American institutional context. *Work and Occupations, 41*(4), 409–439.

Van Hoye, G., van Hooft, E. A. J., & Lievens, O. F. (2009). Networking as a job search behaviour: A social network perspective. *Journal of Occupational and Organizational Psychology, 82*(3), 661–682. https://doi.org/10.1348/096317908X360675

Wanberg, C. R., Kanfer, R., & Banas, J. T. (2000). Predictors and outcomes of networking intensity among unemployed job seekers. *Journal of Applied Psychology, 85*(4), 491–503. https://doi.org/10.1037/0021-9010.85.4.491

Wolff, H. G., & Moser, K. (2009). Effects of networking on career success: A longitudinal study. *Journal of Applied Psychology, 94*(1), 196.

Yakubovich, V. (2005). Weak ties, information, and influence: How workers find jobs in a local Russian labor market. *American Sociological Review, 70*(3), 408–421.

8

Unemployment Experiences During Covid-19: A Little Less Blame?

How has the Covid-19 crisis and the temporary suspension of obligations affected the unemployment experiences and more specifically the ways that people think about their job search and the various ways they can invest their time and energy to get a job? Even for those who are already very actively seeking a job and are quick to write job applications, the suspension of the requirement to apply for two jobs per week does make a difference—not for the pace, per se, but in relation to the quality of job searching. As Else says: "It's been great [laughing] [to get rid of the demands, ed.]; it's not like I have applied for fewer jobs". Maiken finds that job searching has been more meaningful during the period when the claim has been suspended, both because she does not have to apply for jobs, as she puts it, and because she can apply for jobs in a more flexible manner, writing up more applications at times when there are interesting vacancies and doing less at times when there are fewer:

> Well, it's very different, the fact that this feeling of pressure of "I also have to remember to apply for that." It's easier to get it done now, when it's less "you have to do it." Because there isn't the same stress, that "now you have to remember to apply for two jobs", because if I only apply for one job, then I can apply for three jobs the next week, and it's up to me.

Laura is relieved that there is a break from the communications from the employment office and the unemployment fund:

> I actually think it's been a bit liberating that I haven't had to respond to this and that all the time, the regular flood of mails from the employment office, "now you have to check this," and the unemployment fund, "now you have to keep an eye on that", "fill out this" and this and that. There's been much more breathing space.

From Laura's description, it seems that requests and demands from PES are overwhelming and she also needed a break from them.

Maiken states that instead of planning her job search on the basis of activity requirements, she now has the opportunity to focus on the labor market, and only spend time on applications that makes sense to her. The suspension of the requirements makes it more visible to her that the system's demands were associated with 'pressure' and 'stress'. To Maria this is related to the way the suspension has removed the formal element of the job search:

> Generally, I have enjoyed the feeling that there's no superior who's checking whether I fulfill my obligations before May 25th, so you know, not having the superior "Sauron's Eye" on me … I haven't applied for jobs to prove that I apply for jobs. I've applied for jobs because I want to get a job.

Inherent in the activation technologies established by the system is an underlying understanding that unemployed people only apply for jobs if they are required to do so; otherwise, they remain inactive or are perhaps even perceived as lazy. This formal moral assessment or test is also put on standby during the suspension, enabling the unemployed people to experience another way of actively engaging which is more meaningful and autonomous. When the apparatus designed to construct self-responsible, active jobseekers is put on hold, paradoxically, we see active engagements associated with what is described as a heightened sense of agency. The quote also demonstrates that continuous effort to make unemployed active is linked to an experience of being mistrusted and surveilled which

Maria expresses with 'Sauron's eye' referring to an evil character in Harry Potter.

The closure of employment offices and unemployment insurance funds due to the Covid-19 crisis also means that unemployed people do not have to attend compulsory interviews. According to Else, it has been a relief not to have to go to meetings at the employment office: "I've stopped going to job consultations at the employment office. And since I've never experienced the employment office as a helpful institution, that is, it's not something that has helped me in finding a job, then it isn't something I've missed much." To Else, living up to the demands and talking to PES has not been linked with getting closer to finding a job. In a sense, living up to system demands seems detached in relation to the overall goal. However, we also identified unemployed people who felt isolated and abandoned by PES, and thus, unable to 'move on' toward a job as they needed support from job consultants. For a substantial minority of the people we interviewed, it is not simply the absence of the formal dimension of the suspended requirements that provides them with relief, but the experienced pressure of complying with them.

> But immediately, applying for jobs, I can feel that pheeeew, it takes my breath away and I get really sad. I really easily start to cry when I talk about it. I feel them [her tears] now, sitting there, bothering me. And then the corona virus was a bit of a blessing, because it put these demands on hold.

Josefine was overwhelmed by the unemployment experience, and has a hard time living up to the requirements of PES activation policies, so the suspension from the job search provided her with a much-needed break. In another way, it becomes clear that the various strings that attach an emotional burden on unemployed people during corona was relieved a little bit, resulting in a much needed experience of feeling a little less governed. Perhaps inadvertently the employment technologies are translated to technologies of self in a way that become instrumental and a demand 'on top of' qualified job search rather than actually contributing as helpful and supportive activities.

The Continuous Self-Doubt in the Job Search and the Impact of the Pandemic

Overall, unemployed people continuously reflect on their job search strategies they employ in the quest for a job. In alignment with this tendency, most of the interviewees describe continuous reflection and doubt in terms of the specific configuration of their strategy: Am I spending my time in the best possible fashion? Should I put different strategies into use? Can I do more? The Covid-19 crisis adds an extra layer of doubt and insecurity. Below, Maria expresses the personal agony involved in critically reflecting on how to govern oneself. Asked directly about her idea of what she wants to do from now on and what she thinks it will take for her to get a job, she answers, obviously frustrated:

> That's what's on my mind. That's the question I wake up with every morning. Am I doing enough right now? And that's really … I think that's one of the big things that has changed now that the pressure is there too, that there's a dead end, which is, am I following the right strategy? So, I'm spending so much time thinking about my strategy. That is, what is the right strategy? How should I spend my energy? Should I call all my network first? And there's no right answers, you just try to hope.

Engaging wholeheartedly in job search and trying to figure out the best way of investing time and energy without having control in terms of the outcomes makes the unemployment experience exhausting. So far, her plan has failed and that makes her feel unhappy here and now, but she also worries about the long-term effects of her unemployment.

> Well, yes, you're unhappy getting up every day not knowing what to do. But the long-term consequences of how it affects my adult life, and thereby, when can we buy [a house]. We've had meetings with the bank. "When are you getting a job?" Well, I really don't know. I wish I was able to give you an answer. And all that about applying for jobs at supermarkets, well, here during the corona crisis, I've also applied for jobs far away and I've also applied for jobs at schools. But I don't hear anything, I'm getting rejected. Well, okay, I am not useful there, either.

The insecurity about the future again puts pressure on her short-term plan, and at the same time, it postpones major life decisions and puts the long-term plan on hold, mentioned before as unemployment to some extent puts life and life decisions on hold. This makes her ever more flexible in terms of applying for jobs across a wider geographical range and across professions as well targeting lower-ranged jobs. However, being rejected in relation to jobs she did not even want in the first place leaves her feeling even more useless. Downgrading thus comes with an affective price eating away the sense of feeling like having value.

This picture is well-known from this book and also from other studies on unemployment experiences (Demazière & Zune, 2023; Boland & Griffin, 2015).

The pressure of the activation technologies were also documented in prior empirical studies but it is a strong validation when the unemployed people both have experience living up to these demands and not having to live up to them. From a research perspective, this comparison is of high quality. The rather uniform descriptions of being relieved from the demands and perhaps more interestingly, the experience of getting back into the driver's seat of job search testifies to a problematic instrumental way of dealing with the demands, that might in fact damage the job search competencies. When you apply for jobs to satisfy the system and live up to the conditions you need to, to be eligible for economic compensation, you miss out on some important potential qualities inherent in job search which is initiated by the individual on the basis of a sense of agency and personal aspiration.

The Relentless Job Search Leaving No Time for Life

One of the issues of job search is that it is difficult to take time off and thus maintain or establish a work/life balance. Hobbies that used to provide people with a sense of ease are for some difficult to keep up in the everyday life as unemployed. Inge has always enjoyed painting and doing needlework and has considered gathering a group of people around this hobby, but since she became unemployed, she does not "have the mental energy for it" and painting a whole day would give her "a guilty conscience". Thus, activities that used to be enjoyed in the spare time after work are toned down or even prevented as the job search and perhaps especially the bad conscience and fear of the future take up all one's energy. Hence, Inge is only able to conduct herself in a way that prioritizes job search over all other activities. Even activities that used to be located within the 'life' domain in the classical (and perhaps a bit problematic) distinction between life and work, is now somehow off guards living no room for activities that help her relax. These activities no longer provide her with ease; rather, she is ridden by guilt, even though she admits that it is "nonsense". The emotional struggle that unemployed people find themselves in is very evident from this example as it makes visible the emotional labor that goes into thinking and reflecting on the need to take time off and relax and at the same time, this is challenging or even impossible, while at the same time considering this struggle as "non-sense". Either way, she has not been able set up boundaries between job search and time off. Similarly, Maria describes not being able to relax until she gets a job, and thus, the only thing she is able to do is to sit by her computer:

> Well, sometimes I've maybe been sitting and looking [at the computer] and thought, now I really don't know what to do. I always sit by my computer ... I can't do anything else, before I get a job. If I knew tomorrow that from August 1st I'll have a job, then I could say, okay, now I can sew this, I can plant these flowers in the garden, I can go home and visit my parents and just enjoy my time with them. Well, all those things, I can't do those at all. Really, I need a job before I can enjoy myself.

The job search has in effect excluded engagement in other domains of life, which frustrates Maria because she is unable to relax. While job search excludes, we also identify dynamics in which people tweak what used to be hobbies and turn them into part of the job search. For Lene, gardening work is requalified in the job search of developing business ideas. Lene has always enjoyed gardening but after becoming unemployed and participating in start-up courses, she suddenly sees this as an opportunity of developing a business within gardening consultancy work.

> Privately, I have this interest in gardening in general, and hey, if you could … I've made some garden drawings for friends for free and then all of a sudden, I thought, hey, what if you could develop that part? It could just be fun and exciting, and then I could use the qualifications from my higher education and then use the practical part, that I also really like.

Thus, Lene's private interest in gardening that she normally associates with relaxing and taking time off becomes part of job search. The boundaries between 'work' or job search and 'life' can thus be viewed as dynamic or even porous. While job search does not equal going to work, there are resemblances, and tragically, it is often even more difficult to manage the work/life balance as unemployed, even though unemployed people in principle have the necessary time. This struggle adds an interesting perspective on the literature of work/life balance emphasizing the psychological and social psychological dimensions that are sometimes overlooked in studies focusing on a balance between demand and control (Karasek, 1979) or effort and reward (Siegrist, 2016) or similar approaches that center on the working conditions and actual tasks rather than employing a more broad analytical scope looking into the social psychology of everyday life.

Exploring Alternative Values

For some of our interviewees, the Danish government's suspension of rules and demands during lockdown in spring 2020 results in a vacuum that gives space to other kinds of activities and ways of being. These include taking a break altogether from applying for jobs and instead spending more time with one's family, home-educating children during the first Covid-19 lockdown, learning new skills and starting new leisure activities, etc. In various ways, they step out of job search so dominantly prioritized and pushed forward by the activation technologies. A few of the interviewees seem to invest in their current employment situation with a sense of exploration, emphasizing how the slow pace of their current situation has led them to "check in with themselves" on how they want to spend their future (work) lives:

> It was a good opportunity for me to think things through and find out what I should do for the rest of my life. Instead of just doing the same all my life. I actually spend time thinking about "what do I want" and try to ask myself "what would I like"?
>
> I've learnt more this half a year [while unemployed] about work life and my role in being a cogwheel in some machine, or whatever I was … I would never have been able to genuinely feel the pulse of it unless I'd stood where I stand now not having a job.

They both emphasize unemployment as a chance to figure out what they want to work in and what they have learnt about themselves more generally from being unemployed. Jesper and Ole approach the situation with exploration. This involves taking a critical stance to the dominant social values in which paid work is the only way to a fulfilling life. Jesper and Ole's enthusiastic expressions of the meaningfulness of the new insights about their lives and confidence that in time they will find a job illustrating emotional benefits from this way of conducting oneself. They have qualified their situation as one of (self) discovery providing new exciting insights about themselves. Jesper even expresses that had it not been for his time of unemployment, he would not have been able to pause his high-speed work life, "driving on a career track at 100 km per hour", as he put it. More concretely, Ole and his girlfriend dream about moving abroad, so Ole takes advantage of his time out of work to explore future possibilities for that, while Jesper explores mindfulness, meditation, and Buddhism and has taken up an old passion for gymnastics. He stresses how his time being unemployed has taught him to explore and do things solely out of desire and interest contrary to doing things for the sake of achieving something (in work life). In short, he is exploring a meaningfulness of life that does not depend on employment status and that entails taking a critical look at his former work life.

While we have seen that some of the participants engage in their state of unemployment with exploration, for others the suspension gives space to a stronger investment in family life, often referred to as 'life' in work/life dichotomy.

Some of the unemployed people enjoy this uniquely 'demand-free' period and take a break from applying for jobs altogether. Instead, they spend time with family, helping family members or friends with practical issues, babysitting relatives' children, home-schooling their own children or spending time on practical projects in their gardens or apartments. To give an example, Søren, a 40-year-old journalist, decides to not apply for jobs and instead focus on home-schooling his son, who is sent home from school as part of the lockdown.

> I think it's been a huge gift to be able to spend so much time with my boy and home-educate him. I'll actually compare it with back when I was on parental leave with him, which was an amazing time. It is so lovely to have the opportunity to be so close to your child, right. And it also makes it possible to get a huge insight into where he is at in school. You do not get the possibility to explore that so closely during everyday life, right. In that way it's actually been an oasis.

Describing his time home-schooling his son as a "gift", "an oasis" and a possibility to get "close" to his son's everyday school life points toward a sense of ease and intimacy. Thus, prioritizing family life is expressed through presence, intimacy, and relaxation, that unlike living up to the demands embedded in the activation technologies does not have a functional/instrumental quality to it. Somehow they avoid the emotional debt and thus feel free to be governed a little less, without receiving money from the state and paying back in affective currencies.

Unemployment as a More Legitimate Position: But for Whom?

Finally, job search failure can switch into reflections both about oneself (inward) or critical thoughts of the system (outward). The failed job search leads to doubts about one's own abilities, which gives rise to a sense of inferiority or self-blame. For some, this involves downgrading one's value in the labor market, for example by seeking more widely in terms of geography, profession, or salary, or seeking unpaid work. However, we also see that the Covid-19 crisis can provide the occasion for a reevaluation of the worth of the unemployed themselves. For instance, the crisis offers an opportunity for Maria to openly talk about her formal status, as she experiences a greater understanding of being unemployed during Covid-19 and she explicitly remarks that the link between unemployment and lack of competences has been loosened:

> Even though I didn't get hired, then I could kind of say, "Oh, I was just about to do a business Ph.D., but then corona came". So it has become a quite nice narrative. Somehow, it is not about not being able to do anything. It is about "oh, but it was just external circumstances which caused that, it was such a pity".

The pandemic thus allows Maria (and others) to speak of unemployment as an accident beyond her control in opposition to the individualized and responsibilized understanding of unemployment inherent in the active turn and common in the widespread representation of unemployed people. Before the crisis, Maria did not tell family and friends that she went in and out of unemployment in her precarious working life, but the increased understanding, sympathy and not least legitimacy of unemployment during the crisis, allowed her to show up more honestly in relation to family and friends. As mentioned in Chap. 6, among artists, cultural workers and other professionals belonging to labor markets with a lot of precarious positions, it is rather common not to identify nor communicate the formal status of being unemployed but rather hiding under the umbrella of "freelancer". This strategy was identified as an answer to the deal with the sticky shame that comes with the unwanted identity of being unemployed. Interestingly, COVID-19 posed an alternative way of conducting oneself. In that sense, this self-governing makes visible the intricate ways that there is no direct relation between unemployment and status/dignity, but that this relationship in fact emerges as a complex relation between unemployment, employment policies and how they are administered at PES, social values in society and a representation of unemployed people that can actually change. Even though the understanding of unemployed people has almost been cemented and sedimented during the last many decades, COVID-19 proved the mantra of social constructionism to be true: everything can always be different.

While we see the contours of an alternative way of ascribing dignity and worth to people whether they have a job or nor, this was not the only pattern, that emerged in response to the changed landscape of unemployment during the pandemic. The increased legitimacy does not seem to be distributed evenly in the unemployed population. Quickly, a distinction emerged through those who were unemployed before COVID-19 and those became unemployed because of it. Others emphasize the increased economic insecurity and the increased unemployment rate making the competition for sparse jobs even fiercer. As an effect of Covid-19, a new distinction between various groups of unemployed people have been introduced. Some distinguish between people who have become unemployed as an effect of Covid-19 and the people who were unemployed before:

> I surely also think that since you hear that there's a lot who got laid off, then it can also cause one to think about those who were available right before corona. Is it gonna get even more difficult for us, really? I think that is a bit tough, or very. It really is.

Lene speculates that there is a difference in worth (and, thus, in labor market value) between the two groups and that especially the pre-Covid-19 unemployed will suffer under these circumstances. This is discouraging to her. Inge speculates that the moral test of people becoming unemployed during Covid-19 will be milder and thus they will be considered more attractive job candidates:

> So, I do know that there are a lot of other newly unemployed people, who will probably be chosen before me, so I also feel that I have been moved a couple of steps further back in the queue ... But it's obviously something that people look for, when they look at these job applications, and then if someone writes that they were fired because of the corona crisis, then the employers are more willing to take them on than someone who's been available before the corona crisis.

According to Inge, Covid-unemployed people enjoy more understanding, but she feels that this change in worthiness is restricted to that group, rather than covering all unemployed people. While we do see that the Covid-19 crisis to some extent shifts or tweaks the moral test of unemployed people, especially for those who became unemployed during Covid-19, the view on the unemployed more generally as a group still reflects the idea that unemployed people are a burden on society (Pultz, 2017). As an example, Else criticizes the unemployment system and how unemployed people "are paid to stay away" instead of being put to use and she advocates for integrating unemployed people as volunteers during the Covid-19 crisis to a greater extent:

> The public authorities could maybe also have done a bit more to integrate unemployed people. And also ask the unemployed people to volunteer during the corona crisis, because it would have helped present a positive picture that they can do something for society. Because, to be completely honest, as an unemployed person you get paid to stay away and not create problems.

Else in a sense problematizes that there is not enough investment in unemployed people as a valuable source for a country when dealing with a crisis such as corona. Being "paid to stay away" is demoralizing to Else.

Similarly, Katrine reconsiders what she understands as a "good quality job" considering Covid-19, and the need to feel "useful" and contribute to society becomes pressing to her, which in some sense indicates that she starts exploring what she wants to do with her life anew: "I felt a strong need to sign up to Covid assistance … It would make so much sense to me to be able to be useful and someone who's beneficial, someone who is needed". Another example of critical exploration is Lene, whose own experiences have led her to be highly critical of ageism in the sense of age discrimination of the unemployed in job application processes:

> There's been an interview with the new Minister of Employment, Peter Hummelgaard, where he is upset about the fact that it's so difficult for people in my age group to get a job. So, I thought, well, if he thinks like that, well that is lovely, then I will just write to him … So I also wrote to

the Ministry of Employment, and they thought, hey, that's a really good idea, go out and find someone who wants to put money into it.

Lene is proactive in trying to address problematic conditions for older unemployed people. She appreciates having a Minister of Employment who is aware and brings up the issue; however, she is disappointed that he is not willing to finance the event. At the same time, this critique can again be tweaked into potential job search, because most likely, if she managed to find funding for the event, she would put it on her CV demonstrating entrepreneurial abilities highly valued in current labor markets. Again, the dynamics between job search and leisure, or "work/life" are porous and one is easily transformed into the other. Especially the enterprise culture has put fuel to that fire.

Surely, the unemployment experience is not suddenly changed fundamentally by policy changes. This notion is also supported by the cross-comparative analysis (Chap. 7) as well as studies focusing on the American context alone (Sharone, 2013a; Chen, 2015; Pugh, 2015; Rao, 2020).

First, being active is not simply an obligation that derives from the instruments of the employment office. Since being unemployed has always entailed a degree of devaluation and a sense of inferiority, job searching constitutes the main means to exit this status regardless of obligations and techniques in the PES. In a country such as Denmark, with a long history of the protestant work ethic, these constitute deep-rooted norms and values. The often instrumental and standardized obligations to job search that seem integral to the active turn thus establish a potential tension with the unemployed person's own sense of a meaningful job search (Demazière, 2020). Second, unemployed people are simply confronted with everyday pragmatic needs to make a living in which getting a job is often one of many other elements such as caring for children and family, social life, paying bills, daily routines, participating in the local community, etc. Both elements of the experience of unemployment mean that complying with obligations and 'playing the role of job-seeker' are not tantamount to acceptance. Unemployed people have been shown here to have deep reflexive critical evaluations of the PES and the situation they are in, and the Covid-19 crisis may amplify these ambiguities.

Summing Up

In many ways the covid-19 was a much-needed pause for unemployed people from being governed through activation policies based on a built-in understanding of the unemployed subject as a priori inactive and perhaps even morally questionable.

All of a sudden, the overlooked power of external causes came into the light and allowed a less individualized and privatized way of understanding the case of unemployment. The responsibility machinery was temporarily paused, leaving room for unemployed people's own sense of agency to blossom. Coming out of one's individual unemployment crisis and being part of a broader crisis encompassing people with and without jobs seemed to pave the way for a new way of representation of unemployed people leaving them with more worthiness. This heightened worthiness was however not equally distributed, as people who became unemployed the pandemic set is in some ways felt more insecure, as they got pushed down the lane with more attractive job candidates marching in front of them.

Under these circumstances some unemployed people were still unable to feel the loosening of the emotional grip. For others, they used this time to explore alternative values and emerge themselves in other activities besides job search forefronting other social identities than the professional one.

Either way, this window of time and the changed social and political conditions made one thing clear: everything can in fact be different. The emotional hooks and the emotional debt are historical, not inevitable.

References

Boland, T., & Griffin, R. (2015). The death of unemployment and the birth of job-seeking in welfare policy: Governing a liminal experience. *Irish Journal of Sociology, 23*(2), 29–48. https://doi.org/10.7227/IJS.23.2.3

Chen, V. T. (2015). *Cut loose: Jobless and hopeless in an unfair economy* (1st ed.. [Online].). University of California Press.

Demazière, D. (2020). Job search success among the formerly-unemployed: Paradoxically, a matter of self-discipline. *Critical Policy Studies*, 1–17. https://doi.org/10.1080/19460171.2020.1746372

Demazière, D., & Zune, M. (2023). When job search is deemed insufficient: Experiences of unemployed people disbarred following compliancy monitoring. *Social Policy and Society*, 22(3), 393–407.

Karasek, R. A., Jr. (1979). Job demands, job decision latitude, and mental strain: Implications for job redesign. *Administrative Science Quarterly*, 24, 285–308.

Pugh, A. J. (2015). *The tumbleweed society: Working and caring in an age of insecurity*. Oxford University Press.

Pultz, S. (2017). *It's not you, it's me, governing the unemployed self in the Danish welfare state*. Københavns Universitet.

Rao, A. H. (2020). *Crunch time: How married couples confront unemployment*. University of California Press.

Sharone, O. (2013a). *Flawed system/flawed self: Job searching and unemployment experiences*. University of Chicago Press.

Siegrist, J. (2016). Effort-reward imbalance model. In *Stress: Concepts, cognition, emotion, and behavior* (pp. 81–86). Academic Press.

9

Synthetizing the Contributions

Reiterating the main purpose of the book, I foreground the dynamics between governmental technologies as embedded in various institutional settings and employment policies, the ways they are administered at the street level by the frontline staff and how they are used by unemployed people as they govern themselves in their everyday life. Policies are not only political documents or formal policy (written policies) but are practiced and performed and come to life as they emerge in the social practices of the welfare state (Lipsky, 2010).

I have foregrounded the individual as embedded in a specific cultural, historical, and societal setting by focusing on the dynamic between technologies of power and those of the self. This choice is not applied to discard the important aspects of various individual psychological trajectories that also largely shape how people experience unemployment. A past record of trauma, attachment style, psychiatric vulnerabilities—all of these matters greatly, however, they are just not the key focus here.

While I rely on subjective perspectives to deduce how unemployed people experience the governmental technologies applied in Danish PES as well as the networking technologies applied in American career centers, I do not aim to make any causal or strong correlational claim about how the technologies of power are connected to those of the self. Rather,

© The Author(s), under exclusive license to Springer Nature Switzerland AG 2024
S. Pultz, *Emotionally Indebted*, https://doi.org/10.1007/978-3-031-57156-5_9

I explore the subjective experiences applying these concepts to enhance our understanding of what happens to people when they become unemployed in Danish welfare state today. That encompasses mapping the subjectification processes, the governmental technologies, and their patterns as well as I have explored how unemployed people experience and handle these—and even transform them—in some cases. I have done so by prioritizing giving attention to those who are not governed quite so much or at that cost.

It is my impression, that it is relatively easy to interpret reactions and emotions within an individual psychological framework in an individualist culture. Hence, I see great value in attuning our perspective so that we become increasingly aware and better equipped at grasping the dynamics that are outside of our immediate reach, but which also have a tremendous impact on us and our well-being, especially when venturing off the normative grid.

I place that focus so that we can better understand how the governmental action field is continuously orchestrated around unemployed people made up of policies, societal values, and discourses to mention a few. Both societal values and employment policies exist outside of the individual (however, not independently of individuals) but they do not work in a monolithic fashion. Their meaning is created at the street-level and through the concrete ways that people deal with them and conduct themselves in today's labor markets in their everyday lives.

Inherent in the activity paradigm shaped by conditionality, a citizen is not deemed deserving or worthy of financial support unless they continuously prove their worth by conducting themselves as active jobseekers who not only seek jobs but also display wanting to look for a job. This shift marks a move away from pure discipline and control of behavior toward a system that is more geared toward targeting psychological and affective constructs (such as motivation, empowerment, and cultivation of passion). The question that arises is then; how do unemployed people relate to and conduct themselves in a time characterized by this psychologizing shift in an affective economy?

Psychologization and the Emotional Debt

Findings from this book include identifying some of the historically and culturally contingent issues associated with currently being unemployed in the Danish welfare state and labor market. It lays visible the various emotional pinches unemployed people are put in and how they manage these. I have termed this "emotional debt" to clarify that the positioning comes from a situation of being unemployed and receiving money from the state, but also not accepting the money as a pure right. Receiving money and being in a position of unemployment in many ways challenge people's fundamental experience of being a worthy member of society with the right to belong to and expect support from the renowned universalistic and generous Danish welfare state. You are entitled to receive money from the state if you do not have a job, but the math is not that simple. By receiving money, you also invite in other demands, not least emotional ones.

Applying a social psychological perspective allows me to address many aspects of the pinch unemployed people find themselves in. This includes understanding the shadow effects of employment policies on the one hand and exploring strong cultural narratives of individualization and self-responsibility on the other evident in the Danish culture and even more so in the United States (Lamont, 2000, p. 52; Wiertz, in press).

Across empirical foci such as self-blame, shame, and doubt, it is noteworthy that unemployed people largely describe that challenges and vulnerabilities come from within. That does not necessarily mean that they only remain self-critical, they also criticize the system in various ways. However, from the narratives and experiences of the unemployed people themselves it is clear, that self-doubt, blame and shame, constitute the main challenge for unemployed people. Engaging continuously in self-critical practices deteriorates life qualify and challenge job search capacity. Krug et al. (2019) show that people who self-report high levels of internalized unemployment stigma engage in more job search activities, but this increased activity does not result in better job outcomes compared to people who report a lower level of internalized stigma. The self-critical reflections do not only wear out people, they also do not improve job search.

Especially feeling ashamed and self-blaming challenge the unemployed people's abilities to cultivate and display the affective currencies of assertiveness, self-confidence, and passion that are required in today's labor markets. I find this point is best illustrated by my current favorite meme; an interviewer asks a young woman at a job interview, "Why do you want this job?" and the young woman replies, "I have always been passionate about being able to afford food". It seems there is no lower limit in terms of what can be translated into an affective vocabulary and that plays a significant role in subjectifying job seekers and especially unemployed job seekers in particular ways through demanding and exhausting emotional labor.

The unemployed people are governed through constricting subjectification processes, and this leaves them in a state of ambivalence and tension. I explore the challenges of balancing between being self-responsible, motivated, empowered, and proactive on the one hand and, on the other, being subjectified as self-blaming, fearful, and ashamed.

These tensions are closely linked to societal tendencies understood as the organization of the welfare state and the active employment policy. At the same time, neoliberal logic gains acceptance and encourages and predisposes self-responsibility in various ways. The job seeker is constructed as a modifiable subject whose self-management is affected by changed rules and demands. The demands placed on the active job seeker draw on neoliberal as well as social investment policies and logics to construct self-managing subjects that can govern themselves not only thinking about the immediate future but also by investing in human capital to optimize labor market chances in the longer run. In different ways policies are geared to orient people toward the future—both in terms of balancing between worry and hope, in terms of managing the risk of becoming long-term unemployed (such as predicted by the profiling tool) and by engaging in continuous labor crafting oneself in alignment with what is needed on today's labor market.

Overall, I find that the unemployment issue is *psychologized* and I follow the various dynamics that encourage people to understand unemployment as being a problem of personal matter thus implying a particular self-work to be the solution to the problem at hand. This psychologization is enabled by governmental technologies that rely on psychological strategies using and weaponizing the language, expertise and practices developed within psychology and adjacent disciplines—what Rose terms the psy-sciences (Rose, 1999). These psychological vocabularies cover working on motivation and empowerment, however psychological narratives are also used to install self-responsibility and the darker sides of affective subjectification governing unemployed people through self-blame and shame.

Psychologization and psychological technologies do not replace technologies developed within a control and discipline paradigm. However, the governmental landscape changes character with these psychological technologies dispersing across the welfare state and in a labor market which is also structured as an affective economy calling for dedication, passion, commitment, and a sense of purpose—sometimes even such a strong sense of purpose that the work in itself becomes pay (enough).

Managing (Self)Blame

This book shows how the emphasis of freedom of choice and self-responsibility often manifests in the promotion of self-blame, meaning that unemployed people are encouraged to look for shortcomings in themselves to understand why they have become unemployed and what they can do about it. This finding thus supports the work of others (Newman, 1988; Sharone, 2013a). The phenomenon of self-blame is neither new in psychology nor is it a neoliberal invention; in fact, it has long historical roots in research literature. Nonetheless, the recent decades' focus on self-responsibility stresses the urgency and timeliness of this specific challenge, as also documented by Sharone (2013b). The aptitude of the concept is also supported by the previously mentioned quote from Michael, who observes, "from everywhere you are told it is your own fault".

The construction of the active job seeker is especially attached to a problematization of unemployment as a matter of motivation, thus making a private site an object of intervention. Relying on motivation and other concepts from *psy*-sciences in the governing practices demonstrates the importance of critically reflecting on the use of psychological research in the welfare state. Both the empowerment and motivation technologies are linked with the documented recoding of the unemployment issue in dialogue with management literature emphasizing understanding oneself through categories of personal branding and through a general promotion of selling oneself as Me, Inc. While I do not challenge the importance of motivation in a job search context, I investigate the effects of applying motivational technologies and of how they come to shape unemployment experiences.

The self-responsibility is also re-configured in relation to the technology of networking which is increasingly propagated as a key point of entry to new employment by the unemployment fund. Consequently, it becomes one's own responsibility to modulate oneself in alignment with traits and virtues valorized in contemporary affective economies resulting in, for instance, a mainstreaming of extroverts and a problematization of introverts. New technologies of the self are required, as job searches call for cultivating and displaying other talents than the ability to write a good application or documenting mere merits. Interestingly, through networking the governing site is expanded. The governing of not only the individual but also that person's network and the potential beneficial effects on job search constitutes another side of the psychologization of the unemployment issue as it brings personality to the fore.

The empowerment technologies can be viewed as a meaningful response to earlier criticisms of welfare institutions for disempowering and subjectifying people as clients rather than treating them as knowledgeable and competent people (Villadsen, 2011). However, well-intentioned motives, approaching the field from a social psychological perspective equipped with governmentality studies, obliges one to investigate many of the effects of empowerment policies in its complexity. Empowerment technologies do not only result in unemployed people feeling empowered or more capable of dealing with their situation. It also results in a feeling of being objectified and pushed in some directions, rather than others. Rather than feeling empowered, some unemployed people feel estranged and exhausted.

Empowerment technologies are linked to the shift in policies that has been described from prohibition associated with discipline and control to instructions or normative ideals (Hjortkjær, 2022). The goal of policies is no longer to prevent or prohibit certain behaviors. Rather, they are aimed at shaping people's desire and will to do something, to be active. In the existing unemployment system, people are governed through disciplinary technologies evident in unemployed people's fear of getting caught doing something they are not allowed to do. At the same time, they are governed through empowerment technologies that encourage people to be ever more active and proactive, with no upper limit to possibilities. Whereas the disciplinary technologies can result in people being afraid of sanctions, the latter can result in people feeling inadequate and install an ever-present sense of bad conscience that prevent them from enjoying 'time off' and maintaining a sense of work/life balance while being an unemployed jobseeker. While the unemployed people are still afraid that they might behave in ways that are not allowed, they are even more afraid that they are not doing enough (Hjortkjær, 2022) and hence the ability to engage in leisure time or any time really, is strained. I wonder how many people who are diagnosed and sick with stress or on the verge of becoming so, dream of having hours with nothing to do, however it seems close to impossible for unemployed people to relax and recharge.

Profiling and Individualized Risk Management

Taking responsibility for oneself does not only cover the here-and-now, but also often involves thoughts about the past, thinking about prior choices that may have affected one's current situation. Increasingly, the self-responsibility also involves the ability to look ahead and be able to identify and manage potential risks.

Profiling systems represent governmental technologies that do exactly that; based on one current and prior life the aim is to predict future outcomes.

While profiling system can best be linked with the so-called dispositive of security it is important to note that while this type of technology gains preeminence in contemporary societies, it does not replace other forms of power such as the law and discipline. The same penal law, the same punishment, the same framework of surveillance and correction exist, but now the dispositive of security has been added. Key to the dispositive of security is a logic of probability and estimated costs embedded in the technologies (Raffnsoe et al., 2014, 2016). The exercise of this form of power establishes a readiness to consider that which can happen and "work on the future" (Foucault et al., 2007, p. 23), and instigates a sense of insecurity in the population, a sense that misfortune and disaster, such as cancer, flu pandemics or terrorist attacks, are ever-present possibilities and only the skill of expert can avert them.

As Foucault noted, an important element in the new professional discourse is risk, and risk is indeed a very pertinent concept for unemployed people regarding both technologies of power and those of the self. Professionals claim that through their knowledge of the past, for example, through epidemiology they can not only identify future hazards, such as lung cancer and other diseases linked to tobacco smoking but can also identify the actions that individuals need to take to mitigate these risks, for example, by not smoking (Burchell et al., 2003). Thus, for Foucault, the central claim of modern professions is that they provide security through the systematic application of statistical technique and their understanding of probability (Foucault et al., 2007). This technology of prediction and prevention is central to the modern states and shares important elements with the technology of risk (O'Malley, 2008), for example, both rely on statistics and probabilistic technique (Burchell et al., 2003) and the ways in which information about a large number of events is collected and ordered to enable experts to make predictions about the future.

In such large datasets, 'irrelevant' information is filtered out in the search for risk factors which will enable prediction. Surveillance of people and their behavior, and registering events as data, is the foundation for this practice. Foucault noted that ever since the nineteenth century, the economic logic has gained a hegemonic position as the political rationality embedded in the governing of societies including areas of welfare. In considering risk, it is important not only to examine the specific technology of risk, for example, the use of statistical methods to develop tools or screening instruments to identify those at risk of a harmful outcome but

9 Synthetizing the Contributions

also to examine how these tools are used (Heyman, 2010; Heyman et al., 2006). In particular, how they shape the experience and anticipation of misfortune and unemployment.

Screening promises to reduce risk by actively managing and preventing the risk of people remaining unemployed. The categorization in risk groups based on risk factors reduces and simplifies the real-life complexity of unemployment and makes it 'manageable'. This practice has some shortcomings. One is that more 'fluffy' factors that are more difficult to measure in a register and through a short survey are not included in the picture. The practice can be viewed as a reproduction and normalization of today's massive gathering of data as part of a security regime with an aim of predicting and controlling citizens' behavior (Dean, 2013; Foucault et al., 2007).

A pivotal notion of productive power is that surveillance is not just about who the state is watching but also about multiple circuits of collective surveillance: it is not just about the act of seeing or noticing or screening but it is also about acts of collecting and tabulating data (Greco & Stenner, 2013). According to political scientist and affect scholar Puar today's surveillance places a special demand on people. Puar states: "The 'democratization' of surveillance works through networks of control and demands we pay even greater attention to the uneven distribution of disciplining, punishment, and pleasure" (2014, p. 1). Data are gathered on all large numbers of people; however, the distribution of discipline, punishment, and pleasure is uneven, and interventions are focused on a small group, namely the 'high-risk' persons. Some unemployed people are categorized as in need of help; however, little is known about the effects of the interventions employed to mitigate the risk. It is not clear whether unemployed in fact become better job seekers by coming to more meetings and participating in more courses or if the opposite holds true: by being identified as 'at risk' they come to relate to themselves through such lens.

Turning the Arrow Outward

Having established some of the key technologies enacted in the unemployment system, I now turn to discuss the implications of these on self-management as well as how some young people, in a way, transcend these conditions. Affective governing does not subjectify people homogenously, as these processes are not determining but rather dispositioning (Foucault, 1982). Accounts of self-blame are present in almost all interviews as well as reflected in the survey and the strong association with self-reported lower psychological well-being. However, self-blame is not a single story (Adichie, 2009) and, and indeed system-blame is also evident in the data.

Current practices result in a growing pressure on personal psychological understandings of unemployment and turning the arrow inward, meaning that self-management among unemployed people often entails working on one's personality and social skills more than improving one's professional or educational competences. Critique is not lacking from the data, though. Seen from the vantage point of the unemployed people, many required activities and rules are experienced as meaningless and out of sync with the contemporary labor market. Applying for jobs through formal hiring systems is often experienced as a 'black hole' with either no feedback or with standardized rejections and overall, it overlooks the potential of people creating their own jobs. Participation in meetings and courses are often described as 'a waste of time', as stultifying and as estranging, which affects young unemployed people negatively, impairing their self-esteem and eroding their imagination and hope.

The fact that Danish unemployed people also point the arrow outward to society in general, the welfare state and PES in particular does not only nuance the dominating self-blame narrative. Being a citizen in the Danish 'competition state' implies a sense of right and entitlement to be economically supported and most participants voiced their gratitude for this security system. Interestingly, none of the (albeit limited numbers of) American job seekers I interviewed criticized the system and most of them were merely positively surprised to experience any sort of social security and support.

Many of the interview participants straightforwardly admitted fabricating lists of job applications to meet the requirements of such activity and many of them describe how they learnt to decode what the job consultants want to hear so that they can repeat it and thus be left alone. Here, social skills and being able to 'laugh at the right times', demonstrates that a considerable amount of immaterial of emotional labor is part of managing the system for unemployed people. Acting a particular role is well-known in other areas of the welfare state, for instance when patients simulate being a good client, or simulate a certain psychiatric diagnosis to gain access to the financial and treatment privileges associated with that diagnosis (Brinkmann et al., 2015).

In fact, the system critique plays a fundamental role when it comes to restoring a sense of worthiness and also in terms of justifying unemployment in general, and perhaps in particular when it comes to the young, creative people who are unemployed by choice. Criticizing the system, in fact, plays a key role in the justification of dealing strategically with the unemployment system. This allows for an identification of a balancing dynamics in which receiving money from the state could be compensated for by contributing with, for instance, art and culture. This balancing is made possible by a postponing strategy meaning that they justify taking from the state now by expecting to be able to able to 'pay back' in a different currency later. In that sense they main idea for the social investment paradigm is evident. Investing in human capital and creative activities today is expected to result in returns in the future. From the vantage point of the people who are unemployed by choice it is not entirely clear whether this return is mainly conceptualized in economic value or whether it also denotes social value (such as producing art and other cultural products).

Managing Shame

The book contributes to the emergent field of the joint venture between governmentality studies and affectivity (Ahmed, 2014a; Probyn, 2004; Sedgwick & Frank, 1995; Tomkins, 2008). Cromby (2015) states that it is notoriously difficult to agree upon definitions of feelings, emotions and affects since an important component is the embodying nature of these complex phenomena and therefore, they are, to some extent, ineffable, that is not wholly representable in words (see also Smail, 2005). Cromby (2012) draws attention to the methodological difficulties in analyzing ineffable phenomena such as affects in qualitative analysis, mainly drawing on explicit linguistic resources. Meaning does not exclusively reside in language but also in atmospheres or moods that affect the production of meaning as well as subjectively experienced feelings. Despite methodological difficulties and a lack of theoretical clarity in the field of feelings, emotions and affects, I argue that the challenges should not result in a reluctance to take these complex phenomena into account. The capacity to affect and be affected in a particular delimited (cultural, historical, political, biographical) context plays a key role in the subjectification of young unemployed people, which ought not to be overlooked. One of the characteristics of subjectification outlined is that these processes do not only work through discursive and self-reflexive repertoires but also by 'sneaking in' and 'sneaking up on' people in a vague sense of feeling that something is going on but it being difficult to pinpoint exactly what and how. The benefit of using a concept such as atmosphere is that it takes hold of a level of analysis that tends to be overlooked in governmentality studies. By using this concept, one can avoid the individualist pitfall characterizing much academic work on emotions and feelings, but also on unemployment. Interestingly, this study contributes with empirical support to the notion that affects and atmospheres are crucial sites of governing. Affects and atmospheres are intentionally manipulated as evident in the field observations, but they are also uncontrollable and linked to the affective economy.

With inspiration from Tomkins and Ahmed, I have analyzed the empirical material through literature on the duality of shame and passion and thus I have followed the productive as well as the detrimental potentialities of shaming. I found that experiences of shame as well as passion were prevalent and significant in both the field observations as well as in the accounts of unemployed people, thus complementing other recent findings in social work (Gibson, 2016; Featherstone et al., 2014). So far, self-blame has been identified as a prevalent self-conscious feeling among unemployed people (Sharone, 2013a; Pultz & Hviid, 2018) but the book offers empirical support for the importance of investigating the role of other self-conscious feelings in addition to self-blame. I add to this by including shame and passion as relevant capacities and sites of governing in the micro-foundations of social interactions. Thus, the book opens up new venues for investigating ways of constraining or encouraging certain actions, as also documented by Voronov and Vince (2012). By more precisely documenting how unemployed people are encouraged to work on and mold their abilities to feel and convincingly display shame and passion in their job search, the study also contributes empirical support for an understanding of shame, not as something dissociated from passion, such as Creed et al. (2014) employ, but as affective capacities that should be explored in their duality.

Self-reflection and self-understanding constitute the foundation for self-management, but the unemployed people are also governed in more diffuse ways through certain attunements and atmospheres and this finding constitutes the empirical motivation to engage theoretically and methodologically with an understanding of how people are affectively situated via their ability to affect and be affected. Related to this notion, self-responsibility has to be managed in a particular affective economy in which receiving money from the state, especially as an unemployed person (vs. receiving money from the state as a student), comes with an 'affective price'. The affective economy is driven by the potent cocktail of interest and shame (Tomkins, 2008). Even though the two would, intuitively, seem disconnected, the literature on shame guides us to understand the double-sided nature of shame as both productive and detrimental, as restrictive and expansive. As Tomkins pointed out, interest and shame counterintuitively reinforce each other, as interest is the prerequisite of shame. Put in other words; we are only ashamed of something that is of importance to us. If we did not care, we would not feel shame. Related to the affective economy, for unemployed people, networking poses a different challenge in comparison with employed people. In Ahmed's term, being unemployed is associated with a certain 'stickiness', meaning a negative representation or stigma (Goffman, 1968) that affects people on an affective and embodied level. This stickiness is reflected in most unemployed people's reluctance or embarrassment in revealing their situation in social encounters, not to mention, for instance, concealing one's formal status as unemployed on a résumé to improve chances in the hiring system.

Shame is by some managed by refusing to identify with the unwanted label and by directing the 'stickiness' to other objects. Some of the unemployed people create a counter-figure that they use to distance themselves from, namely, the 'real unemployed person'. This maneuver allows them to align themselves with the neoliberal idea of shaming unemployed people without themselves being included in the stigmatizing dynamic. In some sense, the present study supports the finding of Mascini et al. (2013) who report that those who suffer under neoliberalism often accept its ideology rather than challenge it.

A good deal of contemporary critical literature joins in an increasingly widespread way of thematizing modern power, that is, by means of the concept of governmentality, but often articles with a governmentality perspective are criticized for being too programmatic and for regarding technologies as too monolithic (Stenson, 2008; Clarke, 2005). By investigating power in situ, that is analyzing governance as it operates through strategies and techniques at the micro-level, it is possible to see subtle acts of what may be termed 'resistance' or unexpected effects, thereby challenging governance studies that primarily view governance as a top-down analysis with little room for agency (Clarke, 2005). I also call this "not governed quite so much or at that cost" quoting Foucault (in Foucault & Lotringer, 2007, p. 45) on the subject.

Resistance and agency are perceived as immanent in power and the activities and actions on a micro-level are part of the construction of governmental practices, and thus it remains imperative to consider the complexity and heterogeneity of conduct (Foucault, 1982). Relying on self-reflective capacities, shame works by making parts of oneself visible and manageable.

This point is crucial in understanding how the proliferation of enterprise ideas and empowerment vocabularies are interlinked with shame as well as the emergent figure, the freelancer. Unemployment is, in a Danish context, recoded in affective self-help and enterprise vocabularies in accordance with what may be termed 'neoliberal virtues' of flexibility and precariousness. Technologies are put in place that shape people's desire to care, to be active, responsible and future-oriented.

The freelancer is a relatively new configuration construction but he or she plays against the disciplinary backdrops of regulations as being on the verge or outside the norms and rules thus risking economic sanctions. In addition, the figure of the freelancer offers entrepreneurial unemployed people an identity more in alignment with the virtues and competencies valorized in the precarious labor market marked by austerity (Fryer & Stambe, 2014; Kalleberg, 2011). Constructing oneself in the image of the freelancer implies a particular affective economy—it demands the ability to perform with intensity and passion and a willingness to stay active, even if this means working voluntarily, and thus outside what is allowed in the unemployment system. However, the practice comes at a price. Receiving the economic income of unemployment benefits while at the same time acting as freelancers invites an ever-present fear of being caught and having to repay the benefits. Work for freelancers is not delimited to paid work or to formal employment but is viewed as practices and assignments that are needed, and thus they challenge the traditional understanding whereby work is defined in economic terms, an issue also taken up by feminists (Hardt & Negri, 2001) and which has received renewed attention in the literature on postwork and less work movements (Weeks, 2007; Srnicek & Williams, 2016). The freelancers are aware that they are more likely to get a job if they get a 'foot inside the door' and keeping active is pivotal.

Expanding on these notions, I have further explored an alternative and subversive practice among young striving artists officially registered as being unemployed and in receipt of benefits. The practice is not restricted to artists but is present across a range of professions. In this dispersion, the romantic figure of the artist who does not need to be paid for his or her work, because the activity in itself is reward enough is also translated into other professional fields. Contextualizing this figure in contemporary labor markets makes it easy to see how this figure fits like hand in glove. The practice challenges traditional borders between work and pay. Passion is not only cultivated but also displayed as visible to others. Oakley and O'Brien (2016, p. 18) point to the necessity of undertaking unpaid work as essential to the cultural and creative industries and point toward the "pleasure" or "psychic income" that cultural workers are said to find in their work. Butler (2006) addresses the psychic life of subjection in relation to subjectification processes and Mackenzie and McKinlay (2021) go on to explore the psychic life of cultural work employing the concept "hope labour". They define hope labor as "unpaid or under-compensated labor undertaken in the present, usually for exposure or experience, with the hope that future work opportunities may follow" MacKenzie and McKinlay (2021, p. 1882). Inherent is an idea about the exchange between labor and pay as more complicated than an exchange here and now as well as it involves a transaction between monetary and affective currencies. Surely this equation encompassing a mix of monetary and affective currencies is not new, but the affective vocabulary helps us disentangle and understand the dynamics and transactions better.

Cultivating new opportunities in the future involves a willingness to accept poorer working conditions: "even when cultural workers appear to have employment status, project work implies a need to be hired for the next project, involving an acquiescence to long hours and an unwillingness to contest unfair working practices" (Mackenzie & McKinlay, 2021, p. 1844). Similarly, Butler and Stoyanova Russell (2018) identify a particular willingness as they explore the emotional labor involved in negotiating pay among stand-up comedians. They argue that freelancers engage in a "labour of love" which make them willing—and willing to display their willingness—to accept poor working conditions such as low salary. Hence there is some evidence that cultural workers invest in their human capital and that this involves a particular "psychic", "affective" or "emotional" dimension. Broadly, this refers to reward that cannot be measured in money or goods but it entails prestige or pleasure.

In general, for some people networking constitutes a much-needed alternative to the formal hiring systems that are often characterized by standardized rejections, lack of in-person contact, and in general, referred to as "the black hole" familiar in the qualitative literature on unemployment (Boland & Griffin, 2015; Sharone, 2013b; Wanberg et al., 2012). Networking, for some, entails benefits such as acknowledgment, social contact, a sense of productivity and comparably, 'being in the driving seat' seen in relation to passively reacting to job openings online.

For others, however, the pressure to take part in networking is experienced as a personal invasion as, to some extent, it erodes the boundaries between the private and professional self, leaving no room off-limits to job search and thus no place for the unemployed subject to "just be herself" as American interview participant Sarah expressed it.

The affective currencies are key in successful networking and cultivating and displaying a conglomerate of positive feelings is conceived of as exchangeable with paid work or as conditional in job searching. The interplay between the monetary and affective economies entails hiding the emotional toll of unemployment and, at the same time, displaying a conglomerate of positive affects/feelings such as passion, enthusiasm, joy, and motivation.

To many, networking raises issues of inauthenticity as potentially it entails an instrumentalization of relationships. The Danish participants raise the issue of nepotism, but interestingly, none of the American interview participants questioned this development as networking is far more integrated and naturalized in the American context.

Freelancers: Working *within* and *against* the System and Values

A substantial group of my interview participants with educational backgrounds in social sciences, humanities, and natural sciences conduct themselves as freelancers. The system increasingly enacts and draws on enterprise and management vocabularies and understandings, and these are actively taken up by some unemployed citizens who use these semiotic resources to govern themselves as entrepreneurs or freelancers using the unemployment benefit system in untraditional ways. Among them, they view employment in a new way less tied to work as a social institution defined by a contractual relationship and salary. Rather than focusing on paid labor, they focus on 'meaningful activity'. Meaningful activity is a subjective concept and among unemployed people, it covers a different set of parameters such as flexibility, experience of control, and experience of creative freedom. This representation of activity is characterized by projects, 'being your own boss' working for yourself rather than for capitalist company. However, the protestant work ethic pervading capitalist culture is also part of the moral economy here. Through activity, one displays being of value to others, as well as the activity demonstrates a passionate relationship to a professional field demonstrating that the activity is enough reward. However, this practice does come at a price, elaborated below. The freelancers embrace the virtues valorized in the precarious labor market such as freedom, flexibility, and self-control and they desire temporary and intermittent employments and can thus be viewed as conducting themselves in complete compliance with the neoliberal virtues that are so very highly valorized in neoliberal precarious labor markets (Hartmann & Honneth, 2006). Dis-identifying with their formal status, they actively enable hiding unemployment and this increasing invisibility through their practice as well as the overall recoding, makes political mobilization difficult. Lazzarato (2009) notes, that this austerity ensures a large pool of workers who apply for and desire even the most insecure, and sometimes even unpaid, positions.

If an unemployed person experience being invested and engaged in meaningful activities, this serves as a protective factor against the deterioration of mental health that is otherwise so widely reported in the unemployment literature. In that sense Jahoda's description of latent functions associated with paid labor (time structure, common goals, activity, social contact, and social status) cannot only be achieved through paid labor (see also Pultz et al., 2020; Wiertz & Chaeyoon, in press).

In various ways, not perceiving oneself as an unemployed was, as emerged in the in-depth interviews, associated with identifying the 'real' unemployed (such as long-term unemployed people, social assistance recipients or middle-aged people who have been dismissed from their jobs). This move, in a sense, allows abiding to social norms while still portraying unemployment as negative and as a sticky matter. The stickiness is, however, no longer tied to them individually. This coping strategy identified among the freelancers is not regarded here as being unproblematic. However, in unemployment research there is also an imperative to focus on identifying factors that help people cope with the challenge of unemployment, as this type of work is essential to develop preventive interventions (Kessler et al., 1988).

What is the reach of these alternative ways of governing oneself as an unemployed? Subcultures and artistic milieus have long existed, but the general restructuring of contemporary society toward becoming increasingly precarious enable this way of positioning tremendously for many groups of professionals on the labor market (Kalleberg, 2011). While unemployment during the last centuries have been thought of in a relatively binary fashion opposing being employed and unemployed, research now shows that there is a gradual erosion of such binary. Building on Chen (2015), Wiertz & Chaeyoon (in press) go so far as to denote a continuum that ranges from being unemployed and not looking for a job toward full and stable employment. I understand this practice, not as an indication of immorality among young people, but rather conceptualize their behavior as conditioned and enabled by modern technologies and contemporary ideologies stressing the self-responsibility as well as self-sufficiency orchestrating unemployment as a painful and sticky affair. The practice of the freelancers in this study underlines the importance of maintaining heterogeneity in the study of unemployed people, as they are not a homogenous group (Wanberg & Marchese, 1994). The freelancers, in a certain respect, make visible the struggles around subjectivity and it demonstrates that subjectification processes are, in no way, monolithic thus contributing to a methodological contribution that highlights the benefits of maintaining empirical sensitivity by investigating the micro-political analysis level.

Norris (in press) explores the identity work among unemployed people who experiences what she terms "mismatches" between their self-perception and how they imagine or experience that other people view them. She identifies two strategies that unemployed people can use in trying to repair the unpleasant mismatch: sustaining and shifting. Sustaining is illustrated by holding on to and continuously performing one's professional identity even though one does not formally work within that field at the moment. This practice involves working for few or no money. Shifting involves forefronting another aspect of one's identity. She provides the reader of an example with unemployed people putting more identity into the role of being a parent. She also notes dominant heterosexual gendered patterns with women having easier access to that shift compared to men in an American heterosexual context. Her gendered findings support the findings of Rao (2020) who also find that job search tend to play a different role in heterosexual families with children. In men's case, job search is prioritized and deemed important, while in the case of women, unpaid reproductive work tend to take over a lot of the time taking care of household chores and caring responsibilities. While the strategy of the freelancer in some sense can be viewed as a shifting strategy, the gendered dimensions are rather unclear at this point. Some people capable of being more explorative while being unemployed and others unable to do, and this finding might be filtered through that gendered notion, however more work is needed to settle these unanswered questions.

The Caring State and the Contours of the New Shadow Sides

Recent studies have also touched upon the various technologies that foreground the relational frontline work associated with ideas such as caring state and enabling state (Morel & Pallier, 2011). In a Danish context, we see a euphemizing of unemployment in the categories applied in the system. Historically groups of unemployed people have been categorized based on their problems (Nielsen et al., 2020). Since 2013 these categories shifted from problem orientation toward resource-orientation introducing categories such as "prepared for education" or "prepared for activity". No existing group was deemed un-prepared. This change can be tracked to the key ideas in social investment paradigm by which the welfare state should set in early and prepare citizens rather than "repair" them when problems arise (Morel & Pallier, 2011; Jenson, 2011). Such discursive change is not considered neutral but in fact carries loads of meaning as it shapes how unemployed people are met at the frontline. While it seems 'morally good' to focus on resources rather than problems, there is a shadow side to such approaches. Nielsen (2019) describes this shift as politics of optimism and notes that such policies can also be seen as manipulative and degrading. For some people in society the resources to work are simply not there and not acknowledging that can be seen as "cruel optimism" (Berlant, 2011). In 2022 a new policy termed "believing in" is rolled out, particularly dealing with social assistance recipients based on studies that showed that social workers' ability to believe in an unemployed citizen and their abilities to find a job makes a difference in terms of job outcome in this vulnerable group (Amilon & Lindegaard Andersen, 2019). Governing unemployed people, and in particular the social assistance benefit recipients, using such believing technologies put more pressure on the frontline workers' ability to conduct relational work. Also, by meeting the citizens with care either instead of or alongside more control-oriented technologies, where does that leave the citizen's ability to resist? Does this type of welfare care dismantle the potential resistance or critique of the system? How easy is it to argue against somebody who truly cares and believes in you?

Yang (2015, in press) similarly describes how the party governs unemployment in China through massive strategies and technologies that aim at governing the heart and Yang similarly asks: does care in effect replace the focus on rights? (Yang, in press). Especially policies that appear to be overwhelmingly 'good' should in fact also be scrutinised to enhance our understanding of the shadow effect of these. This is the case, whether we focus on policies that enable psychologization, emotional debt, or the intricate ways that unemployed people are affectively governed both in terms of being governed more clearly through emotions as well as the ways they have to mobilize emotions and affective currencies in the quest for a job.

Insights from Covid-19

Suspending the activation policies during the covid-19 made it visible that everything can always be different and that policies within the employment field for decades have enjoyed or suffered some path dependence. Living up to the demands and rules is exhausting for many unemployed, perhaps not so much the single activities that need to be done, but more so the symbolic value that they carry. The instruments of PES push toward engaging in job search activities and valuation of the unemployed. On the other hand, for most of the unemployed people, the uncertainty about 'what is' and what will become implies a state of exploring other domains in life. The Covid-19 crisis has also been an event that to a degree has put the activation policies to the test; making it visible what aspects are usually associated with stress, pressure and surveillance and what aspects are missed such as support and sparring. In addition, the Covid-19 crisis has tweaked and turned the moral test of unemployed people, as unemployment has now been associated more with external and structural factors, thus opposing the individualizing and responsibilizing dynamics associated with the active turn dominating the last three or four decades (Hansen, 2019; Pultz, 2017). Hence, it has become slightly more acceptable to say that you are unemployed (Pultz & Hansen, 2021). However, new polarizing dynamics have also become visible between people unemployed before and during Covid-19, with the latter group viewed as more attractive job candidates and issues of worthiness embedded in that distinction, with corona-unemployed people also being viewed as more worthy and less to blame for their misfortune. At the systemic level we find that job search is an exclusive strategy making it impossible to engage in any other domains in life. Activities outside of work or hobbies are instrumentalized to develop new entrepreneurial endeavors. Existing studies have pointed to how the unemployed are thereby encouraged to conduct themselves as small enterprises and in that sense become their own brand or company, eroding the boundaries between private and work life (Pultz, 2018; Vallas & Cummins, 2015). This move involves increasingly requalifying leisure activities such as gardening and absorbing them in job search. Interestingly, we also identified unemployed people who qua unemployment were able to critically assess their work life and appreciate a slow pace and investing more in personal relationships just for the sake of it. Such critical reflections have also been identified before the pandemic in relation to unemployed people but perhaps the context of the pandemic has enabled or facilitated them.

Among our interviewees, the unemployed people who were exclusively able to invest in job search were also the ones who had the hardest time 'taking time off'. Spending time away from job searching and participating in other activities seemed to provide people with a sense of joy. This finding is in line with Pultz and Teasdale (2017), Demazière (2020), and Eschweiler and Pultz (2021). Having hobbies or engaging in meaningful often unpaid activities detached from the job search is identified as important for well-being and agency (Pultz & Teasdale, 2017; Eschweiler & Pultz, 2021). Demazière (2020) identified a successful job search strategy among former unemployed people as investing limited emotional resources in the job search to avoid a strong sense of defeat and rejection thus resulting in making better job candidates. Especially for PES, this might be worth considering, as strategies so far seem to go in one direction: cultivating more and more aspects of life and leaving little or no room free from job searching. Further, in a political context where the unemployed is predominantly portrayed as inactive and passive being in need of firm governing, insights building on the pandemic study points to the agency and reflexive competences of same persons. The study thus accentuates the need to listen to the voices of the unemployed, working with them, not in them in research as well as in policymaking.

The Practical Implications: Where to Go from Here?

Based on this work, I highlight the need to maintain heterogeneity in future research and thus challenge the dominating trend in unemployment research by offering another conceptualization as a foundation to talk about how we want to govern unemployed people. By sensitizing the gaze for practices that indicate that people are not governed one-to-one, but instead manage themselves and the system in strategic and creative ways, I was able to make visible the group of unemployed by choice and freelancers. Importantly, the exploration has been guided by a non-normative approach stressing the aim not of making value judgments, but rather exploring the muddy reality of the everyday life of unemployed people.

I have sought to explore and track how the practice is enabled in relation to a system and a society that conditions and disposes toward such innovative behavior, despite different intentions. The investigation of the freelancers and how they navigate in various welfare institutions in the Danish competition society should be further explored in future studies, especially through longitudinal research design, which could shed light on personal and societal effects of this practice, also in the long term.

This book maps current technologies but the pressing question of what kind of unemployment system we want remains to be unfolded. Lamont (2019) critically discusses the very limited sources that give rise to a sense of worthiness in capitalist societies with grave implications for people who are marginalized on the labor market, and unevenly so. Exploring the (in)dignity experiences among unemployment people is a lens apt to identify problematic practices within the public employment services as well as it informs about promising experiences within the employment system such as counselors that can support unemployed people's sense of respect and agency by listening to them and relating to them as subjects rather than objects. The analysis thus makes visible what is needed to enable dignified experiences and point to the necessity of developing good conditions for counselors who can spend time and resources on relational work rather than focusing too much on living up to demands of process and bureaucratic rules. Supporting unemployed people's sense of agency and treating them as subjects rather than objects provide a better foundation for dignified treatment. The role of social psychology is about identifying problems in society, but it is also about pointing forward in new and improved directions by developing better imaginaries for the employment system in the future.

References

Adichie, C. N. (2009). *The danger of a single story*.
Ahmed, S. (2014a). *The cultural politics of emotion*. Edinburgh University Press.
Amilon, A., & Lindegaard Andersen, H. (2019). Sagsbehandlerrelaterede forhold som påvirker lediges jobchancer: litteraturgennemgang. VIVE—Det Nationale Forsknings-og Analysecenter for Velfærd.
Berlant, L. (2011). *Cruel optimism*. Duke University Press. https://doi.org/10.1515/9780822394716

9 Synthetizing the Contributions

Boland, T., & Griffin, R. (2015). The death of unemployment and the birth of job-seeking in welfare policy: Governing a liminal experience. *Irish Journal of Sociology, 23*(2), 29–48. https://doi.org/10.7227/IJS.23.2.3

Brinkmann, S., Petersen, A., & Joachim Wrang. (2015). Diagnoser, perspektiver, kritik og diskussion (1. udgave). Klim.

Burchell, G., Miller, P., & Gordon, C. (2003). *The Foucault effect, studies in governmentality, with two lectures by and an interview with Michel Foucault* ([Reprint.]). University of Chicago Press.

Butler, J. (2006). *Gender Trouble Feminism and the Subversion of Identity*. Routledge.

Butler, N., & Stoyanova Russell, D. (2018). No funny business: Precarious work and emotional labour in stand-up comedy. *Human Relations, 71*(12), 1666–1686.

Chen, V. T. (2015). *Cut loose: Jobless and hopeless in an unfair economy* (1st ed.. [Online].). University of California Press.

Clarke, J. (2005). New labour's citizens: Activated, empowered, responsibilized, abandoned? *Critical Social Policy, 25*(4), 447–463.

Creed, W. E. D., Hudson, B. A., Okhuysen, G. A., & Smith-Crowe, K. (2014). Swimming in a sea of shame: Incorporating emotion into explanations of institutional reproduction and change. *Academy of Management Review, 39*(3), 275–301.

Cromby, J. (2012). Feeling the way: Qualitative clinical research and the affective turn. *Qualitative Research in Psychology, 9*(1), 88–98. https://doi.org/10.1080/14780887.2012.63083

Cromby, J. (2015). *Feeling bodies: Embodying psychology*. Palgrave Macmillan.

Dean, M. (2013). *The signature of power, sovereignty, governmentality and biopolitics*. SAGE.

Demazière, D. (2020). Job search success among the formerly-unemployed: Paradoxically, a matter of self-discipline. *Critical Policy Studies*, 1–17. https://doi.org/10.1080/19460171.2020.1746372

Eschweiler, J., & Pultz, S. (2021). Recognition struggles of young Danes under the work first paradigm: A study of restricted and generalised agency. *Human Arenas*. https://doi.org/10.1007/s42087-021-00200-7

Featherstone, B., Morris, K., & White, S. (2014). *Re-imagining child protection: Towards humane social work with families*. Policy Press.

Foucault, M. (1982). The subject and power. *Critical Inquiry, 8*(4), 777–795.

Foucault, M., & Lotringer, S. (2007). *The politics of truth*. Semiotexte.

Foucault, M., Senellart, M., Ewald, F., & Fontana, A. (2007). *Security, territory, population*. Palgrave Macmillan.

Fryer, D., & Stambe, R. (2014). Neoliberal austerity and unemployment. *Psychologist, 27*(4), 244–248.

Gibson, M. (2016). Constructing pride, shame, and humiliation as a mechanism of control: A case study of an English local authority child protection service. *Children and Youth Services Review, 70*, 120–128.

Goffman, E. (1968). *Stigma, notes on the management of spoiled identity (1963)*. Penguin.

Greco, M., & Stenner, P. (2013). Happiness and the art of life: Diagnosing the psychopolitics of wellbeing. *Health, Culture and Society, 5*(1). https://doi.org/10.5195/hcs.2013.147

Hansen, M. P. (2019). *The moral economy of activation: Ideas, politics and policies*. Policy Press.

Hardt, M., & Negri, A. (2001). *Empire* (Paperback ed., 4. printing). Harvard University Press.

Hartmann, M., & Honneth, A. (2006). Paradoxes of capitalism. *Constellations, 13*(1), 41–58. https://doi.org/10.1111/j.1351-0487.2006.00439.x

Heyman, B. (2010). Screening for health risks: A second editorial. *Health, Risk & Society, 12*(2), 81–84. https://doi.org/10.1080/13698571003632460View

Heyman, B., Hundt, G., Sandall, J., Spencer, K., Williams, C., Grellier, R., & Pitson, L. (2006). On being at higherrisk: A qualitative study of prenatal screening for chromosomal anomalies. *Social Science & Medicine (1982), 62*(10), 2360–2372. https://doi.org/10.1016/j.socscimed.2005.10.018

Hjortkjær, C. (2022). *Utilstrækkelig: hvorfor den nye moral gør de unge psykisk syge*. 1. udgave. Klim.

Jenson, J. (2011). Redesigning citizenship regimes after neoliberalism: Moving towards social investment. In *Towards a social investment welfare state?* Policy Press. https://doi.org/10.1332/9781847429247.003.0003

Kalleberg, A. L. (2011). *Good jobs, bad jobs: The rise of polarized and precarious employment systems in the United States, 1970s–2000s*. Russell Sage Foundation.

Kessler, R. C., Turner, J. B., & House, J. S. (1988). Effects of unemployment on health in a community survey: Main, modifying, and mediating effects. *Journal of Social Issues, 44*(4), 69–85. https://doi.org/10.1111/j.1540-4560.1988.tb02092.x

Krug, G., Drasch, K., & Jungbauer-Gans, M. (2019). The social stigma of unemployment: consequences of stigma consciousness on job search attitudes, behaviour and success. *Journal for Labour Market Research, 53*(1), 1–27.

Lamont, M. (2019). From 'having'to 'being': Self-worth and the current crisis of American society. *The British journal of sociology, 70*(3), 660–707.

Lamont, M. (2000). Meaning-making in cultural sociology: Broadening our agenda. *Contemporary sociology, 29*(4), 602–607.

Lazzarato, M. (2009). Neoliberalism in action inequality, insecurity and the reconstitution of the social. *Theory, Culture & Society, 26*(6), 109–133. https://doi.org/10.1177/0263276409350283

Lipsky, M. (2010). *Street-level bureaucracy: Dilemmas of the individual in public service*. Russell Sage Foundation.

Mackenzie, E., & McKinlay, A. (2021). Hope labour and the psychic life of cultural work. *Human Relations, 74*(11), 1841–1863.

Mascini, P., Achterberg, P., & Houtman, D. (2013). Neoliberalism and work-related risks: Individual or collective responsibilization? *Journal of Risk Research, 16*(10), 1209–1224.

Morel, N., & Palier, B. (Eds.). (2011). *Towards a social investment welfare state?: Ideas, policies and challenges*. Policy Press.

Newman, K. S. (1988). *Falling from grace, the experience of downward mobility in the American middle class*. The Free Press.

Nielsen, M. H. (2019). *Optimismens politik: skabelsen af uværdigt trængende borgere*. (1. udgave. 1. oplag.). Frydenlund Academic.

Nielsen, M. H., Danneris, S., & Andersen, N. (2020). The silent expansion of welfare to work policies: How policies are enhanced through the use of categorizations, evidence-based knowledge and self-governance. In A. Eleveld, T. Kampen, & J. Arts (red.), *Welfare to work in contemporary european welfare states: Legal, sociological and philosophical perspectives on justice and domination* (s. 163). Policy Press.

Norris, D. R. (in press). Unemployment counseling: An identity-based perspective. In O. Sharone, V. Chen, & S. Pultz (red.), *Handbook on unemployment and society*. Edward Elgar Publishing.

Oakley, K., & D. O'Brien. (2016). Learning to Labour Unequally: Understanding the Relationship Between Cultural Production, Cultural Consumption and Inequality. *Social Identities, 22*(5), 471–486. https://doi.org/10.1080/13504630.2015.1128800

O'Malley, P. (2008). Governmentality and risk. Social theories of risk and uncertainty: An introduction, 52–75.

Probyn, E. (2004). Everyday shame. *Cultural Studies, 18*(2–3), 328–349.

Puar, J., & West, L. (2014). Regimes of surveillance. *Cosmologics Magazine*, 4.

Pultz, S. (2017). *It's not you, it's me: Governing the unemployed self in the Danish welfare state*. Copenhagen University.

Pultz, S. (2018). Shame and passion: The affective governing of young unemployed people. *Theory & Psychology, 28*(3), 358–381. https://doi.org/10.1177/0959354318759608

Pultz, S., & Hansen, M. P. (2021). Arbejdsløs i en (corona)krisetid: et opgør med selvansvaret? *Tidsskrift for Arbejdsliv, 23*(3), 9–25. https://doi.org/10.7146/tfa.v23i3.129426

Pultz, S., & Hviid, P. (2018). Imagining a better future: Young unemployed people and the polyphonic choir. *Culture & Psychology, 24*(1), 3–25. https://doi.org/10.1177/1354067X16660853

Pultz, S., & Teasdale, T. W. (2017). Unemployment and subjective well-being: Comparing younger and older job seekers. *Scandinavian Journal of Work and Organizational Psychology, 2*(1).

Pultz, S., Teasdale, T. W., & Christensen, K. B. (2020). Contextualized attribution: How young unemployed people blame themselves and the system and the relationship between blame and subjective well-being. *Nordic Psychology, 72*(2), 146–167. https://doi.org/10.1080/19012276.2019.166785

Raffnsoe, S., Gudmand-Hoyer, M., & Thaning, M. S. (2014). Foucault's dispositive: The perspicacity of dispositive analytics in organizational research. *Organization*, 1350508414549885. https://doi.org/10.1177/1350508414549885

Raffnsøe, S., Gudmand-Høyer, M. T., & Thaning, M. (2016). *Michel Foucault: A research companion*. Palgrave Macmillan.

Rao, A. H. (2020). *Crunch time: How married couples confront unemployment*. University of California Press.

Rose, N. S. (1999). *Powers of freedom, reframing political thought*. Cambridge University Press.

Sedgwick, E. K., & Frank, A. (1995). Shame in the cybernetic fold: Reading Silvan Tomkins. *Critical Inquiry, 21*(2), 496–522.

Sharone, O. (2013a). *Flawed system/flawed self: Job searching and unemployment experiences*. University of Chicago Press.

Sharone, O. (2013b). Why do unemployed Americans blame themselves while Israelis blame the system? *Social Forces, 91*(4), 1429–1450. https://doi.org/10.1093/sf/sot050

Smail, T. (2005). *Once and for All: A Confession of the Cross*. Wipf and Stock Publishers.

Srnicek, N., & Williams, A. (2016). *Inventing the future: Postcapitalism and a world without work*. Revised and updated edition. Verso.

Stenson, K. (2008). Governing the local: Sovereignty, social governance and community safety. *Social Work & Society, 6*(1), 2–14.

9 Synthetizing the Contributions 211

Tomkins, S. S. (2008). *Affect imagery consciousness, the complete edition.* Springer Pub.

Vallas, S. P., & Cummins, E. R. (2015). Personal branding and identity norms in the popular business press: Enterprise culture in an age of precarity. *Organization Studies, 36*(3), 293–319. https://doi.org/10.1177/0170840614563741

Villadsen, K. (2011). Modern welfare and 'good old' philanthropy: A forgotten or a troubling trajectory? *Public Management Review, 13*(8), 1057–1075. https://doi.org/10.1080/14719037.2011.622675

Voronov, M., & Vince, R. (2012). Integrating emotions into the analysis of institutional work. *Academy of Management Review, 37*(1), 58–81.

Wanberg, C. R., & Marchese, M. C. (1994). Heterogeneity in the unemployment experience: A cluster analytic investigation. *Journal of Applied Social Psychology, 24*(6), 473–488. https://doi.org/10.1111/j.1559-1816.1994.tb00594.x

Wanberg, C., Basbug, G., Van Hooft, E. A. J., & Samtani, A. (2012). Navigating the black hole: Explicating layers of job search context and adaptational responses. *Personnel Psychology, 65*(4), 887–926. https://doi.org/10.1111/peps.12005

Weeks, K. (2007). Life within and against work: Affective labor, feminist critique, and post-Fordist politics. *Ephemera, 7*(1), 233–249.

Wiertz, D., & Chaeyoon, L. (in press). The impact of joblessness on civic engagement: Longitudinal evidence from the United States. In O. Sharone, V. Chen, & S. Pultz (Eds.), *Handbook of unemployment and society.* Palgrave Macmillan.

Yang, J. (2015). *Unknotting the Heart: Unemployment and Therapeutic Governance.*

Yang, J. (in press). Governing Frictional/Structural Unemployment in China: Psychologization of the Heart. In O. Sharone, V. Chen, & S. Pultz (Eds.), *Handbook of unemployment and society.* Edward Elgar Publishing.

Conclusion

Being unemployed in the Danish welfare state is a highly regulated space that involves far more challenges than merely finding a job. Unemployment experiences are shaped by preconceived ideas about the unemployed identity ad underlying value systems that distribute dignity and worth unequally in the population.

First of all the active labor market policies that run as a red thread across the manifold ways unemployed people are governed in the welfare state instigate that unemployed people are not active by themselves, but need particular behavioral and affective pushes to become active jobseekers. There is an inherent mistrust in the policies.

Increasingly the activation instruments rely on and weaponize psychological narratives. The unemployed person has been described as individualized and self-responsible for decades, however, this contribution emphasizes the new ways that the governmental technologies target affective and emotional capacities, rather than strictly disciplining behaviors (such as job search). The psychological narratives involve focusing on motivation, empowerment, and passion and they enhance the dynamic of making unemployment a private issue rather than a public problem.

Receiving money from the state comes with an affective price, and here, some of the key exchanges and dynamics through which the monetary currencies and the positioning as unemployed is accompanied by certain emotional demands resulting in a position of feeling emotionally indebted.

Unemployment invites in fundamental questions of worth, identity and value beyond the challenge of dealing with systemic demands and the quodidian challenge of job searching. The demands involve emotional labor convincing the counselor not only that you live up to the existing demands and thus deserve receiving money and avoid sanctions, but also you want to conduct yourself as an active jobseeker *wanting* to and *willing* to do the necessary self-work. Surely, people who become unemployed are affected as whole human beings; however, employing and weaponizing psychological narratives in governmental practices also encompass shadow sides. When the state cares for you, how can you really be against it and resist it?

The demands from the personalized labor market also increasingly demand that employees show affective currencies such as passion and dedication. Cultivating these affective currencies and displaying them is identified as a key asset in the competitive job market. However, the managing the affective currencies is a demanding task for unemployed people facing nebulous affordances to feel ashamed for being unemployed well as to blame for getting in that mess in the first place.

While the diversification of employments spreads in labor market, the boundaries between unemployed and employed become increasingly eroded, and this constitutes a new landscape for especially professionals to position themselves in. While, dis-identifying with the social identity of unemployed as a strategy for getting rid of the sticky shame works well on an individual level, it is less clear to see from where the struggle of subjectivity and dignity are fought at a political level. If nobody is willing to be open about their situation as unemployed and fight the battle for a more dignified position in society, how will it change? The experiences during the pandemic did show that the dynamics are not set in stone, but rather negotiated in an endless complexity and hence opened a window toward alternatives.

While many people do not agree with the simplistic underlying value system that paid labor is the primary or sole source of dignity in society, it is overwhelming to explore the embodied effects of this system leaving unemployed people to face a much more complex challenge that simply not having and looking for a job.

The first step to change the order of things is to deeply understand how unemployed people are put in a position of debt and which instruments and understandings enable such positioning. For unemployed people it might also be worth something noting that this type of debt can actually not be repaid, and the books will not be balanced either way. Taking that as a starting point might be useful in figuring out the best way to deal with unemployment both individually and as a society.

Index

A

Activation policies, ix, 8, 21, 64, 68, 83, 104, 110, 134, 135, 169, 180, 203, 204
Active labor market policies (ALMPs), xi, 1, 2, 8, 9, 18, 63–65, 67–68, 213
  See also Activation policies
Affective currencies, viii
Affective economy, *see* Affective price; Affective pushes
Affectively subjectified, *see* Subjectification
Affective price, 20
Affective pushes, 19
Affective turn, 45
Agency, 40
Algorithms, *see* Profiling
Ambivalences, *see* Ambivalent
Ambivalent, 110
Applications, 134
Artists, *see* Cultural workers
The art of not being governed quite so much, *see* Resistance
Atmospheres, 46, 114
Attunement, 115
  See also Atmospheres
Austerity, *see* Precariousness

B

Believing in, 203
Belonging, 108
Bio-politics, 37
Black hole, 142
Body, 163
Boundaries, 204

C

Caring state, 202–203
Caseworker, 12
Citizenship, 19

Index

Competition, *see* Competitive infrastructures
Competition state, 63
Competitive infrastructures, 82–84
Conditionality, ix
Corona-unemployed, xii
Covid-19, ix, 67
Critical evaluations, *see* Critique
Critique, 113
Cultural workers, *see* Artists
Culture of insecurity, *see* Insecurity

D
Dating, 143
Demoralizing, 155, 178
Deserving, 19
Deservingness, *see* Deserving
Determining, 192
Dignity, vii
Dirty, 162
Discipline, 40
Dis-identifies, 121
Dispositioning, 192
Doubting, 110
Downgrading, 171

E
Ease, 89
Elevator speech, 157
Emotional debt, *see* Affective economy; Emotionally indebted
Emotional dissonance, 149
Emotional labor, *see* Emotions
Emotionally indebted, vii

Emotions, 48
Employability, 7, 160
Employment status, vii
Empowerment, ix
Enterprise culture, 10
Enterprising selves, 44
Escaping the shame, 120
Everyday life, *see* Social psychology of everyday life

F
Fear, ix
Feeling dirty, 87
Field observations, 142
Flexicurity, xi, 61

G
Good enough job, 89
Governmentality studies, 33

H
Hidden job market, 144
Hope, 130
Hope labour, 198
Human capital, 9

I
Identity, 36, 118
(In)dignity, 206
Individualization, 4
Insecurity, *see* Precariousness
Instrumentalization, 199
Internalized stigma, 185
Interviews, 3

K
Keynesian, 63

L
Latent functions, 85
Lazy, 80
Legitimacy, 176
Legitimate position, *see* Legitimacy

M
Marienthal, 16
Meaninglessness, 135
Meritocracy, 161
Micro-political, 39
Mistrust, ix
Monetary currencies, vii
Morality, 19, 100
Motivation, ix

N
Neoliberal, 63, 186
Neoliberal policies, *see* Neoliberal
Nepotism, 142
Nepotistic, *see* Nepotism
Networking, ix
Normative ideals, 189

O
Objectifying approach, *see* 'Working on'
Organisation for Economic Co-operation and Development (OECD), 5
Othering, 48

P
Pandemic, *see* Covid-19
Pay back, 193
Paying back, 129
Personal failure, 108
Pity, 157
Pleasure, 198
Politics, 19, 34
Postponing, 130
Post work, 131
Potentialization, 119
Power, 36
Powerlessness, 113
Precarious living, 120
Precariousness, x
Predictions, 89
Pressure coming from within, 113
Prevention, 190
Probability, *see* Statistics
Profiling, 89
Protestant work ethic, 104
Psychic income, 198
Psychologization, 4
Psychology, 19
Psycho-political patterns, vii
Psy-sciences, 14, 188
Public employment services (PES), 1

R
Recognition, 133
Rejections, 152
Representation, 48
Resentment, 156
Resistance, 40, 196
Respect, xii
Re-tooling, 38, 104
Return, *see* Social investment

S

Sanction, 119
Screening tool, *see* Algorithms; Profiling
Self-blame, 19
Self-conscious feelings, *see* Self-blame; Shame
Self-marketing, 157
Self-responsibility, ix
Self-responsibilization, *see* Self-responsibility
Shame, ix
Shifting, 201
Single story, 192
Social assistance, ix
Social assistance recipients, 108
Social hierarchy, 116
Social integration, 32
Social investment, 9, 63
Social norms, 100
Social psychology, 2
Social psychology of everyday life, 12
Statistics, 86
Stickiness, *see* Sticky emotions
Sticky emotions, 103
Stigma, *see* Shame; Sticky emotions
Street-level bureaucracy, 10
Structural conditions, *see* Structural factors
Structural factors, 4
Subject, 11
Subjectification, 11, 40
Subjective standpoint, 16
Subjectivity, 9
Surveillance, xi, 36
Suspicion, *see* Surveillance
Sustaining, 201
System-blame, 192

T

Taboo, 116
Technologies of power, 35
Technologies of the self, 35
Tensions, 20, 130

U

Uncertainty, 20
Undeserving, 19
Unemployed by choice, ix
Unemployment benefit, ix
U.S., 143
Useful, 170

V

Value system, *see* Social hierarchy
Volunteer work, 84
Vulnerability, 152

W

Weaponizing, 187
Welfare regimes, 63
'Working on', 12
'Working with', 15
Work less movements, *see* Post work
Work/life dichotomy, 175
Worry, 130
Worthiness, 206